ANTHROPOCENE FICTIONS

ANTHROPOCENE FICTIONS
THE NOVEL IN A TIME OF CLIMATE CHANGE

Adam Trexler

University of Virginia Press   CHARLOTTESVILLE AND LONDON

University of Virginia Press
© 2015 by the Rector and Visitors of the University of Virginia
Printed in the United States of America on acid-free paper

First published 2015

1 3 5 7 9 8 6 4 2

Library of Congress Cataloging-in-Publication Data
Trexler, Adam.
Anthropocene fictions : the novel in a time of climate change / Adam Trexler.
      pages   cm — (Under the sign of nature: explorations in ecocriticism)
Includes bibliographical references and index.
ISBN 978-0-8139-3691-8 (cloth : alk. paper) — ISBN 978-0-8139-3692-5
(pbk. : alk. paper) — ISBN 978-0-8139-3693-2 (e-book)
1. Ecofiction—History and criticism. 2. Ecofiction, American—History
and criticism. 3. Climatic changes in literature. 4. Environmentalism in
literature. I. Title.
PN3448.E36T84 2015
809.3'936—dc23

2014036319

CONTENTS

ACKNOWLEDGMENTS

The research for *Anthropocene Fictions* was partially funded by the European Social Fund, agreement number 09099NCO5. I also wish to acknowledge the University of Exeter, where much of the research for this book was undertaken.

Adeline Johns-Putra saw the early promise of climate change and literature as an area of study. Although our approaches ultimately diverged, I am grateful to her as a research supervisor and colleague.

Many colleagues at the University of Exeter, Cornwall Campus, were instrumental in developing my thinking about climate change. Ilya MacLean and Hilary Geoghegan were tremendous coinvestigators, and Simon Naylor provided important insights into both the history of science and geography. The English, geography, and biosciences departments fostered a remarkable spirit of interdisciplinary exchange, for which I am truly grateful.

I also wish to acknowledge the insights and encouragement of Greg Garrard, Evan O'Neil, Dana Phillips, Sharae Deckard, Jenni Halpin, Richard Kerridge, Heather Sullivan, SueEllen Campbell, and Robert Markley, as they encountered early versions of this work.

I would like to express my very great appreciation to Boyd Zenner for her perceptive, enthusiastic, and patient editorial efforts. Carol Sickman-Garner's copy editing was a joy to receive; any remaining errors are solely my own.

My family showed tremendous endurance and faith during the process of writing this book. My heartfelt thanks to Tom and Lorraine. Fritz and Carlyn's support made the completion of this project achievable. Without Jen, this book would have been impossible, many times over. Thank you.

ANTHROPOCENE FICTIONS

INTRODUCTION
Contextualizing the Climate Change Novel

From 2000, a group of geologists, led by the Nobel Prize winner Paul Crutzen, began to argue the present period of Earth's history should be known as the Anthropocene.[1] Before this, the period from approximately 11,700 years ago to the present was known as the Holocene, an interglacial period after the most recent ice age. According to proponents of the term *Anthropocene*, human activity has so altered the history of the Earth that it has become necessary to declare a new epoch to signify this impact. For Crutzen, the principal impact is the anthropogenic emission of greenhouse gases, increasing atmospheric levels of carbon dioxide by 30 percent and methane by 100 percent, triggering significant changes in global temperature and climate. However, scientists have also cited the rapid expansion of human population, human exploitation of 30–50 percent of the planet's land surface, the disappearance of tropical rain forests, the transformation of waterways through dams, and the exponential growth of energy use.[2] Dating the Anthropocene remains contentious. Possible dates include James Watt's invention of the steam engine in 1784, the increase in background radiation from Cold War nuclear tests in the 1950s, and the beginning of human agriculture ten to twelve thousand years ago. The term *Anthropocene* has appeared in nearly two hundred peer-reviewed articles, become the title of a new academic journal, and is the focus of a study group convened by the International Union of Geological Sciences to decide by 2016 whether the term should be officially adopted.[3] Yet *Anthropocene* is also anticipatory, indicating humanity's probable impacts on geophysical and biological systems for millennia to come.

Global climate change is likely to be our time's lasting legacy on Earth. Future impacts are predictions, not facts. Actual outcomes will be affected by future emissions, human efforts at adaptation, and, to some extent, geophysical forces beyond human control. Yet barring tremendous, immediate, and global interventions in emissions, global temperatures are likely to rise between 3 and 5 degrees centigrade by 2100, leading to a number of predictable geophysical, biological, social, and economic outcomes. Droughts, tropical cyclones, heat waves, crop failures, forest diebacks and fires, floods, and erosion will become more extreme. Inadequate water supplies, malnutrition, diarrheal diseases, and infectious diseases will become more common. Flooding, drought, and water shortages will lead to mass migration and regional conflicts. Low-lying coastal areas, including island countries, will face risks from rising sea levels and more intense coastal storms. Over one billion people will face risks from reduced agricultural production. Traditional ways of life will be disrupted, particularly in polar regions. The Mediterranean, western North America, southern Africa, southern Australia, and northeastern Brazil will face decreased precipitation and desertification. Ocean acidification is already occurring, and much of the world's coral is likely to die. In polar regions, permafrost is already melting. Ice sheets in Greenland and West Antarctica would likely take centuries or millennia to melt, leading to significant rises in sea levels. Weather patterns will be disrupted, including the Gulf Stream, leading to persistent cooling in Greenland and northwest Europe. This warming will lead to the release of further greenhouse gases from permafrost, peat lands, wetlands, and large stores of marine hydrates, exacerbating these problems. There will be significant losses of biodiversity, perhaps even the world's sixth extinction event. Human societies and economies have considerable potential to adapt to these changes, but the economic costs of this adaptation are likely to be considerable and unequally distributed. Earth's biological and geophysical systems have much less potential for adaptation. All of these systems are likely to be further effected by greater warming and more rapid change.[4]

The effects of burning fossil fuels have been studied for over a century. In 1896, Svante Arrhenius made the first calculations of how changes in atmospheric carbon dioxide due to burning coal would impact global temperatures. Few scientists studied these impacts until the 1950s, when new research indicated carbon dioxide levels could increase in the atmosphere and should warm the Earth. Military agencies, with a vital interest in oceans and weather patterns, funded much of this research. In the 1960s, researchers began to model climate mathematically and with computers, but early predictions of temperatures a few degrees warmer in the next century did not provoke immediate alarm. In the 1970s, the rise of environmentalism led to more widespread concern with human impacts on global climate, although there was confusion in the mass media over whether melting ice caps or a new ice age were more likely. In the same period, solar flares, volcanic eruptions, and changes in Earth's orbit were also shown to impact global temperature, while better records of ancient climates were discovered, particularly from ice cores that trapped atmospheric gases from millennia before. Through the 1980s, scientists discovered that the atmospheric levels of other greenhouse gases were rising and that Earth's climate had changed abruptly in the past. In 1988, an international meeting of scientists called for the curbing of greenhouse gas emissions, while industry groups and those opposed to government regulation began a campaign to counteract any such coordinated action. Evidence for direct links between atmospheric carbon dioxide and temperature was reinforced through the 1990s, as the findings of global climate models were confirmed. The Intergovernmental Panel on Climate Change, a panel tasked with reviewing and consolidating the most reliable possible evidence, established a consensus by 2001 that human civilization very likely faced the effects of severe global warming. Since then, better computer models and far more extensive data have strengthened the case that human emissions are likely to cause serious climate change. By 2007, its effects were already being measured in some regions, including more deadly heat waves, stronger floods and droughts, and notable impacts on sensitive species.[5] Some groups continue to spread doubt about the scientific basis of global warming trends or that human emissions are the main cause of climate change, and this activity will undoubtedly persist in some form. Different forcing elements will continue to shape global temperature, and scientists will continue to refine models and experiments to study global climate, perhaps influencing our understanding in unforeseen ways.

Public discussions about climate change have been dominated by issues of evidence, representation, and belief. Popular belief in climate change has been a major focus of media reporting for much of the twenty-first century, justifying further climatic research, sociological inquiry, public relations campaigns, and political platforms. The processes underpinning public perceptions of climate change have been extensively documented in academic histories; in popular science, environmentalism, and political books; and in mainstream and alternative media. This preoccupation with belief was linked to extraordinarily heightened rhetoric: threats of human extinction, the end of the world, the death of our children, scientific and corporate conspiracies, governmental collapse, and totalitarianism have rarely been far from the surface. The term *Anthropocene* may help to move beyond the narrow questions of truth and falsity with regard to climate science.

In its preference for *Anthropocene* over *climate change,* this book emphasizes the emergence of its subject from a scientific theory (contained in models and brains) to a geological process reflected in the atmosphere, oceans, ecosystems, and societies. At the turn of the last century, even the choice between the terms *global warming* and *climate change* was politically contentious, and debate over scientific certainty became a favored strategy for deferring action. The framework of the "Anthropocene" helpfully moves beyond the dead-end debate that dominated environmental politics in that period. *Anthropocene* indicates that atmospheric warming is not merely a theory, but a phenomenon that has already been measured and verified across scientific disciplines and conclusively linked to human emissions of fossil fuels. Thus, *Anthropocene* productively shifts the emphasis from individual thoughts, beliefs, and choices to a human process that has occurred across distinct social groups, countries, economies, and generations: the wholesale emission of fossil fuels that began in the Victorian period and has intensified through the present day. Both *climate change* and *global warming* are easily bracketed as prognostications that might yet be deferred, but the *Anthropocene* names a world-historical phenomenon that has arrived. Despite talk of tipping points, we are in the midst of a historical process of fossil fuel consumption that began before our parents and will continue long after us. Moreover, the effects of these events are superhistorical, affecting the Earth on a geological timescale. Of course, the rate of change may well increase, but later disasters are contiguous with our moment, not events that we can wholly defer. The Anthropocene is also a truly global event, even as it affects local climates and ecosystems in different ways. Too often, climate rhetoric has focused on the power of individual choice: that consuming or voting or communing differently might allow us to avoid the whole problem, like prodigal children. The Anthropocene, by emphasizing a geological process, can usefully indicate the larger, *nonhuman* aspects of climate, as well: the greenhouse gases already in the atmosphere will continue to act, independent of how we "imagine" the "environment."[6] By using the term *Anthropocene,* this study takes the firm position that climate change is upon us. On a geological scale, our emissions *are us,* though they persist far beyond our individual circles of influence, experiences, and lifetimes.

While early climate rhetoric continually raised the stakes on belief and action, it also obscured the imaginative processes that are fundamental to engaging with climate change. Recognizing global warming requires much more than assenting to scientific data. Humanity has discovered itself to be implicated in a geological transformation of the Earth, with profound implications for nearly all our reference points in the world. If *culture* can be used to denote human styles of building, interacting with, and relating to the world, the Anthropocene also indicates a *cultural* transformation that cannot be described through a rubric of belief. Setting aside questions of fact, how has the immense discourse of climate change shaped culture over the last forty years? What tropes are necessary to comprehend climate change or to articulate the possible futures faced by humanity? How can a global process, spanning millennia, be made comprehensible to human imagination, with its limited sense of place and time? What longer, historical forms aid this imagination, and what are the implications and limits of their use? What is impossible or tremendously difficult for us to understand about climate change? How does anthropogenic global warming challenge the political imagination or invite new organizations of human beings to emerge? How does living in the Anthropocene reconfigure human economies and ecosystems? And finally, how does climate change alter the forms and potentialities of art and cultural narrative? These are not questions of bald fact. Addressing them requires an investigation of larger, fabricated systems of expression.

As a discipline, literary studies has long experience with just these sorts of problems. Cultural texts like novels, poems, and plays show complex networks of ideas: history, scientific ideas, political discourse, cultural rituals, imaginative leaps, and the matter of everyday life. Interpreting such texts can be understood as a way of describing the patterning of enormous cultural transformations, such as the Anthropocene. Just as important, literary studies can describe these patterns without reducing their complexity to a monovocal account, a set of bare "interests," an immovable orthodoxy, or a predetermined certainty. It is able to accomplish this by examining a range of preexisting texts, not as mirrors of a culture, but as specific artifacts in wider networks of meaning.

When I became interested in the interactions between climate change and literature around 2008–9, I did not imagine there would be enough literature specifically about global warming to merit a substantial inquiry. After early searches and conversations with colleagues, there did not seem to be more than a handful of novels about anthropogenic global warming. Many of the early narratives I found treated it as an afterthought or a symptom of wider environmental collapse. There were unfocused novels by literary giants (Margaret Atwood's *Oryx and Crake*) and self-published e-books I couldn't ask anyone to read. Other novels achieved critical acclaim and were said to be about climate change but hardly treated the phenomenon itself (Cormac McCarthy's *The Road*). There was entirely too much science fiction, of course. And I worried that the rest would be preachy, politically partisan in the worst sense, apocalyptic rather than scientific, or, yet worse, craven rehearsals of the "facts."

Other directions presented themselves. Perhaps one might comment on the rhetoric of documentaries, nonfiction writing, or Hollywood disaster films. Both documentaries and nonfiction writing are popular sites for exploring climate science and politics and for describing Earth's future. Often, these works are more direct in their warnings, but they also lack the novel's capacity to interrogate the emotional, aesthetic, and living experience of the Anthropocene. There have been far fewer mainstream films about climate change. *The Day after Tomorrow*'s succession of impossible spectacles could only detract from dozens of nuanced novels. There is also a body of verse treating environmental devastation, of course, with a few of these poems directly concerned with climate change. Analyzing the techniques of climate poetry would take this study in a very different direction. Additionally, there are excellent memoirs and journalistic accounts of climate change's effects on different regions around the globe, although their preoccupation with authenticity draws on precisely that which climate fiction fabricates. More generally, these climate texts are worthy of investigation, but a media studies approach could too easily turn climate change into a discourse or a series of representations. Following a cross-genre approach, global warming could become still more dematerialized, even as well-funded media campaigns emphasized climate change as a "construction" to defer action.

While many media studies describe the mutability of events and the interests "behind" form, *Anthropocene Fictions* emphasizes the real agency of atmospheric warming and the novel.

As I went on, my original assumption that there simply wasn't enough climate change fiction was slowly eroded. Simply, more climate change novels kept presenting themselves. Early searches of subject bibliographies and online booksellers had yielded few results, but colleagues and friends-of-friends would suggest half a dozen works, many of them new. Detailed searches of newspaper reviews yielded more. The significant breakthrough came from a rather painful archival search of booksellers' trade publications. In short order, the bibliography grew to 150 novels about climate change, in one sense or another. It has continued to swell, from both the publication of new novels and new leads from the same sources. There were novels by many of the leading figures of "literary" and middle-brow fiction: Margaret Atwood, T. C. Boyle, Jonathan Franzen, Maggie Gee, Barbara Kingsolver, Doris Lessing, Ian McEwan, Will Self, and Jeanette Winterson. There were many more critically acclaimed novels by younger authors, including Rivka Galchen's *Atmospheric Disturbances,* Sarah Hall's *The Carhullan Army,* Sarah Moss's *Cold Earth,* and Tim Winton's *Dirt Music.* A number of the most respected science fiction authors had also made contributions: Piers Anthony, Paolo Bacigalupi, Octavia Butler, Ben Bova, Ursula LeGuin, Kim Stanley Robinson, and Bruce Sterling. Just as important, there were comic novels, thrillers, action-adventure stories, romance novels, mysteries, stories about prehistoric climate change, multicultural novels, last man narratives, quasi-religious apocalypses, monster stories, and teen novels.

The journalistic press has only just begun to recognize this literary movement. In 2009, an *Observer* critic argued that "in these more strained ecological times . . . eco-thrillers have become a more robust genre," noting several recent novels had tackled climate change.[7] Such notices occurred regularly, listing half a dozen novels but not diagnosing a wider movement. In the trade press, however, publishers noted readers' widespread interest in books about global warming.[8] Even so, climate change seemed like a nascent project to many. Andrew Dobson, a professor of environmental politics, reviewed a number of novels, concluding the needed climate change novel had yet to be written.[9] In 2011, a *Guardian* reviewer exclaimed, "Where are those [climate change] stories?" and the following year, Daniel Kramb asserted that novelists "appear singularly reluctant to address it."[10] By 2012, *Kirkus* noted science fiction had "[used] the effects of climate change to spin excellent stories."[11] Rather suddenly, critics recognized that something more momentous had occurred. Perhaps prompted by Dan Bloom's coinage "cli-fi," NPR, the *Christian Science Monitor, the Guardian, the Financial Times, Vice,* and the *New Yorker* reported that global warming had spurred the creation of a whole new genre of fiction.[12] In all these articles, critics named a handful of recent novels and invoked older works but lacked a sense of the scale of climate fiction publication. There remained significant confusion about climate fiction's relationship to the dystopian, science fiction, future speculation, and "literature." And critics continued to have little sense there was an extensive history of the genre.

In fact, there is an considerable archive of climate change fiction. Human-altered climates were of grave concern to authors before greenhouse gas emissions attracted wide scientific interest. Terraforming—the purposeful transformation of a planet's climate (usually) to make it more hospitable to humans—surfaced in science fiction at least as early as 1951, with Arthur C. Clarke's *The Sands of Mars;* Frank Herbert's *Dune* (1965) introduced terraforming to a wide audience. Many, many more novels, such as Philip K. Dick's *Do Androids Dream of Electric Sheep* (1968), explored nuclear winter. Other science fiction novels, such as Brian Aldiss's *Hothouse* (1961), speculated how long-term shifts in Earth's climate would affect human evolution. The first novel directly concerned with an anthropogenic greenhouse effect seems to have been written in 1971 (Ursula LeGuin's *The Lathe of Heaven*), and several others appeared in the late 1970s, but it wasn't until the late 1980s that climate change novels began to be written in significant numbers. The 1990s saw the publication of a wide variety of science fiction novels and more dystopian futures. Octavia Butler's *Parable of the Sower* (1993) and Ben Bova's *Empire Builders* (1993) are examples of early speculative novels from major authors. Through the first decade of the 2000s, climate fiction steadily expanded. Major literary voices entered the discussion around the turn of the millennium, with Kim Stanley Robinson's *Antarctica* (1999), T. C. Boyle's *A Friend of the Earth* (2000), and Doris Lessing's *Mara and Dann* (2000). There was a spike in publications around 2008, likely due in part to George W. Bush's reelection in late 2004, when there appeared to be little hope of American leadership on environmental issues. Many of the novels featured in this book were written in this period, including Julie

Bertagna's *Exodus* (2008), Saci Lloyd's *The Carbon Diaries 2015* (2008), Paul McAuley's *The Quiet War* (2008), Bruce Sterling's *The Caryatids* (2009), Paolo Bacigalupi's *The Windup Girl* (2009), Matthew Glass's *Ultimatum* (2009), and Ian McEwan's *Solar* (2010). Other novels also received considerable critical attention in the mainstream press, including Rivka Galchen's *Atmospheric Disturbances* (2008), James Howard Kunstler's *The World Made by Hand* (2008), Jeanette Winterson's *The Stone Gods* (2008), Margaret Atwood's *The Year of the Flood* (2009), Liz Jensen's *The Rapture* (2009), Raymond Khoury's *The Sign* (2009), Marcel Theroux's *Far North* (2009), and Jonathan Wray's *Lowboy* (2009). Since this period, there has been a steady flow of excellent novels about anthropogenic global warming; a number of these are examined in chapter 4 and the conclusion.

The concept of the Anthropocene helps explain the widespread phenomenon of climate change fiction. Early climate change novels tended to focus on the theoretical malleability of global climate, in terms of terraforming, nuclear winter, or geological processes. Through the 1970s and 1980s, anthropogenic global warming grew as an area of concern, but it was generally treated in fiction as just another environmental problem, alongside deforestation, urban development, toxic waste, and depletion of the ozone layer. Around the time of the formation of the Intergovernmental Panel on Climate Change (1988) and the Rio Earth Summit (1992), sustained, speculative explorations of climate change in fiction began to emerge. Through the 1990s, the body of novels grew, keeping pace alongside firming scientific evidence and increasing calls for international climate policy. Al Gore's 1999 presidential campaign ensured climate change was a central issue in American politics at the same time that a new wave of novels came into print. After Gore's defeat, the subsequent decade was a period of overwhelming scientific calls to action and equally intransigent international politics. To date, nearly all Anthropocene fiction addresses the historical tension between the existence of catastrophic global warming and the failed obligation to act. Under these conditions, fiction offered a medium to explain, predict, implore, and lament.

In the last forty years, climate fiction has slowly come to grips with a world phenomenon. Greenhouse gas emissions are produced in a global economy; political solutions are likely to require international commitments; and those harmed by flooding, food shortages, or violent weather may be far removed from a given smokestack or tailpipe. By contrast, novels are typically national, with a single language of composition, although international characters and settings may extend this reach. Some early novels were distinctly chauvinist, imagining the United States would brazenly solve the world's problems.[13] Many climate change novels continue to be parochial in their concerns, describing the collapse of the global economy and a return to village localism.[14] Over time, other Anglophone novelists have begun to describe the supranational effects of climate change. Various novels explore "natural" disasters originating in Antarctica, international waters, or across continents. Refugee crises trigger conflict between wealthy and poor countries, often reversing familiar emigration patterns. Other novels articulate the political and economic challenges of climate change in Africa, Asia, and South America.[15] Chapter 3 describes some of the literature that investigates political conflicts resulting from human-induced warming. Just as important, climate fiction has slowly emerged as an international phenomenon, with German,[16] Norwegian,[17] Icelandic,[18] Spanish,[19] Finnish,[20] and Dutch[21] novels finding their way into English translation. It remains difficult to locate such novels, although there is a vital need for the cross-cultural insight they could provide and a commensurate need for scholarship by critics specializing in other languages.

As a significant body of climate fiction came into focus, it raised a number of critical questions. The breadth of the narratives was surprising, as was the range of different genres represented. It would be easy to assume that the best novels would be by famous authors writing "serious," "literary" fiction. Reading widely, it quickly became clear that there were many excellent novels marketed as genre fiction. Other novels proved important as test cases, even if they were of dubious literary merit. But the archive also suggested broader questions that could not be answered through close reading. How did the climate novel develop over time? What forms and tropes enabled different aspects of climate change to be articulated? Were there aspects of the contemporary world that simply couldn't be described within the conventions of realism, science fiction, or dystopias? What strategies were available to represent, or even reconfigure, the politics of global warming? What were the limits on representing climate change in fiction? Were there things that simply couldn't be articulated through fiction? And perhaps most interestingly, how did climate change make new demands on the novel itself, forcing formal and narrative innovation? Climate fiction is not the result of a literary "school" of related authors. No singular influence or unitary "idea" connects all climate fiction. Climate change itself is a remarkably broad series of phenomena in the nonhuman world, politics, and the media. Wider, systematic reading would be necessary to describe this literary moment.

Nevertheless, academic criticism of contemporary fiction has been overwhelmingly focused on determining a literary canon deserving of serious study. *Anthropocene Fictions* might have followed the critical norm in "literary" fiction, science fiction, and environmental writing by first excluding all but a handful of works. The critical impetus to the canon is questionable, at best. Other periods of study have largely moved beyond this concern, bringing a wide variety of literary and nonliterary texts into analysis. In contemporary studies, on the other hand, monographs almost universally remark on the gamble of writing about recent literature. Brauner highlights the issue: "Any book of this sort makes an implicit case for the inclusion of certain writers in, and exclusion of other writers from, the canon, and making judgments on the worth of writers before their careers are over is invariably fraught with difficulties, particularly in the field of contemporary American fiction, in which new contenders for the title of Great American Novelist appear almost weekly and often disappear virtually overnight."[22] Criticism of contemporary literature is preoccupied with the business of prediction, treating writers as risky assets in the scholar's portfolio. In practice, nearly all studies play it safe with a mix of "difficult," acclaimed authors and "middlebrow," popular authors. An incredibly small number of writers attract the vast majority of contemporary criticism, and these are nearly all authors that are prepackaged by a handful of publishing houses to be recognized as "great." In earlier periods, it was possible for a critic to read an appreciable proportion of novels published in a year. Now, in the United States alone, there are approximately fifty thousand novels published each year.[23] Publishing houses and marketing departments effectively preempt that age-old critical question—what should we read. The academic promotion system feeds into this model by supporting research on "well-known" authors. Nevertheless, this preselected canon obscures some of the most important questions about climate fiction, excluding wider arguments about how climate change is imagined, the role of the novel in the face of the Anthropocene, and the formal possibilities of fiction in that confrontation.

The principal reason for this is that contemporary literature depends on a model of the canon that has long been discarded by most academic critics. Booksellers claim, implicitly or explicitly, that their list stands along-side the great novels of the past. Although he's contentious, Harold Bloom illustrates that the fundamental issue is one of aesthetic discernment: "Aesthetic criticism returns us to the autonomy of imaginative literature and the sovereignty of the solitary soul, the reader not as a person in society but as the deep self, our ultimate inwardness. That depth of inwardness in a strong writer constitutes the strength that wards off the massive weight of past achievement, lest every originality be crushed before it becomes manifest."[24] According to Bloom, the central act of both canonical writers and aesthetic critics is a forceful separation from society and a renewal of the inward, solitary soul. This has remained relatively intact, even as more diverse authors have been judged worthy to enter the meritocracy. Similarly, politicized interpretation (including environmental criticism) has often supplanted the collection of dead white men with "a *de facto* canon based on preconceived political determinants."[25] One might argue that contemporary critical accounts describe literary production as a dialectical conflict between the literary and popular; between formal experiment and realism; or between the works "routinely celebrated in the press and in the prize awards" and "challenging work from the margin, from the perspective of the other."[26] No matter the outcome, these skirmishes further foreground authorial achievement.

In practice, appealing to the canon constrains fiction. Novels that claim to be serious bear "an essential ingredient," a "low-key self-consciousness, the process by which all 'literary' novelists implicitly evaluate (and stake the claim for) their place in the canon."[27] Much "serious" contemporary fiction is also preoccupied with other times and places. Historical fiction wins a remarkable percentage of literary prizes, and there has been enormous consumer demand for both retro styles and fiction set in a handful of past moments. Such novels further foreground their place in a longer cultural tradition. On the other hand, the contemporary has often been "linked to a sense of endless change, to the rapid turnover of novelties, to the commodification of artistic experiment."[28] The measure of such "experiments" is their alteration of a unitary literary history, their ability to force themselves on the canon. From Bloom's celebration of the sovereign, solitary soul, all these literary values necessarily follow: the privileging of self-reflexivity over reference to the material world; of the historical and literary past over a coherent account of the present or future; of formal innovation over plotting or problems. Canonical criticism can have little to say about a problem like global warming, which undermines any account of souls by foregrounding collective human actions, the material world's agency, the immediate present and likely futures, complex plots among different human interests, and the inseparability of human experience from climate.

More disastrously, such canonical criticism depends on an impoverished model of literary innovation that can exclude the most formally innovative work of a historical moment. Underpinning the canon is a model of imagination whereby the author pulls all the strings, and character is the center of the fiction. In short, it revolves around the human. But this isn't how the world works, of course, and it isn't actually how fiction works. Landscapes, animals, devices, vehicles, geological formations, and buildings are formally constructive entities in fiction. To take an obvious example, the western as a genre doesn't work if cowboys lost in the desert can find a water fountain every few feet. What, then, about more imaginative works? Surely the desert plays a similar role when Moses strikes his staff and water gushes forth. The desert actively provides a ground for despair and magic, a universe in which God intervenes in the real. Since at least Exodus, the desert has been formative in constructing certain kinds of literary meaning that are unthinkable without it. In contemporary literature, melting ice caps, global climate models, rising sea levels, and tipping points have altered the formal possibilities of the novel. To argue thus is to challenge the yet-pervasive origin story of literature, shifting attention from author-geniuses to texts in a complicated material world.

Perhaps the central question of *Anthropocene Fictions* is how climate change and all its *things* have changed the capacities of recent literature. One way to measure innovation is against the backdrop of genre. Many preexisting genres offer extraordinary resources to think about complex issues like climate change. Science fiction has rich techniques to speculate about future technology and conditions, as well as the human experience of new historical moments. Chiller fiction ably evokes the dread and horror of catastrophic events, despite our quotidian desire to avoid them. Teen fiction specializes in describing the inertia and hypocrisy of domestic life, as well as structural tensions between different generations. Suspense novels are all but unimaginable without fast cars and jets—some of the most efficient engines ever invented for generating greenhouse gas emissions. They also specialize in international conflict, the motives of countries and industries, and diplomatic intrigue, all mainstays of the Anthropocene.[29] In all of these cases, the genre helps construct the meaning. And yet, climate change necessarily transforms generic conventions. The Anthropocene challenges science fiction's technological optimism, general antipathy toward life sciences, and patriotic individualism. Chiller fiction becomes wholly implausible when supernatural forces resolve enormous, atmospheric effects. Coming-of-age stories break down when the actions of prior generations trigger insolvable weather disasters and collapse economic opportunities for young people struggling toward independent adulthood. Safe identification with the hero of a suspense novel breaks down when he drives sports cars and exotic yachts, not to mention serves a government that has repeatedly thwarted climate accords. It is even more difficult to condense the distributed, impersonal causes of global warming into a climate villain. In the face of these challenges, climate novels must change the parameters of storytelling, even to draw on the tropes of recognizable narratives. More often than not, the narrative difficulties of the Anthropocene threaten to rupture the defining features of genre: literary novels bleed into science fiction; suspense novels have surprising elements of realism; realist depictions of everyday life involuntarily become biting satire. For these reasons, novels about the Anthropocene cannot be easily placed into discrete generic pigeonholes. Wide reading in this archive indicates recurring challenges to twentieth-century modes of narrative.

Much of contemporary criticism emphasizes authorial creativity in the face of contemporary life. To be sure, there are more and less satisfying fictional approaches to climate change. And yet, the archive of Anthropocene fiction also draws attention to the irreducible role of *things* in literary innovation. By its nature, the novel assembles heterogeneous characters and things into a narrative sequence: not just "solitary souls" but scientists, consumers, politicians, insurers, drivers, zookeepers, children, punk musicians, and bureaucrats are yoked with cars, factories, big box stores, thermostats, oil wells, butterflies, mountains, and glaciers. This complexity allows the novel to explore diverse human responses to peak oil, alternative energy, carbon sequestration, carbon trading, consumption, and air travel, in ways that are difficult for nonfiction or other art forms to portray. The novel can also think about climate change's intermingling with cultural narratives, such as nihilism, progress, collective resistance, and international cooperation. Moreover, the climate change novel can explore the aesthetics of wilderness, gastronomy, domesticity, species, urban life, fast cars, and international life. Climate change is, itself, a complex network of things and effects. (For example, consider the legion sources of greenhouse gas emissions, as well as the wildly varied human needs that justify them.) When the novel incorporates things implicated in climate change—climate models, glaciers, cars, future hopes, weather—it becomes impossible to read without the preoccupation of climate change. At a more theoretical level, the novel is founded on the tension between fact and invention, history and place, society and interiority, and the practice of making a living. These sites are integral to the meaning-making of a novel, and each of them is being radically reordered as we locate ourselves in the Anthropocene. This is not to say that the novels interpreted here are the cipher through which all contemporary literature may be understood or that climate fiction is the preeminent site of contemporary writing. But it can be said without exaggeration that the underlying causes of the Anthropocene have altered the horizon of human activity, as well as the capacities of the novel. As still more novels incorporate the weather, technology, and ideas of the Anthropocene, features of these early climate change novels will be diffused into literature at large.

Accordingly, *Anthropocene Fictions* moves between the overview of groups of novels and close reading of exemplary texts. Broad reading enables patterns in climate fiction to be gathered. A number of central questions could not be answered by interpreting a handful of novels: What specific things are necessary to describe the Anthropocene? How do these things determine narrative choices in climate fiction? What is the theoretical relationship between fiction and the "real" world in the Anthropocene? What preexisting cultural narratives have shaped our understanding of human-induced atmospheric warming? How can novels articulate the simultaneously local, national, and international politics of climate change? To what extent is there a history of climate fiction? Which novels are likely to reward repeated critical investigation? Unlike Elizabethan plays or Modernist poetry, Anthropocene fiction has not been cataloged, sorted, and analyzed over decades. Literary critics have become unused to "descriptive" scholarship, and the result is that contemporary criticism has come to depend on perilously few authors. Contemporary publishing has produced an archive that dwarfs all the historical texts that have been analyzed by literary critics. As they navigate this archive, contemporary critics must begin to show their work, not least so their assumptions can be checked. This study is unapologetically descriptive, in order to construct a framework to gather, evaluate, historicize, and interpret climate novels.

At the same time, novels have agency in their own right. Each novel rearticulates the complex relationships among fiction, humans, technology, the moment of composition, and climate. By necessity, novels composed in the Anthropocene challenge received literary functions, such as character, setting, milieu, class, time, and representation. Different novels address these structures in innovative ways. Indeed, one surprise for me in writing this book was the discovery of so many novels that challenged my expectations, created unexpected sympathies and new emotions, and were genuinely a pleasure to read. Beyond my narrow tastes, dozens of works successfully reconfigure the historical relationship between fiction and truth-telling; alter assumptions of how humans relate to place; reimagine social and political organization; or rearticulate the global, mechanized, consumer economies of the twenty-first century. Some of these novels could reasonably be said to alter the generic foundation of the novel itself or materially contribute to an understanding of our time. Sustained critical attention is necessary to trace these innovations, and so *Anthropocene Fictions* examines a number of novels in much more detail. At times, the novels I have chosen are exemplary of a wider movement. Others complicate a trend or undermine it. Describing these relationships involves continual movement between the wider archive and specific examples, between descriptive and close reading. It seems likely that this strategy could trace similar trends in contemporary literature: those that have a legitimate claim to be new.

Anthropocene Fictions is not solely an archival work, a historicist account, or a study of pure literary form. Two critical discussions, environmental criticism and science studies, have shaped every chapter. Both strongly influenced early discussions of climate fiction, raising fundamental questions and suggesting modes of investigation. At the same time, neither discourse has been able to provide a satisfactory account of Anthropocene literature.

Of course, *Anthropocene Fictions* hopes to contribute to a wide body of literary scholarship that investigates environmental concerns. Environmental criticism encompasses historicist studies, interpretations of environmental themes in literature, and political criticism. Much of this research falls under "ecocriticism," a somewhat narrower rubric of methods and preoccupations, of which this book is often critical. Ecocriticism emerged in the early 1990s, not as a rigorous disciplinary approach, but rather as an interdisciplinary group of researchers interested in literature, culture, and the environment. Initially, ecocriticism was shaped by the political and academic prominence of feminism, race studies, and postcolonialism, which had attracted significant funding and autonomy on North American campuses. Following the lead of these fields, ecocritics hoped to critique current environmental ideas, draw attention to environmental issues, develop new ways of thinking about the environment, and energize activism. The field has also been shaped by interdisciplinary forays into ecology, geography, biology, and evolutionary sciences, but it has shown little interest thus far in climatology. Many ecocritics have also been inspired by English Romantic poets, American Transcendentalists, and ideas of nature inherited from this tradition. Ecocriticism was slow to engage with climate change, but it has recently become a central preoccupation of the field.[30] One cause for the early neglect is that environmental politics bear little resemblance to domestic and international struggles for liberation. The field's preoccupation with life sciences led ecocritics to diagnose climate change as a human incursion into ecosystems or Nature writ large, rather than a process that inextricably binds together human and nonhuman systems. As a result, ecocritics did surprisingly little to analyze anthropogenic global warming for the first decade and a half of the movement's existence.

Many early critical accounts of climate focused on single literary texts, though just as many interpretations of these works ignored climate change altogether. The ecological destruction and the extinction of human beings in Atwood's *Oryx and Crake* (2004) and *The Year of the Flood* (2009) attracted significant critical attention, but climate change was rarely central to their interpretation. Cormac McCarthy's *The Road* (2007) was declared by the environmental journalist George Monbiot "the most important environmental book ever written," but other critics denied the novel was about global warming or ignored climate change outright.[31] T. C. Boyle's *A Friend of the Earth* (2000) was recognized as an important warning of the "dangers of global warming."[32] Other novelists, such as Doris Lessing, Maggie Gee, Will Self, Ian McEwan, and Jeanette Winterson, regularly receive academic interest, yet their climate fiction is just beginning to attract sustained attention. Science fiction has attracted more direct research, particularly Kim Stanley Robinson's "Science in the Capital" trilogy. Other critics argued that historical literature provides a useful means of understanding contemporary global warming and called for an interdisciplinary investigation of how climate and human culture have shaped each other from the development of agriculture to the present.[33] These interpretations were important forays but only scratched the surface of climate fiction.

In 2007, major figures in environmental criticism began to call for greater engagement with anthropogenic climate change. Timothy Morton provocatively argued that ecocriticism's dependence on Romantic, ahistorical notions of nature and literature had made it impossible to address the politics of global warming.[34] The next year, Ursula Heise argued in *Sense of Place and Sense of Planet* (2008) that ecocriticism must balance attention to place with new cultural frameworks for understanding planetary systems, concluding that literature and criticism had yet had limited success in addressing climate change.[35] The same year, a talk by Scott Slovic, the founding president of the Association for the Study of Literature and Environment, sketched a broad project for criticism: critiquing climate deniers, tracing climate science's role in society, investigating historical responses to climatic changes, and interpreting contemporary climate change discourse.[36] Richard Kerridge, the founding president of the Association for the Study of Literature and the Environment-UK (ASLE-UK), emphasized climate fiction must find new means of mediating between "embodied sensuous perception . . . and wider perspectives."[37] Greg Garrard, ASLE-UK's subsequent president, sought to intervene on earlier preferences for detailed, realist representations of nature, arguing different literary forms were needed to articulate climate change.[38]

These pronouncements were followed by a rush of conferences and special issues focusing on climate change. The 2010 ASLE conference in Bath, England,[39] as well as the ASLE-sponsored "Culture and Climate Change" symposium,[40] framed extensive conversations on the issue. The same year, a special issue of the journal *English Studies* and the ecocritical collection *Local Natures, Global Responsibilities* contained a number of essays directly addressing contemporary climate change.[41] In subsequent ASLE conferences, climate change was a major theme running through panels, while workshops and interdisciplinary conferences elaborated the discussion.[42] Very quickly, research in climate change and literature outstripped the handful of critical articles that had first addressed it.

In particular, from 2012 to 2013, there was widespread recognition that literary theory's founding assumptions ill suited it to the Anthropocene. Over three years, a host of essays addressed these shortcomings, including those found in the *Oxford Literary Review*'s "Deconstruction, Environmentalism, and Climate Change" (July 2010) and "Deconstruction and the Anthropocene" (December 2012); *new formations*' "Imperial Ecologies" (July 2010); and the two volumes of *Theory in the Era of Climate Change*, *Telemorphosis*, edited by Tom Cohen, and *Impasses of the Post-Global*, edited by Henry Sussman (2012). Generally speaking, this body of climate change theory was antipathetic to existing ecocriticism, finding that it had focused too much on individual perception and choice and not enough on "the state, ideology, [and] modes of production."[43] These articles brought a wide variety of thinkers to bear on climate change, including Ulrich Beck, Slavoj Žižek, eco-Marxist critics, Michel Foucault, Freud, Deleuze and Guattari, William Morris, Jacques Derrida, Rudolph Boehm, Paul de Man, postcolonial thinkers, and science studies figures like Bruno Latour and Donna Haraway. The body of work represented by these collections bears a number of foundational insights, many of which have shaped the direction of *Anthropocene Fictions*. At the same time, these essays are remarkable for their inattention to literature. Few of the articles offer interpretations of literary works, and virtually none of them demonstrate a wider awareness of the literary project currently being undertaken by hundreds of authors. This book often engages with specific arguments found in these essays, but the rush to pronounce on the ontology of the Anthropocene would seem to be premature.

By contrast, this book suggests possible directions to investigate a moment whose literary, political, cultural, geological, and biological coordinates have not yet fully emerged. The majority of ecocritical studies have been focused on "eco" authors. A sizable proportion of these works focus on an even narrower canon of writers that can be traced back to American Transcendentalists and English Romantics. When critics have been too closely aligned to these traditions, ecocriticism has often become a means to prescribe how to think right about the Earth, instead of a field of discovery and analysis about literature and environmental problems. By taking a broad, archival approach to climate fiction, and by interpreting works of many ideological persuasions and literary backgrounds, this book hopes to suggest a more open and analytical approach to environmental texts and, by extension, environmental practices. *Anthropocene Fictions* also resists the more recent critical trend toward "theories" of climate change inspired by continental philosophers. As I suggest above, the texts of the Anthropocene have only just begun to be read, mapped, and pondered. Early evidence would suggest that they offer vital articulations of climate change. It seemed far more worthwhile to advance this work than to make premature pronouncements about literary and atmospheric phenomena that are still unfolding. But in order to begin to describe the novel in the Anthropocene, it has been necessary to develop some model of the interconnections among texts, sciences, societies, and things in the world.

A second, related issue for environmental criticism is how it might understand science, as it articulates human-induced atmospheric warming. There is no knowledge of anthropogenic global warming without the highly technical field of climatology, while predicting and tracing climate change's effects require ecology, economics, organic chemistry, and dozens of other fields. For over a decade, the politics of climate change were mired in a debate over the accuracy of scientific findings. Evidently, fiction creates "representations" of science, and these choices have implications for the status of fiction, science in contemporary culture, and perhaps the basic tools we use to understand this contemporary moment. (We will have cause to trouble these categories and the rhetoric of representation in chapter 1.) Even these cursory questions indicate a need to understand the relationships between scientific practices, like constructing global climate models, and cultural practices, like reading and writing novels.

Ecocriticism has long struggled with these relationships. From the 1970s through the 1990s, many ecocritics invoked ecological science as a material, nonhuman foundation for criticism.[44] Ecocritics have variously treated science as though it could provide a factual grounding for their own interpretation, a source for deeper ethical truths, or a bedrock for theory. Or, as Dana Phillips trenchantly described, as a "slush fund of fact, value and metaphor."[45] Such an approach catastrophically misses what science is and what it is for. It also tends to result in forgettable criticism. Critics who elevate ecological fact and theory have often wondered what literature might be good for at all, in the face of environmental crisis. Other critics, more influenced by the English discipline's mainstream, tipped their hat to "the virtues of the scientific method," while claiming criticism can gain access to the immaterial emanations of the mind, see through science's "irreducible social embeddedness," or uncover the "hyperreal."[46] Spiritualism, social constructivism, and postmodernism tend to dematerialize scientific findings in order to carve a privileged space for literature. And yet, in the last twenty years, those who would thwart emissions reductions have appealed to religious fundamentalism, attacked global temperature as a social construction, and claimed climatology is a relative truth or even a liberal conspiracy. Evidently, environmentalism is ill-served by further dematerializing scientific findings.

Environmental critics have made significant progress on these issues by incorporating findings from science studies into their accounts of the relationships between ecology and culture. Early on, Bruce Clarke argued that Bruno Latour's *We Have Never Been Modern* could help ecocritics avoid scientism while addressing the central importance of ecological science to the field. Latour denies that science at large or even individual disciplines can be described as a stable "method." Rather, science is characterized by the ongoing activity of creating new methods of knowledge production.[47] As such, it makes less sense to speak of Science with a capital *S*, and more to understand facts as what emerge from ongoing, developing human practices. Many ecocritics have also turned to Latour to understand why facts seem so antithetical to culture in modernity. In Latour's account, modernity is best understood as a style of ontology that artificially separates Nature and Society, objects and subjects. This act of ontological "purification" persists in postmodernism, neoprimitivism, and social-constructivist critiques of nature.[48] However, the rhetoric of modernity has never determined how reality works. Instead, networks of hybrids, "half object and half subject," commonly called "machines and facts," mediate between nature and society.

Latour's account of the ontological interdependence of subjects and objects, society and nature, has proved productive in environmental criticism. *We Have Never Been Modern* has been used to describe human modification of animals' genes and the atmosphere;[49] to escape the binary opposition between scientific realism and antiscientific reaction;[50] to construct a sustainable vision of place;[51] to trace the dynamic historical interactions between culture and climate;[52] to critique representational demands for proof in climate science;[53] and to explore the simultaneously social and natural, political and scientific dimensions of climate change.[54] In such work, Latour's model has helped avoid both naive scientific realism and strong versions of social constructivism, allowing critics to identify things like genes, places, local climates, findings, and anthropogenic climate change itself as hybrids emerging from natural and human agency.

Nevertheless, ecocritics have struggled to articulate how these theoretical insights should lead to a methodology of environmental interpretation. Science and technology studies provides few clues; the discipline's defining focus on "science" has meant that researchers have paid very little attention to artistic forms of cultural production. This is a pity, not least because the disciplinary boundaries of art and science have so often been defined against one another. On the side of literary studies, critics have often continued the practice of celebrating individual "theorists," particularly Latour and Haraway, without fully appreciating their position within a wider field of study. Latour's own *Pandora's Hope* makes these connections much more explicit, an overview that has been all but unnoticed by literary critics. Science and literary studies share a number of questions that are made acute by climate fiction. How are we to understand discovery or innovation, in both climate science and literary experiments? Does climate fiction demand new literary modes? What are the implications of representing, or mediating, climate in different kinds of texts? How are we to understand the relationship between fact and fiction when disastrous climate change, a scientific prediction, is portrayed in a novel? What are the implications of facts circulating in cultural artifacts? Is the politicization of science always reductive? Can climate fiction be said to be politically useful? The field of science studies suggests provocative answers to these questions, but there is no straight path from a detailed case study of climatological computer modeling to climate fiction.

Through the analysis of these novels, *Anthropocene Fictions* hopes to develop the disciplinary relationship between science studies and environmental criticism. Science studies offers vital tools that allow environmental criticism to describe both literary and scientific production and to investigate how meaning and truth exist in the world. Climate change is inevitably tied to science. Without scientific measurement and theory, we can only experience phenomena: weather, not climate. And yet, climate change is inescapably tied to the meaning of human life on Earth, in ways that studies of glaciers, atmospheric carbon dioxide, and global climate models cannot begin to describe. Accordingly, this book draws heavily on science studies, finding new tools to help articulate phenomena that are simultaneously scientific, natural, political, and literary.

Agency is a particularly useful term to describe such hybrids. Things like climate models, species, and bureaucracies are more than human ideas or social constructions: they do things in the world. They stubbornly resist forms of human determination as well: species can colonize habitats or become extinct despite human "management." At the same time, these things exist in relation to human knowledge practices. They are not purely unknowable or inert like the matter of parlor physics, nor do they have interiority, intentionality, or choice. Things can be said to have "agency" as they shape the world in ways that are irreducible to human knowledge or construction. This is not to make an exotic pantheism out of things, but rather to recognize the common sense of what is going on when a scientist or a neighbor asks, "What is the weather doing?" Agency allows an environmental critic to describe nonhuman things as actors in ecosystems, politics, and novels, while maintaining the sense of their categorical hybridity.[55]

Nevertheless, science studies is not a panacea for environmental criticism. Overall, that discipline has been shockingly ignorant of artistic texts and the tools of interpretation, even as it claims to perform cultural studies. Science studies cannot contribute a theoretical model or an ideological checklist to apply to literary texts; novels are artifacts that produce meaning in their own, unique ways. The imaginative capacities of the novel have made it a vital site for the articulation of the Anthropocene. Tracing these articulations is simultaneously a critical undertaking and a study of scientific culture. It is my hope that *Anthropocene Fictions* will contribute to a bidirectional exchange of ideas between literary and science studies, in order to better describe the ever-evolving fruits of cultural production.

The first chapter, "Truth: Science, Culture, and Construction," directly addresses these issues. Often, fiction is understood as something other than fact, a fabrication distinct from the pure representation of scientific truths. A central problem for climate fiction, then, is what it means for a novel to contain facts or truths, particularly those associated with science. Scientists, politicians, and activists have been preoccupied with demonstrating the truth of climate change, while other scientists, politicians, and activists have sought to discredit the entire body of research. In this dilemma, both sides could view works of climate fiction as crude tracts that exacerbate public ignorance by propagating sensational accounts of environmental disaster. However, recent research in science and technology studies disputes the idea that science, public understanding, and culture are discrete categories. Rather, climate change emerges from a host of interrelated sources, including natural effects (solar radiation), industrial processes (car emissions), and scientific practices (climate modeling), but also cultural processes such as popular science writing, policy papers, political speeches, and novels. Even when novels espouse the idea that climate change is either fact or fabrication, as in Michael Crichton's *State of Fear* (2004) and Ian McEwan's *Solar* (2010), the circulation of climate change through the novel shows it is *both* real *and* fabricated. Climate change does not come "into" novels through special pleading on the part of the author. Instead, climate change spans an enormous, heterogeneous terrain that demands formal innovations of fiction. When climate change circulates through the novel, it is reshaped as a material, scientific, and cultural thing.

Superficially, it would seem that the imaginative form of the novel could present any possible idea, yet evidence would suggest that the articulation of climate change is highly constrained by existing cultural narratives. For any novel, the translation of the abstract notion of global temperature into a plot, comprising a limited cast of characters and a horizon of activity, involves either off-stage reportage to characters or implications supplied by the reader. The second chapter, "Place: Deluge, Floods, and Absence," describes how nearly all climate fiction takes this a step further by bringing characters into confrontation with an immediate climatic disaster. Taking this step allows readers to have a personal experience of climate change, glimpsing its effects on local places and individual lives. Surprisingly, this step is highly dependent on existing cultural narratives. A handful of scenarios—desertification, extinction, polar adventure, and flooding—comprise the vast majority of climate fiction. Floods are the dominant literary strategy for locating climate change. Novels about global rises in sea levels were important through the twentieth century. J. G. Ballard's *The Flood* (1962) has acted as an important precursor, indicating that frequently climate change is experienced not within a place but as an estrangement from place. Richard Cowper's *The Road to Corlay* (1976) is an early exploration of anthropogenic climate change, global deluge, and cultural regression, while Will Self's *The Book of Dave* (2006) is a notable example of the genre's satiric possibilities. Another branch of fiction has focused on local floods, using a more contemporary framework of reportage to draw together the diverse impacts on cities, animals, and different social groups. These capacities are most fully realized in Maggie Gee's *The Flood* (2004), which shows the fragility of complex social networks in an anthropogenic age.

In a moment when scientists and activists make fervent calls for drastic emissions reductions, and when other commentators denounce global warming as a conspiracy between big government and big science, it could be argued that any depiction of climate change is implicitly political. Chapter 3, "Politics: Opposition, Bureaucracy, and Agency," argues that both global politics and the novel struggle to articulate the problems of climate change and to develop sufficient agency for a response. Political discussions of climate change have often focused on forcing elite leaders to take action or creating a popular activist movement. In climate change novels, oppositional politics provide an easy source of dramatic tension, from geopolitical stand-offs between nation states, as in Matthew Glass's *Ultimatum* (2009), to radical eco-activism, as in T. C. Boyle's *A Friend of the Earth* (2000). Yet such novels about elite political action and popular uprising repeatedly struggle to imagine compelling responses to climate change, almost always failing on their own terms. Other novels imagine the creation of new bureaucratic regimes. One of the first climate change novels, Arthur Herzog's *Heat* (1977), shows that the "crack team" found in many thrillers enables collective solutions to be envisioned. More recently, Kim Stanley Robinson's "Science in the Capital" trilogy (2004, 2005, 2007) imagines how scientists, politicians, and diverse publics can be assembled into effective agencies. Thus, climate change novels can provide new models of collective organization to address global emissions and local impacts.

Often, political rhetoric calls for climate change to be averted, threatening catastrophe if it is not. Much of climate fiction follows the same pattern, warning readers of an impending disaster, as if all the effects of rising greenhouse gas levels can be reduced to a single tsunami. This literary strategy simplifies the Anthropocene, and it defers it as well. More sophisticated novels incorporate both economics and ecology, describing climate change as a longer transformation of the terms of human life. Early on, novelists recognized climate change could lead to the breakdown of the global economy and the environmental foundations of industrial modernity, a situation captured by George Turner's *The Sea and Summer* (1987), which charts the collapse of twentieth-century "greenhouse culture." In the late 1980s and early 1990s, the end of the Cold War suggested a renewed optimism that capitalism could also overcome global warming. This optimism is exemplified by Ben Bova's *Empire Builders* (1993), which describes a swashbuckling entrepreneur leading the charge against disastrous climate change. For the next twenty years, both novelists and critics shared a remarkable consensus about the economic causes of climate change, believing capitalism would prove far more rigid than global temperature. In the last several years, a new body of climate fiction has emerged, one that begins to describe the complex reconfiguration of human ecology. Among many others, Saci Lloyd's *Carbon Diaries 2015* (2008), Ben Bova's *The Caryatids* (2009), and Paolo Bacigalupi's *The Windup Girl* (2010) suggest an "eco-nomic" mode of reading. Differing from critique, "eco-nomic" interpretation would instead focus on integrating new concerns into an Anthropocene age that has already arrived.

Criticism in the Anthropocene necessarily focuses on literary qualities that have been underexamined in previous periods. First, climate change introduces disproportionate scale effects, so miniscule domestic choices such as car ownership, vacation destinations, choices between suburban and urban homes, and thermostat settings contribute to catastrophic effects. The novel has long spanned the distance between domestic and political worlds, if not typically in single texts. Climate criticism must develop ways to describe this interpenetration between domestic and planetary scales. Second, climate change is already affecting human economy—our collective modes of making a living, whether through crop failures, demand for local produce, hybrid cars, energy taxes, environmental enterprises, municipal amelioration strategies, or emission targets. Early novels imagined either economic collapse or a new sustainable era, but more sophisticated climate novels have begun to describe a complex transformation of human economies, and so human culture. Finally, climate fiction has increasingly allowed nonhuman things to shape narrative. The best Anthropocene novels are not solely "character-driven." Nor do they reduce climate change to a unitary phenomenon, such as the "Great Storm." Instead, they explore how things like ocean currents, tigers, viruses, floods, vehicles, and capital relentlessly shape human experience.

What might be called "eco-nomic criticism" begins to account for each of these senses of *eco:* domestic life, the broad formation of human enterprise, and a heterogeneous world that exists beyond human idealism. Domestic, quotidian experience challenges the parochial focus of science studies, tracing circuits of scientific influence far beyond the lab or even popular media.

Analysis of economic formations challenges the nature focus of much eco-criticism but also allows environmental critics to more specifically describe the causes of environmental degradation and the opportunities for sustainable living. Accounting for things in fiction challenges canonical criticism's preoccupation with authentic character, author-geniuses, and master texts. Even so, eco-nomic criticism is not a theory of Anthropocene criticism, but rather a starting point for an innovative body of works.

The corpus of climate change fiction represents an enormous and growing archive. There cannot be a single history of these works, based on a corresponding history of climate science or climate politics, because the novels in question have continually reconfigured what it means to live in the Anthropocene, to be part of a self-conscious species that is actively transforming conditions that have reigned throughout its evolutionary history. Every month, more novels are published that address this situation. In the early 1980s, novels about anthropogenic climate change speculated on a possible future and warned humanity to change its course. Authors continue to issue this call, but the Anthropocene has arrived, and *all* contemporary fiction could be said to reflect a condemned "greenhouse culture." Climate fiction can convey cultural narratives, create detailed speculation, incorporate diverse points of view, and hold a multitude of things, from species to machines, places to weather systems. These features make the novel a privileged form to explore what it means to live in the Anthropocene moment.

ONE

TRUTH
Science, Culture, and
Construction

Hysteria, phrenology, the geocentric universe, genetically modified food, vaccines, Prozac, fluoride, DDT, and climate change. We all know those scientific things that we should not believe, technologies that hide the bare interests of patriarchy, cultural bias, religion, social hierarchy, the Enlightenment, corporations, and governments. Other things we cling to as the unobjectionable products of scientific truth. The poles of this argument can certainly be more nuanced, but the dilemma between scientific constructivism and scientific realism pervades early-twenty-first-century political debate.

Fiction also bears the mark of these divisions. In contrast to "nonfiction," fiction is understood as the product of social ideas, cultural beliefs, and individual imagination. And yet, fiction is said to express truths that cannot be described by direct, declarative writing. In a moment characterized by its uncertainty over scientific knowledge, the novel maintains a problematic relationship with the truth of climate change.

Incorporating climate change into fiction is not a straightforward task. To explore how global warming impacts human character, the future, imagined landscapes, the political realm, or culture, the novel must bring fact into dialogue with fiction. The contentiousness of climate change makes this task yet more difficult. From the first plot choices, a novelist faces legion questions about the relationship between climate science and the novel. Which set of predictions should the novelist follow? Should the novel be set in the near future, when changes might be harder to discern, or in a distant, harder-to-predict future, when changes might be undeniable? Which threats are most serious or most likely? How do changing predictions about "tipping points," extreme weather, desertification, raised sea levels, or the Gulf Stream affect the novel's imaginative possibilities? Is it acceptable to oversell the threat or compress the timescale to provide more dramatic possibilities? If the climate has indeed changed in the fictional world, how will characters know about it? Will scientists explain things, or the media, or will civilization be so decimated that scientists and reporters are neither possible nor needed? The novel could focus on the human practices that exacerbate the greenhouse effect—carbon dioxide emissions, energy corporations, individual consumption—or the meteorological details of future climate. Some novels have adopted an elegiac mode for the loss of our present world, while others have investigated amelioration strategies, like carbon sinks, cap-and-trade schemes, and alternative energy. Beneath all of these choices lies an even more fundamental problem: the way that science enters fiction. This issue gets to the heart of what it means for science to be true and what it means for fiction to be distinguished from fact.

Many excellent novels pointedly avoid the tension between scientific prediction and fiction by making climate change self-evident in the novel's world. In T. C. Boyle's *A Friend of the Earth,* violent storms threaten a rock star's compound, where a broken-down environmentalist tries to keep the last surviving members of several species alive. In Paolo Bacigalupi's *The Windup Girl,* a fragile network of sea walls, levies, and pumps keeps a Thai city from being flooded by the swollen ocean. In Will Self's *The Book of Dave,* extreme flooding has turned Britain into a series of backward, medieval island tribes. And in novels like Maggie Gee's *The Ice People* and Doris Lessing's *Mara and Dann,* the very issue of human responsibility for the climate is superseded when anthropogenic global warming is replaced by a new ice age, leading to the collapse of European civilization. In such novels, scientific predictions are embedded in the novel's setting. The climate may be influenced by humans, but the novel's conflicts run along familiar plotlines of humans combating nature and other humans who would further upset a "natural" balance. Even though such novels seem to make science transparent, a key critical question remains: Are the nuanced, evidence-based predictions of climatology altered by being portrayed as fictional facts?

Other novels avoid representing scientific uncertainty and practice by turning thick scientific predictions into tomorrow's scientific givens. In the last two decades, public debate has included the detailed techniques of climate science: Antarctic ice cores and carbon dioxide counts in Mauna Loa have come under scrutiny; surveys of glaciers and species have been folded into the controversy; polls of scientists have explored the importance of scientific consensus; studies' origins in corporate or environmentalist money have been unearthed; conspiracies by university scientists have been alleged; and so on. Matthew Glass's *Ultimatum* avoids this complexity by setting the novel several decades in the future. In the first few pages, a very minor character delivers a classified report to the incoming president detailing rapidly intensifying feedback loops, leading to sea-level rises, enhanced storm activity, altered rainfall and growth patterns, desertification, and new disease ranges, predicting these outcomes with a 90 percent level of certainty. For the rest of the novel, the president and his team can focus on striking a diplomatic deal with China over reduced emissions from the standpoint of scientific certainty. In Susannah Waters's *Cold Comfort*, the teenaged protagonist keeps a scrapbook of newspaper stories about climate change, delivering much information, even as part of her family's home sinks under the thawing permafrost and Native hunting patterns change due to the unprecedented breakup of sea ice. In James Herbert's *Portent*, an omniscient narrator describes natural disasters across the world, divorced from the plot's characters. Scientific knowledge can be put in the mouth of future technicians, newsreaders, Native elders, or the narrator itself, making fictional climate change an unquestionable certainty for the reader.

Despite these strategies, the majority of novels about climate change include at least one scientist. There are crude ways to use such a character: dumping information on the reader, foretelling plagues on humanity to build suspense, granting the sheen of respectability to wild speculations. But in many more novels, scientists play a fundamental role, developing the meaning of climate change while helping to frame questions about both knowledge and the novel as a formal entity. There is a wide variation of the types of science practiced by characters, as well as the roles they play in the novel. In Clive Cussler's *Arctic Drift*, the novel's heroes are marine biologists who chart changes in chemical composition and plankton levels in the Pacific Ocean; their scientific skills help them discover that an energy magnate is dumping greenhouse gases while pocketing the Canadian government's sequestration subsidies. Also, a minor character discovers an efficient way to break down carbon dioxide using the rare element ruthenium, before nearly being assassinated by the energy magnate's henchman. These scientists allow *Arctic Drift* to explore the economic interests in the current energy regime, as well as proposed strategies for emissions reductions. In *Carbon Dreams,* by Susan M. Gaines, the protagonist is a biological chemist in the 1980s using tiny plankton as a biomarker to understand the last 150 million years of global climate. Her relationships with oceanographers, botanists, chemists, geologists, and paleontologists, as well as a romantic interest with an environmental campaigner and organic farmer, allow the novel to explore the emergence of a scientific consensus about climate change and the resulting duties to the scientific community, political environmentalism, and impartial "pure" research. In Liz Jenson's *The Rapture,* a physicist character helps the novel negotiate between rational and theological explanations for natural catastrophes, a pattern repeated in many other novels. In such works, scientific characters play a fundamental role in the investigation of the meaning of climate change for the wider public.

Other novels use scientists to explore what it means to be human in a climate-changed world. A surprising number of climate change novels are also preoccupied with genetics. In Margaret Atwood's *Oryx and Crake,* one of the main characters engineers new animals and humanoids, perfecting them after the collapse of human and "natural" animal populations. In Patrick Cave's *Sharp North,* climate change has precipitated a dictatorial government in Britain. Cloned humans of the society's most important families are raised to be ignorant of their purpose as expendable organ donors. And Maggie Gee's *The Ice People* features a nanotechnology engineer who helps build "Doves," self-replicating robots that replace babies in a world of plummeting birth rates. Social scientists are also common. In Robinson's "Science in the Capital" trilogy, one of the main characters is a sociobiologist investigating what makes for rational behavior in the face of our evolutionary heritage, extreme weather, and the need for a scientific response to rapid climate change. In Sarah Moss's *Cold Earth,* a team of archaeologists explores the fate of Greenlanders who faced a historic shift in weather patterns, even as they are accidentally trapped in similar conditions. Novels such as these may not be particularly interested in the science of climate change per se, but they use science to unpack global warming's meaning for human beings.

Such literary strategies indicate the importance of science to Anthropocene fiction. Environmental criticism has been preoccupied with the theoretical relationship between science and literature. One approach of environmental critics has been to argue interpretation can originate in science and nature, rather than human beings and culture. For instance, ecocritics have suggested that biomes have a primary physical reality and a transhistorical certainty, arguing it is prejudicial to treat them as interior or social constructions.[1] Many ecocritics have concluded that science's methods of investigation are "the best means we have for understanding our world, and for thinking our way toward solutions to the problems of pollution, population, and despoliation."[2] Certainly, it is preposterous to think that the antiscientific bias of so much literary criticism could meaningfully engage with the actual phenomena of climate change. Nevertheless, a transhistorical, natural subject cannot explain how authors shape their material, why biomes pass in and out of literary fashion, or how human technology and pollution have shaped their meaning.

Since the late 1990s, another group of environmental critics has argued that literature is best read using established theoretical and historical methods. Such critical tools are designed to explore the role of society in creating reality, whether they originate in a form of pragmatism, Marxian cultural history, or postmodernism. Thus, Jonathan Levin has argued that there is an "always permeable boundary between science and culture," because scientific and intellectual practices are irreducibly socially embedded.[3] Similarly, Dana Phillips has defended both ecology's ability to convey the real world and critics' access to the "hyperreal."[4] Less controversial is Jonathan Bate's method, tracing historical shifts in the meaning of the key words *culture* and *environment* as they detach from each other and become oppositional terms. For Bate, literature and language are preoccupied with consciousness, not the nonhuman.[5] Levin's argument borrows from the philosophy of science, Phillips's argument is grounded in postmodernism, and Bate's methodology can be traced to Raymond Williams's Marxian historicism, but all of them redirect critical attention from scientific things to the cultural basis of environmental awareness. For these critics, textuality subsumes substance, and things are never really things in literature. Such a position is eminently respectable within wider critical circles, and it also provides an engaged mode to critique the assumptions that lead to environmental degradation. On the other hand, these approaches struggle to describe the way material and natural things, like climate, resist the interpretations humans might choose for them, even when they are found in literary texts.

It would seem, then, that there is a clear set of critical alternatives for reading climate change fiction. Either the novels should be read as more or less factual representations of the scientific phenomena of climate change, or they should be read as cultural texts that represent the collective imagination about global warming. If the first set of critics base their interpretation on a version of scientific realism, the second set of critics depend on social constructivism for interpretation, even if they concede science may do something else. Nevertheless, climate change novels show up serious problems with both scientific realism and postmodern critique.

In the first section, we read the notorious climate change novel *State of Fear,* by Michael Crichton. If ecocritics like Carroll and Love hold that scientific realism leads to a positive engagement with the environment, and Levin, Phillips, and Bate hold that social critique indicates the investments that perpetuate environmental destruction, *State of Fear* uses postmodern ideas and textual strategies to critique the political investments of environmentalists and scientific realism to argue climate change is a postmodern conspiracy. In the novel, scientific realism and postmodernism bolster each other, suggesting they are not the argumentative poles so many ecocritics have claimed. Worse, *State of Fear* indicates that both theoretical positions can be adapted to skepticism of climate change rather easily, suggesting they are not the critical trump cards that critics have hoped.

In the second section, we read a much more respectable defense of scientific realism, Ian McEwan's *Solar.* If science is our only hope for understanding the objective reality of global warming, perhaps a more sophisticated, literary novel could give insight into climate change. Through Michael Beard, a selfish, Nobel Prize–winning physicist, *Solar* suggests that the selfishness of human character, dictated by evolution, makes it extraordinarily unlikely that individual action or voluntary, collective movements will allow us to address climate change. At the same time, the novel holds out the hope that science will solve the crisis with new technology. This literary defense of scientific realism pointedly rejects ethical arguments about individual responsibility, denies the novel political agency, and satirizes the humanities' attempts to engage with climate change and science. In an important sense, *Solar* can only conceptualize fictional accuracy at the expense of meaningful engagement. Even more important, *Solar*'s defense of scientific realism, in which geniuses have great insights into nature, cannot come to grips with contemporary scientific practice, including climate science.

The aim of this chapter is not to discover a novel that perfectly represents contemporary science, but rather to describe the ways science and fiction interact in climate change novels more generally. The third section draws on the heterogeneous discipline of science studies to trace these interactions, making special use of Bruno Latour's synthesis of a number of areas of research. While science studies cannot provide a readymade foundation for a particular brand of literary criticism, it can bring a more sophisticated, detailed account of scientific production into dialogue with the fruits of literary production. As the field is articulated by Latour, science studies denies that the pure social explanations of postmodernism or the purely natural explanations of scientific realism can offer satisfying accounts of scientific practice. Instead, scientific knowledge emerges as things are circulated through laboratories, instruments, competing scientists, institutions, and the public. By returning to *State of Fear* and *Solar*, it becomes possible to see that climate change literature fundamentally depends on these circuits, even when a novel resists Latour's conclusions. Reading in this way also gives new meaning to climate change novels. Instead of fiction being read as attempts to seize the arbitrary meaning of climate change, or as literary representations of scientific representations, climate change novels are best understood as a force that interacts with climate change, remaking what we know about the climate and the novel at the same time.

State of Fear

Although Michael Crichton's *State of Fear* is neither high literature nor scientifically accurate, it may well be the most important climate change novel yet written. Driven by Crichton's reputation as the author of *Jurassic Park* and creator of the television show *ER*, over 1.5 million copies were printed in the United States alone, making it the most popular climate change novel to date.[6] The novel is unapologetically polemical, weaving the set pieces of a thriller with arguments among Evans, a young lawyer with environmental sympathies, Nicholas Drake, an environmental campaigner secretly funding an ecoterrorist organization, and John Kenner, an MIT professor and federal agent trying to prevent Drake's artificial disasters. Despite this controversy, the novel captured the imagination of US senator James M. Inhofe, an Oklahoma Republican who had previously declared global warming "the greatest hoax ever perpetrated on the American people." Inhofe made *State of Fear* required reading for the Committee on Environment and Public Works and then called Crichton to testify before it, to the scorn of the committee's Democratic members.[7] If it seems strange that Inhofe invoked a novel to support his arguments, the novel seemed to encourage a factual reading: Kenner's arguments are backed up with footnotes apparently proving anthropogenic global warming isn't happening.

Critics focused on the novel's footnotes, leading to mixed reviews. Some critics were dismayed to find their thriller slowed down by "facts" and found the arguments silly and "ill-digested," but most reviews declined to comment on the novel's factuality.[8] Scientific reviewers were less charitable. They interpreted the novel as an attack on scientific authority and counterattacked it as a factual argument. In a review in *Nature*, Myles Allen read the novel as an argument that scientists were collaborating with the environmental movement by bending and inventing facts. His counterattack focused on the footnotes and appendices, which were "clearly intended to give an impression of scientific authority," and found the novel's argument depended on cherry-picked data, straightforward scientific errors, and illogic. *State of Fear* undermined the legitimacy of scientific review and reduced climate change to "a matter of political taste," rather than a difference between good and bad science.[9] Prominent scientists weighed in to dispute the novel's account of their data.[10] Scientists were within their rights to dispute Crichton's misrepresentation, but they badly misread Crichton's investments toward science. In public speeches before the release of the novel, Crichton defended a realist account of science, which should be a search for objective facts, and he inveighed against postmodern relativism, which claimed science was "just another form of raw power." Even so, the debate around climate change, with its dependence on scientific consensus rather than verifiable data, suggested postmodernists might be right.[11] Crichton's simultaneous belief in scientific realism and skepticism about climate change made for a difficult argument: a critique of climatology would seem to undermine the scientific realism he would defend. Instead of writing a novel with a realist or postmodernist sense of science, Crichton constructed a thriller in which both sensibilities operate at the same time. As we will see, their coexistence suggests they are not the polar opposites contemporary criticism (and Crichton) assumed.

The plot of *State of Fear* stages an undecideable contest between scientific realism and postmodern relativism. On the one hand, Nicholas Drake is a reluctant political relativist who believes science and environmentalism are naturally allied, even though Crichton never permits him evidence or footnotes. Under Drake, the National Environmental Resource Fund (NERF) bankrolls a lawsuit by the island nation of Vanutu against the United States for causing rising sea levels, even though the action is a media stunt that will never reach court. Drake also creates a major climate change conference, while secretly planning artificial "natural" disasters by the Environmental Liberation Front (ELF) to galvanize public opinion.[12] NERF gains media attention with Hollywood spokesmen like Ted Bradley, who plays the president on TV, rather than scientific data. Science has its uses: NERF funds research into fields like glacier geology but pressures scientists to adopt findings that are consistent with climate change. For Drake, objective research is out of date, because environmentalists are in "a global war of information versus disinformation," fought in newspaper op-eds, television reports, scientific journals, Web sites, conferences, classrooms, and courtrooms. The enormous resources of huge, global corporations force science to be shaped by environmental aims, in order for the truth to emerge.[13] As a media-obsessed critic of capital, a relativist in the name of objectivity, Drake is the perfect postmodern villain.

Against Drake stands John Kenner, who holds a PhD from Caltech in civil engineering, a law degree from Harvard, and a chair in geoenvironmental engineering at MIT and *also* works for the "National Security Intelligence Agency" (NSIA), apparently hunting ecoterrorists through the "web."[14] Not only does his center examine risk to corporations, but he's also a world-class skier and mountaineer and has a Nepalese sidekick who agrees with everything he says. Kenner's unlikely affiliations nominate him as the representative of the Enlightenment's institutions, able to pursue truth in the laboratory and the courtroom, on behalf of the democratic state and private wealth. After a billionaire environmental patron suspiciously disappears and the fresh-faced young lawyer and environmentalist Peter Evans is made his executor, Kenner drags him around the globe, uncovering the truth about NERF's secret plot. This is stock-in-trade for the thriller genre, but *State of Fear* doubles the drive toward revelation through dialectic. On the long plane trips between exotic locations, Kenner asks Evans to explain why he believes in global warming and then systematically dismantles his responses by citing scientific studies. By foiling Drake's plot and converting Evans, Kenner defends the establishment's claims to produce truth and justice, even as he denies that universities, courts, and governments have a responsibility to confront climate change. This plot structure, pitching Drake the postmodern environmentalist against Kenner the scientific realist and establishmentarian, made it too easy for early readers to interpret the novel as antienvironmental propaganda. Nevertheless, scientific objectivity does not win the day. Kenner operates in an undeniably postmodern world, defined by simulacra and pastiche, controlled by hidden interests, and ruled by terror.

The novel's whole argument against climate change depends on a realist view of science but operates in a thoroughly postmodern world. Underlying the novel is the contradiction that science uses reason to represent external reality but that climate itself may be indeterminate. In arguments with environmentalists, Kenner repeatedly denies that what "lots of people think" has anything to do with science. Instead, science is a matter of dividing human opinions between fantasy and what can be verified in the objective real world (*State* 504). The trouble starts when characters begin to examine scientific data. Members of the Vanutu legal team show Peter temperature charts that seem to confirm there is no warming, but subsequent charts show that the data can be massaged to support almost any interpretation (447–49). The lawsuit itself captures this tension between objective and power-based truth. Initially seeming to establish climate change's real costs, it is shelved when the issues become intractably muddled. Kenner's scientific realism would seem to depend on an objective, representable climate, but the novel repeatedly notes ecologists have abandoned the idea that climates reach equilibrium, describing them instead as unstable, chaotic systems (481, 538, 578). Kenner uses this observation to dismantle environmentalist claims of Earth's permanent harmony and the International Panel on Climate Change's (IPCC's) warnings about future climate, but he doesn't seem to notice this instability is precisely what makes the dumping of greenhouse gas so dangerous. In short, the indeterminacy of climate undermines both objective science and the ideologies that would deploy it.

Climate science is just one example of *State of Fear*'s postmodernism. For Crichton, one of the most important features of the decline from objective facts into postmodern relativism is a dependence on simulations and models, which are neither human representation nor objective facts. Climatology, of course, depends heavily on global climate models (GCMs), which allow scientists to study the complex interactions among the ocean, land, atmosphere, flora, fauna, clouds, and human industry. GCMs are built from empirical data and experimentally determined processes, are run hundreds of times to study relative probabilities, and are matched against actual temperature data. Even so, George Morton proposes a stamp, "WARNING: COMPUTER SIMULATION—MAY BE ERRONEOUS AND UNVERIFIABLE. Like on cigarettes" (673). Apparently, the impurity causes cancer, but models also allow the police to uncover a staged car wreck and Kenner to sift enormous amounts of Internet traffic to find ecoterrorist agents. Kenner himself says computer models are "*de rigeur* for the modern organization," usefully altering "your version of reality" and even superseding "the data from the ground" (496). Here artificial simulacra produce knowledge, rather than being transparent, ineffectual representations of the real world.

There is a similar problem with *State of Fear*'s footnotes and bibliography. The ungainly academic apparatus seems to be an effort to stabilize the disembodied, immaterial, nonfactual novel. While fiction is (apparently) elusive, disembodied, and nonfactual, footnotes are pure forms of realist reference, directly indicating facts in the world. Kenner's use of footnotes makes clear he speaks the truth, while Drake isn't permitted citations. There are no references to the thousands of studies confirming climate change, which would be needed to form a balanced opinion. This one-sidedness produces a curious effect: citations often admit opponents, counterarguments, and authorities, but Kenner isn't able to locate a scientific foundation for climate doubt. Just as important, footnotes are used in intellectual communities where readers have the expertise to evaluate the data, but neither Crichton nor his readers could usefully participate in this evaluation. The result is that Crichton's footnotes read as evidence of bias, a pastiche of academic authority reminiscent of the postmodern novel. If models are stable when they shouldn't be, apparently stable academic references fail to point unambiguously to the real world.

Underlying the pastiche of references is a central anxiety about authority and reason. Apparently, *State of Fear* is a celebration of scientific reason: Kenner is an independent thinker, espouses surprising opinions, and argues using facts. However, the thriller's individualistic, iconoclastic hero is impossible without a status quo; his objectivity depends on the ignorance of climatology. Partly, Kenner is positioned against popular ignorance: Peter stumbles over the particulars of global warming, suggesting public belief is irrational (95–97). But more important, Kenner stands against the scientific establishment: a member of the Vanutu legal team claims that "the raw temperature data . . . is tainted by the very scientists who claim global warming is a worldwide crisis" (455). (If the lawyer thinks this is "the fox guarding the henhouse," it's unclear who else would create the data.) Some characters allege conscious conspiracy, while others cite psychological studies showing "confirmation bias" and that "expectations determine outcome" (456–57). Crichton is dismissive of science's relationship to consensus, decrying a "herd instict."[15] As McElroy and Schrag observe, "Scientific reputations are made *not* by reaching conclusions drawn by others earlier, but rather by challenging the status quo."[16] However, scientists tended to miss that, within the novel, Kenner is the perfect challenger to the status quo, a dispassionate hero using facts to uncover a social conspiracy. Representing the ideal agent of scientific realism seems to depend on the postmodern tropes of conspiracy and paranoia, suggesting scientific consensus cannot be wholly understood in either schema.

Although environmentalists have denied the novel's claims of environmental conspiracy, *State of Fear* exposes the contemporary contradiction between institutions as places for producing truth and as sites of corruption. In Crichton's narrative, universities discover facts about the world, the media brings truth to the public, government committees and agencies establish the truth for political action, courts seek legal truth, and wealth enables private citizens to pursue the truth. Characters are defined by their relations to these institutions, so Kenner is marked as a likely hero because of his accelerated path through graduate school, while ecoterrorists are dismissed as uneducated (283–84). At times, the novel defends these functions: a scientist refuses NERF's pressure to alter his results, the frivolous Vanutu lawsuit folds, the NSIA uncovers ecoterrorists' Internet activity, and George Morton's wealth allows him to unravel NERF's plot. Nevertheless, the novel indicates these are exceptions in a general state of institutional failure. Most scientists are corrupted by funding, the media reads press releases rather than investigating truth, governmental hearings are used to advance scientific careers, NERF simultaneously sues and receives grants from the Environmental Protection Agency, rich donors fly to NERF's lavish fundraisers in private jets, and Morton's wealth is subverted to fund the terrorist plot in the first place (111–12). Kenner, however, should be just as corrupt, given his affiliations. Scientific realism, postmodern relativism, and the novel itself have no resources for explaining the impure agency of these institutions.

Instead, *State of Fear* zealously exposes acts of mediation in an attempt to defend scientific realism. Realism depends on making the means of conveying truth transparent, obscuring form to focus on content. *State of Fear*, then, is obsessed with forms of mediation that stand in between people and things. The case for anthropogenic climate change is poisoned by its association with the media: James Hansen's 1988 testimony to a joint congressional hearing was "unquestionably manipulative," since it was scheduled to coincide with a heat wave (291). NERF seeks sensational coverage at the expense of the truth, trying to structure information so that normal floods, freezing storms, cyclones, and hurricanes confirm the message that climate change is the cause (372); Drake hardly believes in the real threats of extinction, diseases, and sea-level rise (351). The use of schoolchildren, politicians, actors, and a multicultural audience (not to mention engineered natural disasters) also indicates NERF's obsession with mediation over realism. The media is equally to blame: *Time, Newsweek,* the *Economist,* and *Paris-Match* all accept NERF's story for their covers without any independent verification (427–30). In the novel's postmodern preoccupation with the media, NERF's manipulation of the medium makes the message inevitably false. This is rather ironic, of course, for a mass-market paperback claiming to popularize facts.

Money is another kind of mediation, contradictorily arousing desire and suspicion. On the one hand, *State of Fear* celebrates wealth: the billionaire philanthropist George Morton is portrayed as a hero, his ability to fund research and thwart NERF only just as admirable as his mansion, Gulfstream jet, and collection of Ferraris. California's tech entrepreneurs are similarly lionized. As a corporate lawyer, Evans doesn't do poorly for himself, either, and his love interest drives a black Porsche convertible and comes from California aristocracy. On the other hand, money indicates corruption. Drake rants about "the tremendous amount of money" at the disposal of "disinformation groups funded by industry" that are "intent on destroying the environmental movement" (51, 356, 551), and initially Evans thinks the same thing. Apparently, they are paranoid, but money is also used to impugn environmentalists: Drake hides that he is paid a third of a million dollars a year (151). He also worries about bringing in the forty-two million dollars NERF needs every year (351). NERF spends almost 60 percent of its money on fundraising, and Kenner raises suspicions about how the rest is spent (216–17). Similarly, wealthy environmentalists appear hypocritical consumers for attending NERF's lavish fundraising ball, and their mansions, private jets, and hybrids come in for ridicule (150). In this way, *State of Fear* whets a hunger for capital even as it pushes the critique home.

Bureaucracy is the third casualty of *State of Fear's* attack on mediation. Predictably, the novel impugns environmental organizations as unnecessary impediments between science and environmental action. The US Environmental Protection Agency comes under attack for giving money in lawsuits and grants to the same environmental organizations. The United Nations Intergovernmental Panel on Climate Change is similarly unacceptable, "a huge group of bureaucrats, and scientists under the thumb of bureaucrats . . . a political organization, not a scientific one" (292). Through mediation, bureaucracy pollutes the purity of science, which should be set beyond human organizations (680). As a counterproposal to such bureaucracy, Morton sketches out a new kind of environmental organization in the final pages of the novel. Run as a business, with no bureaucracy and minimal administration, it will use a scientific, iterative approach to manage wilderness. It will also fund science anonymously, so bureaucracy doesn't influence findings (671–73). Morton's vision for an unmediated, objective environmental organization has a significant blind spot: external assessment of programs and a "new mechanism to fund research" are calls to greater bureaucracy. Despite its hostility to mediation, more mediation seems to be the only alternative.

In an expression of postmodernist critique, *State of Fear* unmasks democracy, courts, the media, and universities as irremediably wedded to terror. An eccentric, famous sociologist, Professor Hoffman, explains to Peter that the "PLM," or politico-legal-media complex, rules society with a "State of Fear." Invented fears keep politicians in control, lawyers litigating, and the media selling fear. Universities manufacture fears to increase social control (542–46). Like Y2K, killer bees, and nuclear winter, global warming is "really" an imagined threat to keep society in check. Following politicians on the Right, Professor Hoffman and *State of Fear* worry about religious terrorism and ecoterrorism. On the other hand, Hoffman's ideas have an uncanny resemblance to those of critics on the Left: one reviewer noted similarities to Michael Moore's *Bowling for Columbine,* but the sense of invented dread also owes much to Gramsci and Baudrillard.[17] Rather than assigning the novel a political position, it makes more sense to note its intimate dependence on terror: uncovering global warming as a terrorist tactic; thwarting ecoterrorists; and inventing new terrors, including an artificial tsunami, assault with a tiny octopus, storm control using ammonia-oxidizing bacteria, and live burial in an Antarctic crevasse. With form following content, *State of Fear* participates in the government of terror that it apparently critiques, its appeal based firmly on the thrill of fear.

At times, this terror is deployed against romantic environmentalism. Environmentalists, such as the actor Ted Bradley, locate evil in modernity. He believes that when capitalism depersonalizes humans, they collectively degrade the environment, while (traditional, evolutionary) village life nurtures human beings and protects nature. In response to this view, the novel's climax is designed to show violence actually originates in nature. Bradley, Kenner, Evans, and the love interests are captured by villagers on Pavutu, a Pacific island where ecoterrorists are planning to trigger a tsunami. Bradley is beaten with a rifle butt and kicked in the face. After they are tied up, Kenner resumes the argument:

> "What's your impression of village life so far, Ted?" Kenner said. "Still think it's the best way to live?"
> "This isn't village life. This is savagery."
> . . . "You just don't get it, do you?" Kenner said. "You think civilization is some horrible, polluting human invention that separates us from the state of nature. But civilization doesn't separate us from nature, Ted. Civilization *protects* us from nature. Because what you see right now, all around you, this *is* nature. . . . Some people *like* cruelty, Ted." (627)

In a moment of terror, Kenner tries to break Bradley's belief in a natural harmony between human beings and the environment. Immediately after, Bradley is dragged into a crowd of villagers who beat him with baseball bats and metal pipes; tie him to a stake; and cut flesh from his cheek, underarm, eyes, and genitals. Falling unconscious, he is literally consumed by the crowd. Thus begins the climactic fight sequence: Jennifer Haynes (a love interest) cuts the throat of a fourteen-year-old would-be rapist, Kenner fires on a charging crocodile, and Evans pushes an ecoterrorist into a cavitation machine, pulverizing his body. The good unleash violence onto the uncivilized, the ecoterrorists, and malign nature itself, becoming more sexually desirable in the process (424–27). Despite their disagreements, when the advocates and critics of modernity survey human beings, they find violence under all. Certainly Kenner and Drake disagree about its origins: Kenner locates violence in individuals, while Drake traces it to corporations. But Drake's prognostications are eerily confirmed: flash floods, electrical storms, and the collapse of Antarctic ice all happen, though they are caused by the conspiracy of ecoterrorists rather than automobile and petroleum corporations. The threat of Vanutu disappearing beneath the waves is realized as Pavutu is washed with an artificial tsunami. In either case, nature's horror is displaced onto human beings as a justification for escalating violence. For Drake, this takes the depersonalized forms of lawsuits and ecoterrorism, while Kenner kills Pacific islanders and ecoterrorists in hand-to-hand combat. In *State of Fear*, violence structures both modern scientific realism and postmodern environmentalism.

Above and beyond such violence, *State of Fear* suggests neither scientific realism nor postmodernism can provide a satisfactory engagement with nature. There is no obvious incompatibility between scientific realism and environmental management: *State of Fear* celebrates research-based conservation of specific habitats, which can be carried out by a heroic individual who recognizes the truth of "external" things.[18] The trouble is that climate change (like much of contemporary science) is incompatible with such heroic individualism. If Kenner declares it is "arrogant beyond belief" to think that humans can control the climate, he mistakes intention with impact: many, many people affect the climate without any control at all (670). No single scientist could meaningfully review research in the dozens of disciplines that impinge on climate change. Tackling climate change requires even greater collectives of scientists, diplomats, energy groups, markets, and households across the world. By ignoring collective human action, Crichton's scientific realism founders on climate change.

Drake's postmodern environmentalism also struggles to engage with climate change. Of course, Drake is a ridiculous parody of a postmodern environmentalist, but *State of Fear* gets at something important. Drake locates power in social organizations, like corporations, courts, bureaucratic agencies, media companies, and NERF itself; individual action doesn't figure. This leads to conspiracy talk, as we have seen, and it denies the role of individuals in creating change. Drake's postmodernism also makes it difficult for him to articulate nature's agency as anything other than a passive recipient of society's violence. At the NERF fundraising dinner, Drake paints a nearly hopeless picture of disappearing forests, polluted lakes and rivers, and unprecedented extinctions, with climate change driving crop failures, rising sea levels, and extreme weather (150–51). The result is a model of activism that struggles to articulate its own tremendous successes. Lacking a way to describe nature and human agency, postmodern environmentalism can only repeat its indictment of impersonal forces.

Clearly neither John Kenner nor Nicholas Drake, scientific realism nor postmodern environmentalism, offers a coherent resource for thinking about anthropogenic climate change. Of course, *State of Fear* designates Kenner as the hero, Drake as the villain, but their similarities destabilize each other beyond Crichton's intent. While Kenner lacks the basic categories that make climate science, greenhouse gas pollution, and climate change prevention possible, Drake struggles to encounter scientific accounts of a real environment. While Kenner strips away the collective political power of democracies, obscures the success of environmental litigation, and impugns the social function of the media, Drake sells a story of collective victimization and powerlessness, leaving no room for positive environmental action. Rather than relying on facts and rational argument, both Drake and Kenner stack the deck by arguing the other side is the result of a corrupt conspiracy of shadowy interests. Neither side knows what to do with the public, either. Drake makes terrifying claims that are hopelessly mediated, while Kenner's refusal of mediation eliminates any connection between science and society. In their worst moments, both Drake and Kenner accuse the other side of terrorism, an indictment borne out by the violence each brings to the discussion. And both parties evince an ignorance and horror of nature. Drake's and Kenner's shortcomings suggest that attempts to found criticism on a realist account of science or to supersede science with postmodern critique both fail to offer a satisfactory view of anthropogenic climate change.

Of equal importance, the novel suggests that both scientific realism and postmodernism are so dependent on each other that neither can offer a coherent foundation for environmental criticism. Mimesis and pastiche, authoritative argument and laughable parody, circulate freely together. Perhaps, though, Crichton's satire lacks teeth, because neither environmentalists nor many scientific realists (who would tend to believe in climate change) recognize themselves in its world. Despite its vast popularity, the novel is too easily dismissed as pulp fiction, climate denial masquerading as scientific argument. But the problems of *State of Fear* are endemic to climate change novels and to climate change discourse more generally. Novels struggle to describe what it means for climate change to be real. They also struggle to envision how human beings might respond to its challenges. In the most serious contemporary fiction, these shortcomings reveal the instability of both science and the literary in the face of climate change.

Solar

If *State of Fear* is likely to be the most popular climate change novel so far, Ian McEwan's *Solar* is likely to be the most lauded. McEwan is regularly called the UK's foremost living novelist, and critics often marvel that his serious, literary fiction attracts prizes, academic criticism, and millions of readers at the same time. The differences between the novels are immediately obvious: *State of Fear* is an unapologetically populist novel that earnestly encourages skepticism about global warming, while *Solar* is a literary comedy that takes anthropogenic climate change as a given. However, Crichton and McEwan share a commitment to scientific realism that is explicitly positioned against postmodern literary criticism. *Solar* is strongly informed by this commitment. As we will see, the novel's protagonist, Michael Beard, is built up from scientific accounts of evolutionary psychology. Instead of representing character as an immaterial subjectivity capable of self-transcendence, Beard is driven by evolutionary impulses to eat, reproduce, and dominate. The plot follows the necessary effects on Beard's body, society, and environment. This account of human character refuses to provide a vision for a sustainable Utopia; Beard's character suggests that calls to curb personal consumption and join in collective action are scientifically uninformed approaches to climate change. If many literary characters are modeled on a spiritual interiority, Beard is instead a variety of scientific allegory. For the solution to climate change, McEwan turns to science as the best hope for creating sufficient quantities of sustainable energy to continue to feed human economic development. Michael Beard is heavily parodied, but he bears a striking resemblance to Albert Einstein, suggesting that human ingeniousness, through science, is needed to overcome our evolutionary shortcomings. *Solar*'s account of genius is not without its problems: it rejects collective political action and the insights of the humanities, while science is left so ignorant of individual motives that fiction becomes essential once again.

In climate change novels, scientists typically appear as either Earth-saving heroes or minor characters that allow the author to dump masses of data on the reader. By contrast, *Solar*'s scientist, Michael Beard, is a gluttonous, lecherous, and narcissistically self-centered physicist and therefore a character study in his own right. Having won a Nobel Prize for work done in his twenties, he is now "a man of narrowed mental condition" and allergic to "the vale of swot." Despite his laziness, the prize lets him fly business-class between well-paid speaking engagements and institutional sinecures, including a position as the head of a new renewable energy research center. At "The Centre," Beard meets a young scientist, Tom Aldous, who has made revolutionary breakthroughs in solar technology, potentially eliminating the need for oil and coal. After Aldous is killed in a bizarre accident at Beard's house, Beard steals Aldous's ideas and tries to become a solar energy magnate. Throughout the novel, science remains the least of Beard's concerns: the novel's comic force comes from Beard's self-centered preoccupation with his next meal and the repercussions of his last, foggily fighting the effects of drinks he didn't mean to take, pursuing women and mitigating the effects of his affairs, keeping sinecures and securing patents, and attracting undue credit to consolidate his reputation, even as the fate of the world apparently hangs in the balance. And this is much the point of the novel: Beard's immediate desires continually displace action that would prevent climate change.

McEwan has been an outspoken proponent of evolutionary biology, particularly as it has been articulated by celebrity scientists like Steven Pinker, E. O. Wilson, and Richard Dawkins. For McEwan, evolutionary biology, genetics, and neuroscience explain humans far more effectively than traditional humanities, if "a little less than the exponents of the 'just so' stories of evolutionary psychology would want."[19] *Solar* continually thwarts the reader's desire for rich, private subjectivity by exposing the reciprocal effects of genes and culture on character.[20] Despite his genius intellect, Michael Beard is relentlessly conditioned by the experience of inhabiting an evolved body. He sweats and fumbles, he seeks sex and revenge against his better judgment, he craves salt and grease, and he succumbs to engineered tastes with a chemical inevitability. In all these cases, Beard is hardwired by evolution to find these impulses irresistible, despite rational knowledge of the consequences. And *Solar* relentlessly catalogs the material effects of these evolutionary urges, as he vomits, urinates, gets drunk, and is "draped" in "human blubber."[21] Beard's doctor, like the narrator, describes the medical results of his obesity with a "disengaged, insulting frankness" (*Solar*, 239). Socially, Beard's relationships are overdetermined by an evolutionary drive to compete and dominate against members of the same species.[22] Beard feigns sex with his fifth wife to hurt her, plagiarizes his research assistant's work to efface his memory, frames another love competitor for murder, betrays his research center by setting up competing companies, switches political persuasion as a matter of exigency, and refuses to help the man he framed even when it leads to the destruction of all his efforts to ameliorate climate change. This willful, self-sabotaging vindictiveness is of a piece with Beard's gluttony and greed, the result of evolutionary instincts operating just beyond his awareness. Although Beard is monstrous, the narrator would seem to agree that "human imperfection [is] a large subject," suggesting it is improbable that humans will suddenly engage in selfless collective action to ameliorate climate change.

The evolutionary past of humans has significant environmental implications. At a local level, Beard is a slob, letting his apartment break down. From the view of an airplane circling London, Beard wonders, "How could we ever begin to restrain ourselves? We appeared, at this height, like a spreading lichen, a ravaging bloom of algae, a mould enveloping a soft fruit—we were such a wild success. Up there with the spores!" (111). There is a complex irony here: human slovenliness is not so much a sign of decline, but instead the result of extraordinary evolutionary success. Beard's wealth and social standing allow unrestrained environmental devastation, as he jets around the globe to call for carbon reduction. Further human advancement only speeds the destruction of humanity's environmental preconditions.

The tensions between Beard's personal failings and Western society are brought to a peak in the question of whether *Solar* is an allegory. Almost all reviewers recognized it as such, and characters' names raise the expectation of abstract qualities. Nevertheless, *Solar* interrogates allegory's promise to expose the ideas underpinning human reality. Certainly, the portrayal of Beard is less schematic than the giant Monopoly set for the Tate Modern, which is supposed to be "an indictment . . . of a money-obsessed culture"

(51). Nor is he merely an archetypal example from "the collective bloody unconscious" (158).[23] The novel also resists the apocalyptic note that so often gives allegory its urgency: Beard compellingly mocks the "plague-of-boils and deluge-of-frogs" of environmental warnings (15–16). Not even Beard is so vain as to believe he is a Last Man or an everyman. Instead, Beard is a specific case that is productively representative of the wealthy West at this moment in history. *Solar* is undergirded by a scientific account of the human mind, rather than the ideal moral order of classic allegory.[24] The novel's humor indicates our ability to identify with Beard, suggesting a common human inheritance that supersedes individual subjectivity.[25] If Beard is uncomfortably familiar, even in his excess, this indicates a vast obstacle to addressing climate change.

In an allusion to Milton, the differences between an ideal, knowable order and a scientific conception of knowledge are made pointed. As an undergraduate, Beard memorizes several lines of *Paradise Lost* to seduce a literature student:

> . . . thou Celestial light
> Shine inward, and the mind through all her powers
> Irradiate, there plant eyes, all mist from thence
> Purge and disperse, that I may see and tell
> Of things invisible to mortal sight. (201)

For Milton, poetry is objective knowledge received from the divine, spiritual light, in contrast to subjective, "blind" experience. For young Beard, on the other hand, observational reasoning about the material world requires no Celestial light; he will soon discover the theoretical foundations for replicating photosynthesis by seeking vegetative levels of intelligence. Beard's contempt for Milton's moral insight is made pointed when he deploys the poet's language of Enlightenment as a means to sexual conquest. In the world of *Solar*, subjective experience is a weak and untrustworthy guide to human truth. Attempts to regenerate human morality, even on pain of apocalypse, are doomed to fail; genes don't grant humans the foresight to prevent extinction. Beard is the ideal exponent of this perspective, wholly lacking as he is in self-control or moral vision. Instead, *Solar* pins its hopes on a realist model of science, with culture and human nature left largely intact.

Early reviews of the novel disagreed about whether *Solar* gave any hope of overcoming human evolutionary drives. The question remained open because *Solar*'s reviewers did not follow up McEwan's high acknowledgment: "Above all, I owe a debt to Walter Isaacson's fine biography *Einstein*." Michael Beard bears surprising similarities to Isaacson's respectful portrait of the world's most famous physicist. During their studies, both men seek relief from physics in a bohemian lifestyle. Both men are first married to "exotic, intellectual, and complex" women and then bourgeois, matronly women who can cook.[26] After youthful bursts of genius, both men seek sinecures and witness a decline in their creative abilities, before pushing for massive research programs later in their careers. These similarities suggest a whole line of interpretation for the novel. Isaacson argues that Einstein's personal failings were the direct result of the character traits that made him great. Einstein refused to recognize "merely personal" commitments to family, friends, extramarital lovers, home, and country, not because he was a monster, but rather because of his moral insistence on freedom and individualism.[27] Similarly, Beard's solipsism produces both extraordinary selfishness and the scientific capacity to develop new forms of sustainable energy. Thus, *Solar* suggests that environmentalist efforts to curb human appetites may also disable the creativity needed to address humanity's deepest problems.

The tension between Beard's scientific genius and personal selfishness makes an arresting portrait, but it also disguises a deep investment in scientific realism. Among all the meteorologists, climatologists, biologists, and zoologists in climate change novels, *Solar* is nearly unique in featuring a physicist. By basing Beard on Einstein, the novel builds a case for realist science on a paradigm that is almost a century out of date. In a wine-sodden conversation with a Spanish ice sculptor, Beard quotes Isaacson's Einstein, proclaiming, "There was out there a 'real factual situation'" (65). The "real factual situation" is the lynchpin of the myth of scientist-as-genius, promoted in Isaacson's rather old-fashioned biography. Einstein's great work occurs alone in the study; he shuns material experimentation, preferring "thought experiments." Genius, here, is the almost magical ability to create a mental image that corresponds with unobserved, material reality "out there." For Beard, mathematics acts like an extraordinary form of painting; the Dirac equations are "a thing of pure beauty," predicting the spin of electrons (41), as a portrait can capture the previously unobserved meaning of a face or landscape. Beard understands science as a representational activity, where pure mentality forms theories that are confirmed in the preexisting world, even though this demands an anachronistic rejection of quantum mechanics. Indeed, *Solar* repeatedly invokes even older examples of genius: Aldous's technical drawings are quite like Leonardo's sketches (30), while Beard is repeatedly, if comically, compared to Newton (284–89). Such genius is emphatically single, vigorous, and immaterial. It might be just possible that a theoretical physicist could still express his vocation in this way, but climate modelers, geneticists, and conservationists invariably rely on teams of researchers, a wider scientific community, extensive equipment, and physical data collection. By polarizing science into the genius mind and the real, natural world "out there," *Solar*'s scientific realism excludes the material practices of empirical research.

Solar must take extraordinary steps to separate and purify mental genius from reality "out there." In the first half of the novel, Beard's sustainable energy research center is productive precisely to the extent that it ignores thousands of proposals from self-taught inventors that violate basic laws of physics (16–19). The message is clear: innovation originates with physicists from elite universities, not engineers and tinkerers from the public. Also lacking genius, Beard oversees a project for an urban wind turbine that cannot be rescued with any quantity of research specialists. The Centre's farcical attempt to make the idea good is intended as a cautionary tale against invention through collaboration and experimentation. By contrast, Aldous's ideas for "nano-solar" are the work of pure, private genius. Beard tries to justify his plagiarism with all the "hard work" he does on the project: the experimental, legal, corporate, and financial aspects of making things in the world (186). Ultimately, the Centre's lawyers and Beard's own lies catch up with him, confirming a "real factual situation" out there at the level of the plot. In *Solar*, genius is all; "construction" is an illusion.

Perhaps the main purpose of the novel's insistence on scientific realism is to avoid the quagmire of climate skepticism. *Solar* refuses to represent a character that disbelieves in climate change and only once allows them to form an audience, when Beard speaks to a group of investors from "the solid institutions of the City" (London's financial center), which "nurtured a vigorous culture of denial" (150). Beard's response is to narrate a cumulative history of atmospheric science, arguing anthropogenic climate change is a "scientific fact": "The science is relatively simple, one-sided and beyond doubt. Ladies and gentlemen, the question has been discussed and investigated for a hundred and fifty years, for as long as Darwin's *Origin of Species* has been in print, and is as incontestable as the basics of natural selection" (152). Despite Beard's moral unreliability, the narrator gives no reason to disagree with the "plain fact." Rather, Beard's moral shortcomings are caused by a progressive narrative of industrial revolution and globalization, "lifting hundreds of millions of us out of the mental prison of rural subsistence." Beard argues modernity has two causes: the inventiveness of "very clever monkeys" and "cheap, accessible energy" (148). Thus, Beard's narrative of progress reproduces the basic structure of scientific realism, separating human genius and the preexisting facts of the material world. Beard's opponents are subject to a pincer attack: the material world disowns them even as society, in the voice of "the scientists," calls them ignorant. Extraordinarily, *Solar* pulverizes climate deniers, despite the considerable political, financial, and media power they have wielded in the real world.

Solar's proposals are also determined by scientific realism, falling neatly between the social and the material, "very clever monkeys" and "cheap, accessible energy." Beard's insatiable appetite lends him eloquence when he advocates renewable energy as a means to slow down greenhouse gas production, sustain civilization, and bring millions out of poverty. "Turning down the thermostat and buying a smaller car . . . merely delays the catastrophe by a year or two"; a new energy revolution is needed, which will make many people rich (149). Beard also hopes to lead the way on carbon capture technologies, particularly using iron filings to stimulate plankton growth, which will then pull carbon dioxide out of the atmosphere (187). Underlying these solutions is a belief that human nature is less changeable than the material, natural world, and an evaluation that holds that "for humanity en masse, greed trumps virtue" (149). On the other hand, *Solar* suggests the need for purely social solutions. The most noteworthy episode occurs in the ship's bootroom on the Arctic expedition. Each passenger starts with an organized cubby, but a series of small errors and insignificant acts of theft quickly add up to missing, broken, and misallocated equipment: "By midweek, it was no longer possible for more than two thirds of the company to be outside at the same time. To go out was to steal" (78). As many reviewers noted, the bootroom is an obvious parable for the West's consumer society, and in interviews, McEwan has called for better "bootroom rules," apparently a market economy with government regulation to ensure the equitable, efficient distribution of goods.[28] Thus, *Solar* suggests scientific realism could allow humans to manage both the material world and society, each in their separate realms, without the need for utopian vision.

If *Solar* displays a qualified hope that science will discover objective solutions to climate change, it is scathing of the humanities and social sciences. McEwan himself has often bemoaned the direction of humanities research, publicly expressing a wish he had pursued science at university. Beard's experience as a student in the 1960s convinces him that English and history require neither intelligence nor hard work, while social theory and feminism merely lead to dropping out. As an adult, Beard is thrown together with artists on a polar voyage to witness climate change. He is shocked into "silent wonder" at their belief that aesthetics can meaningfully address climate change, effectively silencing the reader's hunger for artistic unification in the Anthropocene (77). Science studies comes in for even more scathing criticism, when a feminist scholar picks a fight with Beard to advance her own career. Supposedly, Nancy Temple's scholarship endorses postmodern textuality over representation, blank slate arguments over evolutionary psychology, and social constructivism over scientific fact (135). Temple describes her work as an offshoot of social anthropology, following geneticists working in a laboratory to show that genes are socially constructed with "entexting tools," scientists' hypotheses, and a small group of other geneticists, instead of being an objective entity (131). Temple's account of her research is ridiculous: in proving the nonexistence of scientific things and the nonobjectivity of science, social texts become a very spectral sort of reality. It seems scientific realism is the only game in town.

Even as *Solar* seems to valorize science at the expense of art, the narrow definition of science serves to justify fiction as an essential means of understanding the world. Although Beard is both a philistine and a chronic self-justifier, his public pronouncements about climate change indicate the need for greater self consciousness: "It is not in other people, or in the system, or in the nature of things that the problem lies, but in ourselves, our own follies and unexamined assumptions" (155). In this account, climate science can provide a high level of certainty about the dangers of burning fossil fuels, and evolutionary psychology can indicate the behavioral problems that make climate change hard to address, yet neither can provide the kind of self-reflection enabled by narrative.[29] McEwan's scientific realism grants absolute truth to scientific claims but makes them too general, too inhuman to apply to human experience. The novel's *literary* realism allows it to trace the subtleties of a mind preoccupied with the quantum principles of photosynthesis and the self-satisfaction in a packet of crisps. The novel also traces the complex effects of six-figure salaries, stipends, and business-class travel; relationships with civil servants, postdocs, and builders; romantic attachments to shop owners, scientists, and waitresses. Scientific realism is too abstract to deal with such human minutiae, necessitating the novel. In short, science holds reality, while art stands above it. For all its differences with *State of Fear*, *Solar* finally agrees that scientific fact must defer to the omniscient discourse of the novel.

Literary Constructions and Scientific Networks

It would seem that neither postmodern social constructivism nor scientific realism can provide a satisfactory account of climate change. In *State of Fear*, postmodernism and objective science are supposed to be intellectual alternatives, but they depend on each other to a surprising extent. Scientific reference gives way to postmodern pastiche, and conspiracy theories replace reasoned argument or critique. While scientific realism would make the means of representation transparent, and postmodernism would show that form determines content, *State of Fear* displays its paranoia about mediation, disabling any positive proposal. Most damningly, neither postmodernism nor scientific realism seems to be capable of delivering the "objective" truth that climate change is a real threat, and both depend on terrorism. *Solar* is similarly suspicious of postmodernism and celebratory of science. McEwan's evolutionary allegory of Michael Beard may be compelling, but it also disables ethical injunctions and collective approaches to climate change. Rather disturbingly, the novel dispatches climate skeptics and the humanities without so much as a glance. McEwan's proposed solution, technological advancement and better "bootroom rules," is fraught within the novel. Outside of it, McEwan's scientific realism leaves little room for hope.

Postmodernism and scientific realism also aren't very helpful for thinking about what climate change does in literature. Unlike postmodern metafiction, climate change novels don't make much sense as a series of power interests. In *State of Fear*, Kenner's political position becomes entirely mixed up, and the novel winds up advocating more environmental action while criticizing the establishment's interests. *Solar* is even less interested in political power, alternately parodying and celebrating Beard's individualism as the source and potential remedy to climate change. At the same time, both novels are far more complicated than simple repetitions of scientific representation. Climate change draws innovative, unprecedented literary performances. The thriller's tense admiration of science breaks down in *State of Fear*'s case for climate conspiracy, yielding a literary ambiguity uncommon for the genre. In *Solar,* the basic unit of realist fiction, the three-dimensional character, breaks under the strain of understanding climate change. Both novels actively, pointedly seek a relationship with scientific reality and become deeply implicated in science's methods of constructing truth. Engaging with climate change leads the novel to unprecedented literary performances, but tracing these innovations requires a different set of tools.

Although we have followed the argument between postmodernism and scientific realism through environmental critics, a low thriller, and an acclaimed "serious" novel, the terms of the debate have become somewhat outdated. Crichton's fear of social constructivism, actively advocated by Nancy Temple in *Solar,* is the stuff of a particular moment in the 1990s. Popularly referred to as the "science wars," the controversy was sparked when the physics professor Alan Sokal published an article in *Social Text* that was complementary to postmodernism and epistemological relativism but filled with basic errors of science. The so-called Sokal hoax provoked several years' tiresome debate between ill-informed humanities scholars and scientific realists. In relatively recent interviews, McEwan has come out very much on the "side" of scientists, inveighing against "social constructivism."[30] To be sure, many academic critics committed to the idea "that science was just one more belief system, no more or less truthful than religion or astrology," a characterization Beard thinks "must be a slur against his colleagues on the arts side" until he meets Temple (132). *State of Fear* is preoccupied with just the same anxiety, that "postmoderns" might be onto something in their denial of scientific truth. Many literary critics invoked science studies to prove that science itself was socially constructed, justifying textual scholarship as the key to all such discourse. However, most science studies scholars tired of the so-called science wars quite quickly: literary critics had badly misunderstood the field, which was heterogeneous in both method and aim, was far more interested in research than merely attacking science, and had long ago moved beyond the ridiculous social reductivism for which it was praised.

In *Solar*, Nancy Temple's description of "her" field confuses the different approaches of a heterogeneous discipline. Beginning in the 1980s, the subfield of the sociology of scientific knowledge (SSK) challenged the scientific realism that had dominated previous histories of science, which tended to paint a portrait of science "[advancing] steadily in the direction of greater accumulations of factual knowledge," explaining "good" science as "the revelation of a natural order that is pre-given and independent of human action" and "bad" science in terms of errors from society and material conditions.[31] Instead, figures in SSK argued both successful and unsuccessful science should be explained in the same terms, a "pragmatic or methodological deployment of relativism."[32] Such relativism was only mistakenly confused with postmodernism, the generalized relativism that "all claims to knowledge are to be judged equally valid" and that science can be reduced to a "social or linguistic level . . . with no relation to material reality."[33] Moreover, the portrait of Nancy Temple confuses sociological approaches to science with the ethnographic origins of "actor network theory," suggesting confusion about a discipline with diverse and mutually exclusive methods. Like Temple, scholars such as Bruno Latour and Michel Callon also had a background in anthropology, which led them to follow scientists into the laboratory, investigating their day-to-day practices for constructing scientific knowledge. Their findings led them to break with the sociological accounts of SSK, emphasizing the materiality of laboratory technology, the skills of scientists, data and scientific results, and the "things" being studied. Although Temple argues a gene could not be said to exist apart from technology and groups of scientists (*Solar*, 131), "actor network theory" emphasize that both humans and scientific things are irreducibly important elements in creating knowledge.

Unlike Temple, Latour draws on a wide body of science studies research to argue that technological instruments, measures and standards, laboratories and fields, data and results are unexplainable simultaneously social and natural artifacts. Postmodern or social explanations cannot describe the resistances scientific things make to the will of scientists and the assumptions of society, while a naturalistic, representational model of science cannot explain the human labor that helps construct these entities.[34]

Turning the sources of explanation on their heads, Latour argues both society and nature emerge from a common source, in scientific practice. If Temple thinks the gene doesn't exist, Latour argues scientific practice allows a gene to express its agency against scientists and the experimental conditions, even as the scientists become the representatives of the gene. Facts are fabricated to be independent of scientists; they are both objective and made to convince.

Precisely because science creates new networks of humans and non-humans, literary theories that preemptively try to fix them into known constellations are doomed to fail. Since the turn of the millennium, Latour's account of science has strongly influenced literary critics, providing the means to describe emergent relationships between real scientific, natural, and cultural artefacts.[35] In terms of ecocriticism, early ecocritics often deployed an opposition between nature and society, privileging texts and methods that gave access to pure nature. Other approaches to environmental literature, like primitivist nature appreciation, postmodern theory, and critiques of nature as socially constructed, continue to purify nature and society as separate entities.[36] By contrast, Latour suggests that nature and society are ontologically similar, in that neither is of our fabrication, and both emerge as the consequence of scientific practice.[37] Following Bruce Clarke, many ecocritics have seen actor network theory as a means to avoid scientism, "the appropriation of science within a non-scientific context," while acknowledging the field's dependence on (apparently natural) things that emerge from science.[38] Environmental critics have invoked Latour to examine human modification of animals' genes and the atmosphere, to escape the binary opposition between scientific realism and antiscientific reaction; to construct a sustainable vision of place; to critique representational demands for proof in climate science; and to explore the simultaneously social and natural, political and scientific dimensions of climate change.[39] Anthropogenic climate change is evidently a hybrid of the sort described by Latour: naturally produced, it is an effect of nature operating beyond human understanding or control; socially produced, it is the result of human actions.

Interestingly, Latour invokes global warming as a foundational example of the interpenetration of nature and society, arguing that anthropogenic climate change demonstrates the impossibility of dominating nature or society separately.[40] The specific implications of global warming deserve further consideration. Certainly, the warming effect of greenhouse gases is natural, long preceding human beings and making life on Earth possible. At the same time, it is distinctly not natural, as human mining and combustion of fossil fuels creates a new source of greenhouse gases. At the same time, the sheer scale of this process—involving industrialization, mass transport, global mining efforts, and so on—far exceeds individual agency. After the discovery of anthropogenic climate change, nature and society emerge afresh: society is blamed and then invoked as the space for positive action, and nature is cited as the preexisting state and ultimate goal. However, both constructions emerge from the fact of anthropogenic climate change. Actor network theory is not about providing a theoretical account of the single source, but rather provides a means to trace the extraordinary number of actors that together create what is commonly referred to as climate change. This account begins to suggest the real importance of climate change fiction: nature and humans, science and fiction emerge anew from the phenomena of global warming.

Despite such research, questions about the relationship between Latour's version of science studies and literary texts have remained all but unexamined. If facts are both real and fabricated, what is the status of scientific truth in a literary text, itself fiction? How do scientific things come into the novel, and how does truth come out? Underlying these questions is a problem with mediation. As we have seen, literary critics influenced by scientific realism have argued nature could be brought directly into literary texts, unmediated, while critics influenced by poststructuralism have argued there is no essential relationship between text and world; literary texts do not mediate, but operate according to their own rules. Science studies suggests a very different set of relationship to mediation, rejecting the language of representation and mimesis, as well as pure textuality. Scientific practice actively constructs a relationship between scientific data and studied things that is sufficient to force the reader's acceptance, while maintaining productive differences between them. Local temperature records, transcribed into an electronic database, are unlike the human experience of weather, but a painstaking process of transcription and their ability to be shared with other scientists make them eminently useful in forming global climate models. Tracing mediation, in this sense of the constructed, artificial relationships between text and world, is a way of reading that can account for the complex relationships among things, authors, formal conventions, and innovation.

Even so, these networked relationships upset the poles of mimesis and discourse that are typically used to understand literary texts. Instead of depending on an opposition between text and world, science studies has come to some consensus that scientific meaning is produced by circulation. Synthesizing a large body of science studies research, Latour has offered a model that traces the processes of constructing scientific knowledge. The model is comprised of five circuits: one central circuit and four loops that move through the center and also overlap with each other. The central circuit, "links and knots," is what has traditionally been called pure science. The difference between Latour's model and a realist approach, however, is that Latour argues that the other four circuits also shape the center, which binds them together. If any of the circuits were severed, the science would wither and die off (*Pandora's,* 106–7). For a literary critic, Latour's model may be irritatingly schematic; certainly its details may seem cumbersome. Even so, it provides an extraordinarily useful way to understand both the ways literature brings science into itself and, separately, the tensions between science and literature as ways of knowing the world.

The first loop of Latour's model, "mobilization of the world," encompasses the scientific instruments and tools that load nonhumans into discourse and are also tested themselves (*Pandora's,* 99–100). Alongside scientific facts, scientific tools themselves are also tested. Ice cores, foreign weather stations, and remote carbon dioxide detectors have been mobilized to trace the global aspect of climate. Similarly, global climate models, average temperatures, maps, grid resolution, and species predictors have all been themselves debated, compared, and deployed to construct "facts" about global warming.

In the second loop, "autonomization," scientific fact is directly related to the processes of replicating findings and developing certainty among scientific colleagues. Many studies have found that this process is both social, insofar as it involves negotiation between scientists, and material, since data forms the basis of these negotiations, driving the emergence of new social groups of consensus. Autonomization has also been central to climate change discourse: arguments and surveys debating scientific agreement on climate change have been used by climate skeptics (both the *Times* and the

Bush administration described climate change as a controversy), but recent surveys proclaiming 97 percent agreement among climatologists have also been deployed.[41]

The model's third loop traces science's alliances with nonscientific entities. Science is shaped by governments, universities, funding agencies, private corporations, entrepreneurial laboratories, and political movements. As with the other circuits, the influences move in both directions: alliances may provide the capital, personnel, or prestige to shape research, but science also frequently creates new social groups. Of course, "alliances" have also been central to climate change science: the United Nations Intergovernmental Panel on Climate Change, low-lying coastal countries, American and European political parties, environmental NGOs, oil and energy corporations, industry lobbies, and others have contributed materially to the construction of climate change. At the same time, climate change itself is responsible for unprecedented social arrangements (e.g., the IPCC, climate protestors), calls new political groups into existence, and forges unprecedented political alliances. As we will see in subsequent chapters, literature can help to trace and even to create these alliances.

Finally, Latour draws attention to the role of public representation in scientific knowledge. Much science studies research describes how scientific fact and scientific practice have been fundamentally shaped by class, gender, status, and wider social codes. Another major subfield investigates the public understanding of science. Of course, media accounts of climate change, in newspapers, blogs, television reports, and documentaries, have become standard fare for the public. But at the same time, public uncertainty and confusion around climate change has driven further research. Indeed, more certain and precise climatic predictions—better science— have been crafted in the name of further involving the public, even as public uncertainty continues to be a matter of concern for climatologists.

Rather surprisingly, climate change fiction doesn't fit into any one of Latour's circuits of exchange. The most obvious place to situate it would be in "public knowledge"—it is not difficult to imagine a public understanding of science analysis of the literary phenomenon. However, only the most tendentious reading could trace the influence from climate science to fiction. The most cursory perusal of climate change fiction would reveal that it is only problematically interested in facts: scientific knowledge is discarded, ignored, exaggerated, reimagined, and counterinterpreted, for narrative, imaginative, and political reasons. If at times the "links and knots" of science dictate fictional content, just as often novels seem to be able to bypass it completely. The reader's reflex to assess the scientific truth of these narratives is quickly abandoned: not only does climate change fiction thwart attempts to measure its scientific adherence, but different works break with science in very different ways. Although it sounds good in the making, there can be no simple league table of novels' adherence to scientific fact, nor could science studies use novels to trace a linear progression of climate change knowledge into the public. This public encounter between novelists and scientists also begs the question of how (very different) novelists and readers might constitute such a public. If novels don't represent the public, tracing influence back onto science is equally problematic. Some scholarship has shown popular science fiction influenced the direction of astronomy, physics, and aeronautics, but there is no evidence that even the most important novels, like *State of Fear* or *Solar,* are likely to make any such impact on scientific research.

Even so, it would be a grave error to think global warming novels are imaginative products unconcerned with science. Indeed, climate change fiction is intimately bound to the circuits traced by Latour. Instead of being confined to a single loop, fiction seems to trace, or even fabricate, the path of scientific knowledge through the entire model. Some climate change novels explore more of these interconnections than others. Kim Stanley Robinson's "Science in the Capital" trilogy, for example, assembles a complex network of entities to suggest how humanity might respond to global warming. Biologists and mathematicians carry out basic research into lichens that could draw down carbon dioxide; zoologists try to preserve endangered species set loose in Washington, DC, parks; an evolutionary psychologist explores how basic human impulses determine social behavior. The drama of these endeavors relies on the actual, instrumental processes of interacting with single-cell organisms, equations, and the hand ax. Complex alliances of scientists, from universities, federal agencies, and private labs, emerge to carry out specific research, approve grants, and confirm results.[42] The novel's network grows even more complex when several of the protagonists, working at the US National Science Foundation, spearhead efforts to restart the stalled Gulf Stream; field a hypothetical candidate for science in a presidential election; covertly support an actual candidate; and interact with research labs, insurance multinationals, the United Nations, and rival governmental agencies. But the novel also explores what science and technology means for the general public, from a Buddhist communal home to a family with a stay-at-home father, from neighborhoods that coalesce to dig each other out of a snow storm to "feral" communities that cooperate to throw parties and find free food, from a middle-class man convinced to live in a tree by evolutionary biology to homeless people who choose to wear artificial fibers when wool would keep them warm. As much as the novel is a utopian vision of how society might respond to climate change, it is also a realist novel that uses climate change to explore the complex network of people, institutions, and things that are being reformed under its pressure.

The "Science in the Capital" trilogy might be an exemplary means of demonstrating Latour's arguments about scientific networks. Certainly, the novel offers a thorough investigation into the relationship among climate change, science, and politics (for a more complete discussion of this, see chapter 3). The argument here, however, is not that climate change novels should be ranked according to their adherence to science studies, but rather that all climate change novels construct these networks, even when their rhetorical efforts are directed at obfuscating this. Strikingly, this seems to be the case regardless of the quality or seriousness of the novel. It is true of thrillers, science fiction, teen novels, and realist novels, whether humorous or serious. It is true of novels like *Solar*, which refuse to question the truth of anthropogenic climate change, and it is true of novels like *State of Fear*, which express extreme skepticism. Even so, the ways that climate change fiction follows these circuits are highly individual and cannot be reduced to a theoretical schema. On the surface, neither *State of Fear* nor *Solar* should be amenable to the sort of reading suggested by Latour's model of science studies research. As we have seen, both are polemically invested in a realist view of science, excluding the "context" that science studies argues circulates through the heart of science. This scientific realism also leads to a repudiation of both "theory" and social constructivism: nature, not social forces, is responsible for facts. Nevertheless, their investment in science "itself" seems to force inclusion of the instruments, colleagues, alliances, and publics that circulate through science. The novels' contentions are overrun by the literary possibilities of constructing science, fabricating fiction.

The novels' internal tensions can be seen in their approach to constructivism. *State of Fear* offers a paranoid preoccupation that well-funded environmental interest groups and self-interested scientists are manufacturing climate change. Even so, scientific realism leads Kenner to argue that non-human things can't lie. Facts are facts, and so the novel also invokes studies that apparently cast doubt on anthropogenic climate change. When Evans suggests these studies might be funded by industry, Kenner attacks him for impugning the integrity of legitimate scientists with slimy characterizations (232). Context is irrelevant! Read separately, the bad science is a warning about postmodernism, and the good science is a prescription for pure knowledge. Put together, though, the novel suggests that nonhuman things speak honestly precisely because of human investments. *Solar* evinces a similar paradox. McEwan's investments in science, materialism, and literary realism enable him to engage with climate change but also compel a portrait of scientific processes. As we have seen, Beard's genius is taken very seriously, while all that would undercut it is satirized. Even so, *Solar's* satire traces the culture of scientific institutions, providing the megaphone for the lone genius behind the curtain.

State of Fear would suggest scientific knowledge is the product of Kenner's pure rationality, but the novel is shaped, to an extraordinary extent, by scientific mobilizations of the world. Temperature charts of weather stations, numerical data giving geographic locations according to the Universal Transverse Mercator grid, and the footnotes to scientific papers mobilize locations. When Kenner and Evans jet to exotic locations chasing baddies, they follow the same paths as field scientists, to Antarctica, Greenland, and a small Pacific island.[43] The novel's violence, as well, is determined by instrumental technology. The ecoterrorists try to kill the heroes with a chamber to study lightning, a wave generator, a mining cavitation machine, and a rare specimen of tiny octopus, deploying the mobilizations of meteorology, oceanography, geology, and biology. The good guys fight back with applied technology, notably the Taser and the sport utility vehicle. Like those of most thrillers, the plot of *State of Fear* is determined by these strategies for involving nonhumans, Latour's first circuit.

In one of *Solar's* strangest scenes, Michael Beard's instrumental relationship to the world confirms a constructivist view of science. Detective fiction is often seen as a celebration of scientific reasoning: by finding clues and making extraordinary leaps, the ingenious sleuth imprisons the base appetites of the murderer and demonstrates the power of inductive and deductive reasoning. Sherlock Holmes, then, is the fictional equivalent of

Albert Einstein, a genius who makes extraordinary guesses about the factual situation out there. However, when Aldous slips on a polar bear rug and splits his skull on a glass coffee table, Beard is dumbstruck, recognizing he will be accused, falsely, of murder. His solution perfectly inverts the brilliant detective: "His body had a plan. And he walked through it as though experimentally." Having noticed Tarpin had left a bag of tools in the house while having an affair with his wife, Beard finds a hammer "with a narrow head that seemed about right," a comb, a used tissue, and an apple core and uses them to create a crime scene, a murder weapon, and DNA evidence (91). Disposable gloves and kitchen cleaning products allow him to erase the evidence of the original accident, and by fulfilling preexisting obligations, Beard finds an alibi. Unlike in a detective novel, Beard's scientific training doesn't allow him to construct the perfect argument to demonstrate his innocence. Rather, his personal hatred and the incidental, material things around him together construct an alternate narrative, convincing not just the police and court but even the framed man himself. The "facts" of this case emerge from both Beard and the material circumstances, an artful combination of human and nonhuman agency.

Indeed, *Solar* carefully traces how material things are recruited as instruments for producing knowledge. With haunting resonance, Beard uses another brown apple core, this one reclining in a sand-filled ashtray, as the only recurring landmark as he wanders lost through a hotel's many long corridors. The materiality of the thing makes it sordid, not unlike the improvised solutions in Beard's decaying flat: "A large vase collected raindrops in the spare bedroom, an iron footscraper held the fridge door closed, a frayed and curling length of grubby string substituted for a chain on the ancient lavatory cistern" (221). In contrast to the perfect ideation of the scientific or domestic genius, the grubbiness of mobilizing things is a sign of their own agency, emphasizing their resistance to our aesthetic will. Beard's solutions are all the more disgusting because they are not just material: sleeping in a spare bedroom with a leaking ceiling and a vase full of rainwater, dragging a footscraper across the floor to open the fridge, and pulling the curling string to flush the toilet involve the user in a less than dignified negotiation with Beard's muck. The novel is compelled to admit the effectiveness of such practices, even beyond the domestic sphere. Innovations in solar panels require the same sort of improvised construction:

> Tom Aldous had been correct in his general assumptions, and wrong in certain particulars, though Beard could hardly complain now that he owned seventeen patents. For a long time the little lab model that split water in 2005 could not be scaled up or made to work faster. The light-sensitive dyes that drove the process had to be reconsidered. The catalyst was not derived from manganese, but from a compound of cobalt, and another from ruthenium. Choosing and testing the right porous membrane to divide hydrogen from oxygen should have been easy but was not. (212)

The invention of solar panels apparently springs from Aldous's mind fully grown, but the details of making them turn out to involve mobilizing the agency of light-sensitive dyes, rare elements, and other engineered instruments. Transforming the separate parts into a working prototype requires all the genius of a Nobel Prize winner (not to mention the alliances he is able to form). At the same time, Beard is transformed into the interested owner of the processes, an ownership as sordid as the grubby string hanging from the lavatory cistern. The reader is led to expect that Beard will receive his comeuppance for perverting the course of justice, and for justifying his plagiarism with the difficulty of assembling the panels, but a higher truth never springs from the machine.

If instrumental practices construct scientific facts, the process of autonomization socializes them. As we have seen, State of Fear's advocacy of scientific realism leads it to sort natural things as facts and social things as artifacts. The internal contradictions of this move are exposed by the novel's treatment of autonomization. The certainty of global warming is undermined by treating it as a social phenomenon: scientists are politically motivated, selfishly interested in their own funding, bribed by environmental groups, experiencing mass delusion, and more divided than has been claimed. In Nature's review, Myles Allen reads State of Fear as raising the issue of "whether there is any such thing as a dispassionate scientific review."[44] At times, the novel seems to believe that scientific fact stands beyond the processes of replication, peer review, and confirmation by other research. "Consensus is irrelevant," Crichton claims, and "what is relevant is reproducible results."[45] But by cutting the process of autonomization down the middle, dividing the opinions of scientists from the results they seek, Crichton's critique makes it impossible to envision who would confirm facts. *State of Fear* is aware of this problem, to the point where the novel's conclusion must imagine a new social organization, a business for reviewing environmental studies independently. And yet, this social organization merely replicates the investments of current scientists that are hostile to competing assertions and amenable to verifiable, useful claims. Curiously, *State of Fear* confirms that facts are made as they are socialized through autonomization and that fiction can also provide hostility to make scientific findings more real.

In *Solar*, the process of autonomization is turned to humor and irony. Perhaps the most important event in Beard's life is the Nobel committee's independent verification of his contribution to science, opening the door to a series of lucrative sinecures. Beard has also developed a hunger to see his own name and theory in print, exhibiting a narcissism that cripples his concentration (49). The same hunger leads him to plagiarize Aldous's research and to ensure that his colleagues from Golden and MIT, Caltech and the Lawrence Berkeley labs, are present when "his" solar panels are unveiled (213). By becoming autonomous, Beard's theory transforms him again and again into a grasping, failing celebrity. Even lower are readers, who merely reproduce the facts of others and make them our own. Whether science or fiction, reading seems here to be a conflation of narcissism and envy, a satire of the process through which science is detached from its originators.

As has already been suggested, *State of Fear*'s suspicion of context leads to a heavy critique of scientific alliances, Latour's third circuit. For Kenner, environmental groups skew the facts, the US Environmental Protection Agency has been compromised by pressure groups, supposedly scientific bodies like the UN IPCC are really composed of bureaucrats, and environmental funding of scientists creates pressure to falsify data; all such alliances lead to the pollution of fact.[46] Curiously, the "Author's Message" acknowledges the inevitability of this: "Nothing is more inherently political than our shared physical environment, and nothing is more ill served by allegiance to a single political party" (679). For a novel that creates suspense around the intrigues of various interests impinging on science, this is a strange admission, suggesting political investment in material facts is inevitable. The solution, it seems, is egalitarianism. "Stable management of the environment requires recognition that all preferences have their place: snowmobilers and fly fishermen, dirt bikers and hikers, developers and preservationists" (680). The function of politics is to resolve these incompatible goals, the afterword proclaims. Applied back to the novel, particularly clear is the critique of NERF-like organizations, which use courts rather than democratic process to achieve protection, create fear with media campaigns, and may even encourage terrorism. But as we have seen, Kenner's violence is equally suspect, undermining the liberal republic he would protect. Thus, *State of Fear*'s critique is unraveled by its own need for alliances. This is no less true of libertarians, corporations, and academics in risk management than it is of environmental protesters, law firms, and climatologists. In climate change fiction, then, global warming is not merely a set of facts to be espoused by scientists but a strategy to fabricate linkages between unconnected interests.

It would be simple enough to conflate Latour's sense of alliances with an outdated reading strategy that unmasks the social forces beneath character. In *Solar,* a section retracing Beard's childhood provides all the material that would be necessary. His father is a private, meat-and-two-veg man who serves as an officer in the Second World War, who works in a merchant bank and then as a partner in a law firm in Essex, and whose main hobby is keeping up a second-hand Rolls Royce Silver Cloud. Avoiding physical affection, he buys his son scientific toys before sending him to public school and university with a generous allowance and a split-screen Morris Minor. His mother, "an angular beauty who doted on him," encourages a love of food and confesses a remarkable string of affairs to young Beard before dying of breast cancer (193). Here are all the ingredients to explain Beard's sexual appetite, hunger for maternal partners, gluttony, craving of status and recognition, and specific blend of egotism and aloofness. Even more, the passage provides all the proof usually needed to justify a psychoanalytic reading, explaining Beard in terms of his parents; a Marxian reading, explaining his science in terms of class privilege and anxiety; *and* a feminist reading, describing both his personal and scientific life in terms of patriarchal violence. The intentions of these readings may be good, but they are problematic in their dematerialization of Beard's alliances. Even as a child, Beard is shaped not just by maternal pride but also by the "cordon bleu" cookery his mother provides. Reducing Beard to a set of class interests neglects "the Meccano and chemistry sets, build-it-yourself wireless, encyclopaedias, model airplanes, and books about military history, geology and the lives of great men." These toys are signs that express the work ethic and aspirations of the postwar generation, but also a set of facilities that coconstruct the young man's scientific interests, his ability to fix the radios of his social superiors at university, and his lifelong facility with using physical knowledge as capital. The resulting alliances Beard forms at Oxford, with humanities students and his future wife, are no less comprehensible without reference to these nonhumans.

When Beard is a professional scientist, his success depends on such alliances. Even so, there is an incompatibility between *Solar's* theory of character, which paints humans as "very clever monkeys" (echoing the primitivism of *State of Fear*), and the actual work of building technology. Beard calls his business partner a genius, apparently knowing Toby Hammer will return the compliment, but Hammer's facility with alliances, bringing together lawyers, accountants, state legislature, go-betweens, foundations, venture capitalists, patent officers, engineers and material specialists, and federal administrators, is incompatible with an Einsteinian model of genius (210–11). Even so, the ties created by Aldous's original idea indicate literary realism is wholly different from scientific realism. *Solar* lives on such networks of people, but these are inexpressible without matter as well; Beard's connections to venture capitalists and politicians are just as incomprehensible without artificial photosynthesis as hippy friends are without a remarkable allowance from his father. Nor is character a stable entity on which to build a reading: it is not merely hypocrisy that transforms Beard's political self from one who sees no significant difference to the world at large if Bush or Gore finally wins the US election in 2000, to a "lifelong Democrat" who describes the same election as a time "when the earth's fate hung in the balance, and Bush snatched victory from Gore to preside over the tragedy of eight wasted years" (39, 218). Rather, the photosynthesis technology Beard steals from Aldous remakes his inner affections and his political alliances, forming an alliance with his brazen self-interest. *Solar,* like *State of Fear,* is not an example of social, political, or human realism, but rather a network of humans and nonhumans assembled by the force of climate change.

Where, then, does the public sit in this network? Climate scientists, politicians, and novelists claim to speak for the public, or in the name of the public, but the public itself is notably absent. Scientific things are socialized into public consciousness, but the public also provides funding and the presuppositions of science (Latour, *Pandora's,* 106). Rather strangely, Latour's model speaks of "public representation," even as the model of scientific representation is undone by actor network theory. This public seems to be a mental phenomenon, a receptacle for socialized scientific knowledge, even if scientists themselves form a part of it.

The difficulties of representing the public are central to *State of Fear*. Most often, the public is dismissed by Drake and Kenner alike as ignorant and malleable, their opinions formed by the manipulations of the media. On the other hand, there is a belief in common rationality: the difficulty of building a case that global warming will cause Vanutu to be submerged agrees with the skepticism of the novel, even as lawyers concede a real case would be subject to manipulation on both sides. The real jury, however, never appears, because the case is shelved. Then there is Kenner's single-handed educational campaign to convince those he meets that climate change is false. Even as his (supposed) scientific education is unavailable to all, the independent-mindedness he encourages indicates a wider belief in science education and a return of the media "as an independent assessor of fact."[47] *State of Fear* seems to be an effort to encourage the same traits in the public, to turn a confection of academic papers and libertarian moral instruction into something more substantial than airport fare. Despite these aims, *State of Fear* is far too invested in scientific networks to be a representative of the public in the way Latour describes.

If *State of Fear* indicates the difficulties of representing the public, *Solar* makes public representation central to the novel's claims to objectivity. Beard's hunger for fame allows the novel to trace the path from science to the wider public. As Beard demonstrates the scientific truth of the solar process through papers, patents, and confirmation by independent laboratories, he generates spectacles to organize the public. At the novel's climax, the revolutionary power plant is to be switched on for a large audience of national reporters, entrepreneurs, energy executives, scientific colleagues, and the public of Lordsburg, New Mexico, drawn by an air force flyover, a vast marquee and champagne reception, and "a giant neon sign that says Lordsburg, exclamation mark" (213). The public spectacle, with a crowd to report it and the media to replicate it, is not merely a vehicle for public triumph but also an important ingredient in realizing the central project. *Solar*, of course, creates suspense around these spectacles, suggesting fiction is a means of communicating science to the public. Even so, the other half of the circuit, from the public to science, is more difficult to trace.

By circulating climate change as a scientific thing, *Solar* reinforces its factual status. In recent interviews, McEwan has described how his understanding of fiction changed from an emphasis on the imaginary to "the specific, the local, the actual, the naming of things," an aesthetic that has also led him to "[make] use of real events, real people."[48] Nevertheless, climate change is not subject to individual, personal experience: when Beard goes to the Arctic "to see global warming for himself," cold weather prevents the glacial walls from shearing into the ocean (69). Rather, climate change is perceived by groups and reported to broad publics, a process that is unthinkable without the circulation of scientific and popular media like temperature readings, data sets, scientific papers, review papers, popular science magazines, and newspaper stories. As a result, *Solar*'s objectivity is built on a broader circulation of the media, as Beard consumes stories relating to the US presidential contest between Bush and Gore, Blair's fourth successful election, the 2004 Indian Ocean tsunami, and the parliamentary expenses scandal. These stories extend beyond the fictional frame of the novel. By forming a background to his thoughts, they anchor the novel's actions in a recognizably real landscape of media events. In such moments, the media is credible because it represents the real, and this objectivity is extended to the novel. Other events are directly based on media stories to do with climate change: an expedition of artists and intellectuals goes to the Arctic to see global warming for themselves; freak summer storms delay Beard's flight; solar panels spread across the American Southwest. These events, as well, are part of a larger strategy to bring the objective fact of climate change from science through the media into fiction, preserving its objectivity even as it enters the novel.

Although *Solar* maps the importance of the public to scientific research, it is deeply uncurious about the public itself. As noted before, the public is invited to contribute ideas for renewable energy research to the Centre. The move is designed to generate public support but winds up wasting months as the Centre's scientists reply to the thousands of proposals that violate basic rules of physics or demand a secret meeting to protect the inventor from a conspiracy. Here, the public is made to seem irrational, paranoid, and overconfident, a distraction from real science. Beard's alternate proposal for roof-mounted wind turbines also never comes to public evaluation. The theft of the Centre's claim to Aldous's ideas denies the British public a return on their investment, and when Tarpin smashes the

panels, the Lordsburg demonstration is canceled. A sense of the public finally reappears in the form of Beard's daughter, Catriona. Before she is
born, Beard hopes to "command this child's early annihilation" (176), but
he enjoys telling her he is saving the world, with her generation the obvious
beneficiary.[49] Beard's vacillation between self-aggrandizement and annihilation concludes the novel: Beard swells with emotion as Catriona runs
toward him, even as he prepares to use her to manipulate his angry lovers.
The future public is innocent and naive, the passive recipient of Beard's
manipulations. These representations of the public as irrational, absent,
and powerless indicate a deeper problem with representing the politics of
climate change, one that will be taken up in chapter 3.

What can be said at this point is that fiction traces the circulation of climate change through its instruments, scientific associations, alliances, and
public awareness. Rather than forming a single circuit between the imagined text and the real situation of climate change, novels instantiate climate
change by tracing how instruments, data, and scientific tools, like GCMs,
temperature records, ice cores, carbon dioxide levels; groups of scientists,
like evolutionary biologists, meteorologists, physicists, engineers, oceanographers, and mathematicians; associations with nonscientific groups, like
the IPCC, the US Environmental Protection Agency, heads of state and leg-
islators, universities, automobile manufacturers, energy companies, and
armies; publics, like newspaper readerships, television audiences, teenagers, musicians, fishermen, Buddhist monks, Pacific islanders, law firms,
Americans, Chinese citizens, Democrats and Republicans, aristocrats and
the English middle class; and the basic things of science, like fish, plankton, feral animals, carbon dioxide, ocean levels, glaciers, and polar bears,
among other things, are involved with climate change. All of these things
help create the meaning of climate change, and are reshaped by it, within
climate change novels. Climate change and climate change novels are neither fact nor ideation. Categorically impure, they are artifacts assembled
from heterogeneous things in the world.

The relationships between a climate change novel's things and their connections to the world are negotiated through reading. Things that appear
to be purely scientific—temperature measurements, climate models, ice
cores, carbon dioxide levels, extinction rates—are designed to travel beyond
the laboratory or the field, to prize committees, policy documents, newspaper stories, town hall meetings, and dining room tables. When they appear

in novels, these things are recognized and evaluated as they would be in other environments. Literary form and genre may influence this process of recognition, and aspects of the "fictional thing" may be different from the real, but the circulation of the thing between the field and the page allows this shaping to take place. (The next chapter explores an example of this process.) Of course, things like sport utility vehicles, light bulbs, polar bears, heat waves, and glaciers have been contested texts at the center of a major project of reinterpretation. In novels, objects are revised by being received with other things. For instance, *State of Fear* tries to wrest suspicion of sport utility vehicles from liberal critiques of their inefficiency by pressing them into the war with ecoterrorists, while climate predictions come off badly from their association with lawyers and Hollywood celebrities. Novelistic situations like these make it possible to follow the dynamic contests over scientific objects, as well as the reinterpretation of the world that these things make possible.

Often, environmental critics have tried to argue that literature has a link to real nature, while other literary critics have argued texts are discourse, determined by literary conventions rather than the putative real world. In accounts of climate change novels, there is a related temptation to understand fiction against a realist model of science or a postmodern dismissal (or suspension) of objective reality. Although novels like *State of Fear* and *Solar* take positions on these issues and the underlying question of climate change's reality, the things in novels are only recognizable because they circulate among scientific, media, and fictional contexts. Recently, following Latour, critics have begun to recognize that climate change itself is a hybrid of natural and social things. Even so, science studies scholars have displayed almost no interest in artistic forms, and there are important differences among the organization, objects, and practices of science and criticism, even as they influence each other. Science studies will never be a panacea for criticism's theoretical difficulties. Without confusing scientific practice and novel writing, however, it is possible to see that climate change circulates from scientific to popular cultural contexts, including fiction. Fiction is an impure collection of scientific, social, and natural things, and climate change makes meaning among these things, in fiction no less than the laboratory, field, or paper.

The dilemma between scientific realism and postmodern social constructivism has also been fundamental to how the agency of authors and readers is understood. Scientific realism gives novels like *Solar* the ability to invoke, and even contribute to, knowledge and truth, but at the expense of eliminating action. In interviews, McEwan carefully divides facts and human agency: "I don't think [art] can do much . . . about climate change. I suppose it can reflect the problem and pose the problem in terms that might be useful to people. I think we *do* face a test of our nature, and the more we know about that nature, the better we'll be able to face that test. . . . But, no, when I'm writing this novel I don't think I'm going to save the world, that's for sure."[50] By reflecting the problem of climate change, the novel loses any capacity "to save the world" or even to influence human choices. For the scientific realist, art's accuracy comes at the expense of being able to "do much" at all. *State of Fear* starts from a different premise, that social constructivism determines public and scientific discourse in the contemporary world. In Crichton's postmodern account of science, fictional inventions—literature, mass-market novels, and the daily media—create reality. To be more precise, though, this is an unreal reality, devoid of non-human things that resist our capricious interpretations. If *Solar* suggests that fiction dooms the author and reader to a state of passivity, *State of Fear* suggests novels shape a reality that is hardly worth the fight.

But by understanding novels as collections of things in the world, it becomes possible to describe the agency of climate change fiction. Indeed, science studies also faced this dilemma, struggling between accounts of science as powerless knowledge and science as pure social power. Rouse has argued that this is a definitional confusion. Scientific models "are transformations of the world," and they also "transform the available possibilities for acting . . . by materially enabling some activities and obstructing others, and also by changing the situation that some possible actions or roles lose their point, while others acquire new significance."[51] Thus, climate models predicting future temperature give an intellectual basis and argument for funding studies of extinction threats and ocean levels, even as they make assessments of future property damage from natural disasters more difficult. Climate models also make a long cycle to the office or the identity of a "climate activist" comprehensible, even as they question the wisdom of flying to academic conferences and developing properties on low-lying land. If climate models transform the world, so do novels. Although the Republican Party has gained a reputation for philistine dismissals of art,

Senator Inhofe recognized *State of Fear*'s ability to make a wholesale dismissal of climate science and environmental politics seem legitimate. By calling on Crichton to testify to his committee, Inhofe also completed a circuit in which science shapes the novel, and the novel then influences the articulation of science. Of course, *Solar*'s model of climate change is very different. By valorizing Aldous's ideas and satirizing Beard's appetite, *Solar* calls for renewed scientific and entrepreneurial energy to create sustainable resources, even as it makes the current fruits of these activities—private intellectual capital, excessive consumption, and vindictive social power—pointless anachronisms. By assembling diverse things in the world, novels transform it in unforeseeable ways.

If climate change novels do alter the world, critics could worry this signals a return to reading for that dried and shriveled fruit: the message. To the contrary, climate change only appears in novels through a complex, unstable negotiation among texts, readers, and things. When climate change is made manifest in the landscape of a novel, it necessarily alters longer traditions of narrating space, place, and disaster (chapter 2). Narrating climate change also reconfigures expected connections between characters, exposing the limits of interpersonal conflict and the potential for new human organization in the Anthropocene (chapter 3). Similarly, the Anthropocene forces a reconsideration of the character-driven novel, demanding analysis of not just a cast of connected characters, but rather wider groups of human beings, plant and animal species, geophysical events, weather, and technology (chapter 4). The formal innovations described in the subsequent chapters are not predetermined: the Anthropocene has dragged formal history, readerly inventiveness, and the resistant stubbornness of things into a new crisis. Neither postmodernism nor actor network theory can schematize this process. As we will see, unprecedented things force unprecedented literary acts, with new formal techniques and new relationships between text and things emerging from the encounter. Tracing these networks through the novel makes fiction both more real and more powerful.

TWO

PLACE

Deluge, Floods, and
Absence

For the majority of the public, climate change has remained an abstract, remote prognostication. Emerging from computer models, specialist journals, and university press releases, global warming appears first and foremost as a scientific proposition requiring elite, privileged knowledge to evaluate. As a global, rather than local phenomenon, involving changes in climate over decades rather than from month to month or year to year, the very scale of climate change challenges people's capacity to understand it. Activists, policymakers, and scientists themselves have been understandably concerned that climate change has been all but inaccessible to the voting, consuming public. Political campaigns against major emitters, tax rebates for insulation and energy efficiency, and popular science reporting have made but marginal gains in the public's interest and consumption. This presents a dilemma for the truly concerned, since the global, long-term scale of the problem demands a greater mandate from a public unmoved by remote threats. In this context, there has been not a little desperation for art to bring home the risks of greenhouse gas emissions. Fictionalizing climate change is not about falsifying it, or making it imaginary, but rather about using narrative to heighten its reality. The vast majority of novelists have responded to this challenge by rendering climate change as an immediate, local disaster.

By setting climate change in a specific place, such novels would seem to dwell within a long tradition of Anglophone environmentalism. American and British environmentalists have often argued that a sense of place is central to the project of conservation. In contrast to "space," "geometrical or topographical abstraction," place is "space to which meaning has been ascribed," a center of "felt value." Place is simultaneously physical, "inseparable from the concrete region in which it is found," and also defined by individual emotions and social bonds.[1] Environmental critics have found an extensive rationale for place in authors like Wordsworth, Emerson, and Thoreau; the deep ecology of Arne Naess; the phenomenology of Martin Heidegger and Maurice Merleau-Ponty; anthropological accounts of indigenous cultures; and studies from social geography. For first-wave ecocritics, literary articulations of place suggested an ethic of nonexpansionist patriotism, an alternative to metropolitan modernity, and a battleground to conserve both nature and poetry.[2] By arguing that one's survival, history, identity, and affect are intimately connected to place, environmentalists have hoped that conservation would come to seem a natural, intrinsic, and self-preserving impulse for all people, mobilizing resistance against industrial capitalism and "spatial colonization." Climate change literature would seem to concretize global warming by setting narrative where climate change creates floods, storms, wildfires, and droughts, and people suffer from famine, lawlessness, exile, and war. Creating a connection between the reader and characters immersed in disastrous global warming, readers could immediately experience climate change as a threat to their centers of felt value. Thus, fiction would reposition climate change as a fundamental concern for the wider public.

More recently, however, critics have begun to recognize that a celebration of place cannot fully answer contemporary environmental problems. Advocates of environmental justice have pointed to the geographical and racial assumptions underlying celebrations of wilderness and also drawn attention to the environmental importance of urban spaces as sites of degradation or more sustainable living.[3] This impulse has also led to arguments that ecocriticism should address more than nature writing, that it should "recover the environmental character or orientation of works whose conscious or foregrounded interests lie elsewhere."[4] These insights are particularly relevant to climate change fiction. Instead of focusing on wilderness or a pastoral landscape, the vast majority of climate change novels are set in urban centers. Cities are, by definition, extraordinarily dense networks of affective bonds between people and place. These bonds are frequently disorganized and overlapping: people have millions of different associations with New York City's Central Park or the banks of the Thames in London. Other features of the city are designed to organize social affect: monuments, skyscrapers, public buildings, and authorized views of geographical features, like riverbank parks or scenic viewpoints. However, urban spaces give the lie to the assumption that emotional bonds to place are natural, transparent, or straightforwardly progressive. Place is inescapably histori-cal and political, in addition to being material and personal. Urban climate change fiction is able to draw on popular symbols in its descriptions of destruction—London flooded, the US Capitol razed—and thereby engage with a much wider readership. Characters in these novels display varying attitudes to nature and rural areas, but their dense interconnections also allow a novel to trace the social, economic, and interpersonal impacts of anthropogenic warming. Not only does the alteration of global weather pat-terns challenge the Romantic poet's discovery of pristine nature, but the world's urban and rural poor would seem to feel its impacts more acutely. The very notion of localist "place-attachment" has been challenged by other critics, since global warming, like many other environmental problems, de-mands engagement beyond individual locales. This has led to calls for new forms of planetary belonging or eco-cosmopolitanism, creating "imagined communities" of humans and nonhumans at the planetary scale.[5] On the strength of evidence, novelists have often thought computer programmers, urban citizens, journalists, activists, and politicians are better placed to con-struct these communities. Given these considerations, it is little surprise that so little climate fiction can be taken as a reaffirmation of the pastoral or wilderness.

If anything, climate change would seem to challenge not just the limits of lyrical poetry or nature writing but also those of the traditional novel. As Ursula Heise has argued, climate change, as a global transformation, "requires the articulation of connections between events at vastly different scales."[6] In addition to dealing with individuals, families, and the destiny of nations, the narrator's voice would also seem to need to encompass eco-nomic processes, the incremental emissions of every grocery run, chemi-cal and meteorological variations, the life cycle of phytoplankton, and any number of other systems not typically incorporated into the novel. What narrative could possibly span these scales or make their interrelations com-prehensible? Moreover, as Heise points out, these climatic conditions have not been experienced on Earth for millions of years, challenging any novel-ist's capacity for speculation.[7] Although most novels find ways to allude to these conditions, in practice they turn out to be all but unnecessary: readers have little problem inferring that a local disaster is part of a global alteration of the climate or imaginatively dwelling in an unprecedented atmospheric setting, even if it is never spelled out for them. While some novels actively focus on the planetary and cross-cultural implications of global warming, and we are urgently in need of developing cultural means to construct an ethical relationship to the planet, this is not necessarily the most pressing or difficult problem facing an author writing about climate change.

Rather, the first hurdle faced by a novelist is to construct a fictional space where climate change presents itself as an immediate problem. The impacts projected by the Intergovernmental Panel on Climate Change stretch to multiple volumes, and every region and ecosystem will face alterations from significant planetary warming. Intuitively, it would seem that a global process like climate change could be described anywhere and that there would be hundreds of strategies an author might adopt in a climate change novel. In practice, both the spaces and the specific effects of climate change are highly circumscribed. The narrative work of any such novel is to maintain the plausibility of its setting while also describing its transformation, most often through present or future catastrophe. Although there are hundreds of climate change novels, only a handful of transformations cover the vast majority of them: direct heat, catastrophic storms, arctic switches, and floods. Other catastrophes, though equally disastrous, are hardly represented at all. Sudden climatic shift, caused by the release of methane from melting permafrost, is only described in one novel I have been able to find, Paul McAuley's *Quiet War*. Ocean acidification is only even mentioned by Kim Stanley Robinson's "Science in the Capital" trilogy, despite its real potential to decimate life on Earth. The loss of biodiversity is also strikingly underexamined in the wider literature, although a handful of novels, like T. C. Boyle's *A Friend of the Earth*, Paolo Bacigalupi's *The Windup Girl*, and Barbara Kingsolver's *Flight Behavior* (all discussed in subsequent chapters), interestingly explore the subject. The reasons for these patterns are fundamentally connected to genre.

To the extent that the "literary" novel about contemporary society is set in bourgeois spaces, it seems all but unable to register the different scales of climate change. Ian McEwan's *Solar* can only bridge the absurdities between personal choice and planetary fate—potato chips and saving the world—through comedy, suggesting our social real itself cannot survive the present challenge. Jonathan Franzen's *Freedom* comes closer, exploring the environmental obsessions of one character as part of a larger political and social moment of the early 2000s, but extinction and overpopulation are for the most part the verbal and political obsessions of a particular character, tolerated or occasionally indulged by the people around him. If the political and environmental climate of the novel is broadly "real," it is also highly social and grounded in a circumscribed present. Many more well-regarded novelists have written about climate change, but their works venture into "planetary transformations" that have not yet happened, violating a defining feature of literary realism.

On the other end of the spectrum, there is no shortage of novels that use climate change to envisage an end-of-the-world scenario. Perhaps the most well known of these, Cormac McCarthy's *The Road*, pitches father and son in a scorched landscape devoid of the temporal, geographical, and social markers necessary to experience place. While this creates a harrowing narrative, the drama revolves around the father and son avoiding cannibals, scavenging food, and walking south. There is nothing in the book that directly engages with the specificities of climate change, either its causes before the disaster or the specific destructive outcomes afterward. Instead, *The Road* focuses on biblical questions of cosmic justice and the end of time and simplifies social relationships to a matter of paternal succession. In the nameless disaster of *The Road*, the familiar, emotional markers of place are also eradicated, to the point that the novel's geographical location has become a matter of critical speculation. In effect, the novel's apocalypticism actively excludes the social, political, and atmospheric dimensions of climate change, replacing them with a fable calculated to produce maximum horror. Ultimately, such apocalyptic novels fail to place climate change or create a meaningful connection between it and the reader.

Other novels directly try to describe the effects of a warmer climate. In Saci Lloyd's *Carbon Diaries 2014* and *2015*, characters swelter in a London heat wave, water rations are imposed, citizens riot, and civil wars begin in the spreading desert of the Mediterranean. In novels such as Julie Bertagna's *Exodus* and J. G. Ballard's *The Drowned World*, parts of Britain have been changed into tropical climates, with diets, fauna, illnesses, and predators to match. Yet what is striking about these novels is that warming itself does not form the most striking change or precipitate the novel's climax; catastrophic floods provide the main dramatic force. Although a vision of London flooded with rice paddies is striking, humans have lived in warmer climates for millennia, and it is difficult to create a convincing account of human disaster from a shift in climate, even if the real costs of human adaptation and nonhuman extinctions are likely to be disastrous. A handful of other novels describe the effects of desertification. In Octavia Butler's *Parable of the Sower,* California splinters into small militia-controlled farm communities after decades of drought, while in Doris Lessing's *Mara and Dann,* spreading drought turns a brother and sister into refugees flung across future Africa. In both cases, not drought but broken rule of law and crazed, dehumanized ransackers are the real impetus to flight. Of course, climate change has often precipitated the collapse of societies in the past, but the few novels that have tried to describe desertification have quickly veered away from a consideration of place, devolving to rather simplistic accounts of social conflict.

If heat itself lacks a narrative punch, extraordinary storms appear with predictable frequency in climate change novels. The hurricane, cyclone, or peculiarly intense rainstorm is an almost irresistible plot device, ratcheting suspense, destroying communities' infrastructure, and plunging characters into dramatic crises. Storms, however, face narrative difficulties of their own. Humans have recorded accounts of extraordinary weather since the beginning of the written word; storms were already frighteningly unpredictable before climate change. The intensity of storms is expected to increase in the next decades, but neither the terror nor the telling is changed by a footnote to increased global temperature. When the storms are more regular, as in Julie Bertagna's *Exodus,* they produce a sort of drudgery from being trapped inside the house and having to constantly fix the family dwelling, until the inevitable tempest finally arrives. One exception is Bruce Sterling's *Heavy Weather* (1994), which follows a "troupe" of cyberpunk tornado trackers thrilled by global warming's superstorms. If anything, the first decade of the twenty-first century is notable for producing a superfluity of "perfect storm" novels and films that studiously *avoid* any reference to climate change, fully absorbing the event as an unrepeatable singularity to heighten its narrative appeal. By contrast, climate change novels must work against this impulse, almost always by locating the storm against another effect more responsible for determining the quotidian future.

In the first decade of the twenty-first century, media coverage of climate change was dominated by images of the Arctic and Antarctic, leading to a panoply of novels focusing on polar landscapes. However, the various effects of climate change on polar landscapes, present and projected, led to different kinds of narratives. Antarctica was the site of important scientific breakthroughs connected to climate change, including ice cores that linked atmospheric carbon dioxide concentrations to temperature over geological periods of time. Warming is expected to be greater at the poles as well, and calving icebergs and retreating glaciers have become established symbols of global warming. Thus, there have been a number of novels set in Antarctica's scientific community, such as Kim Stanley Robinson's *Antarctica* (1998), Brian Freemantle's *Ice Age* (2002), Sarah Andrews's *In Cold Pursuit* (2007), and Jean McNeil's *Ice Lovers* (2009). All of these use mysterious deaths to create an inquiry into the motives connected to global warming. Other narratives have characters travel to the poles to "witness" climate change: *The Day after Tomorrow* (2004) opens with the dramatic breakup of an Antarctic ice sheet, while *Solar*'s bumbling protagonist goes to the Arctic "to see global warming for himself," with laughable results (59). It should also be noted that Robinson, McNeil, and McEwan were the recipients of grants to write about polar research. Other novelists have been drawn to the poles as a setting that can show climate change without excessive references to science. Often, these novels have been concerned with the loss of traditional ways of life. Robert Mann's *Where the Ice Never Melts* (2011) is about an Inuit boy in a postapocalyptic future. In Susannah Waters's *Cold Comfort* (2006), an Alaskan teenager collects articles about climate change and sees her house collapse with the melting of the permafrost, the dissolution of her working-class family, and the end of traditional Inuit fishing; her boyfriend tries to preserve Native traditions by sleeping in a refrigerated trailer and eventually leads a raid on a perceived climate criminal. Johanna Sinisalo's *Troll: A Love Story* (2004) offers a different take on such traditions: trolls, affected by climate change, are driven into urban areas of Finland. The folkloric monsters exact a kind of revenge on the self-interested, aestheticizing urbanites. John Minichillo's *The Snow Whale* (2011) offers a sardonic take on such narratives: a suburban white man, trusting a DNA report of Inuit ancestry, travels north and bankrolls a quixotic and illegal hunt for a white whale, which is captained by a half-mad, Native Ahab. Undermining assumptions about culture and authenticity, the novel suggests deeper questions about our attachment to place in an Anthropocene era. Taken together, these accounts of science and tradition in the Arctic try to locate meanings in climate change by taking the reader to the ends of the Earth.

The limits of a polar setting are best seen in extremis. Yet another group of novels draw on prehistoric ice ages and the tipping point of world climates: Jean M. Auel's *The Land of Painted Caves* (2011), Stephen Baxter's series of novels about woolly mammoth, and Joan Wolf's *The Reindeer Hunters* (1994). By invoking past changes in climate, such novels can draw on historical certainties and deeper questions of extinction. The disaster of a future ice age also informs Maggie Gee's *The Ice People* (1999) and Doris Lessing's *Mara and Dann* (2000), both of which imagine the collapse of European culture as the continent is engulfed in ice. Another kind of regression is envisioned by Marcel Theroux's *Far North* (2009), which describes a frozen wild west, complete with gunslingers and slave traders, after the world's population flees to Siberia. Poised between past and future, Sarah Moss's intriguing *Cold Earth* (2009) gives a ghostly account of the participants in an archaeological dig haunted by a collapsed community they are researching in Greenland, even as they lose contact and fear the worst about contemporary civilization back home. Separated by extraordinary stretches of time, these novels are extraordinarily ominous, but they struggle to connect to wider implications of climate change around the world, as well as the causes that might still be addressed. Even as they attempt to give an immediate sense of the Anthropocene, the glacial setting makes global warming more remote. The problem is not that readers cannot understand ice, or cold, or the implications of changed weather patterns. Instead, the problem seems to be embedded in the literary history of Anglo-American polar exploration, which paints the landscape as a vast, empty wasteland fit for adventure. This impulse is best seen in novels like Kim Stanley Robinson's *Fifty Degrees below Zero* (2005) and Adam Roberts's *The Snow* (2004), in which the zest of arctic adventure overruns consideration of the snowy disaster that befalls Washington, DC, or London. Both novels would seem to be rooted in a relatively short-lived concern that climate change was altering the Atlantic's salinity, shutting down the Gulf Stream that makes much of the US East Coast and Western Europe habitable. The concern reaches its apotheosis in the popular film *The Day after Tomorrow*, when a sudden, unprecedented cold snap forces a polar scientist to recreate Scott's survival trek by walking from Washington to New York City. The march is dramatic, nonsensical, and wholly unrelated to climate change. While few novels are as crude as the film, these polar novels always struggle to connect change to more familiar and affective places.

Over the last forty years, the dominant literary strategy for locating climate change has been the flood. The reasons for this are simultaneously scientific, geographical, historical, and cultural. As long as there has been the threat of significant planetary warming, scientists have foreseen the possibility that melting polar caps in the Arctic, Greenland, and Antarctica could significantly raise sea levels. As evidence of higher oceans in previous geological periods emerged, the possibility of a world-changing deluge seemed yet greater. Current forecasts project rises of less than a meter for the twenty-first century, but novels have little trouble looking further into the future, when tens of meters are possible. Flooding is also a compelling subject for geographical reasons: 23 percent of the world's population lives within one hundred kilometers of the coast and less than one hundred meters above sea level, with 60 percent of the world's largest cities also near the coast.[8] New York, Washington, DC, and London all sit just above sea level, making for a tantalizing combination of familiarity and disaster.

At least as important, flood narratives readily tap into an existing literary tradition that extends back thousands of years. The story of a global deluge devastating the entire world was circulated in a number of early civilizations and is now commonly thought to have roots in historical fact. This complex background of history, myth, and the rise and fall of nations introduces another fundamental issue into the consideration of climate change: time. The changes wrought in global warming novels invoke questions of *when* such changes might occur and also how time might be marked in a social order radically different from our own. Novels that draw on the historical resonances of the flood have rich resources to think about both of these questions. In a similar way, the cultural resonance of floods offers a more familiar entrée to climate change. We simply do not know how to think about methane, ocean acidification, and biodiversity, but twentieth-century reinterpretations of Genesis were popular before greenhouse gases became a matter of public concern. So, too, factual reports of devastating floods have been an enduring feature of newspapers since their beginning, and the contemporary hunger for disaster reporting only feeds a wider trade in flood narratives. With climate change, stories about floods take on new significance, indicating a global problem ultimately traceable to human actions.

Floods offer a rich, literary means of rendering climate change in a local place, as a tangible concrete effect. Before the advent of anthropogenic climate change, flood narratives offered a striking metaphor for evolutionary processes and nuclear war. These literary forebears shaped early climate change novels, particularly J. G. Ballard's *The Flood* (1962) and Richard Cowper's *The Road to Corlay* (1978). The deluge continues to inform climate change fiction, most notably in Will Self's *The Book of Dave* (2006), a novel that ironically questions humans' capacity to contemplate climate change at all. Other excellent novels neglect the global awareness of the deluge narrative, focusing instead on a more immediate, local flood. George Turner's *The Sea and Summer* (1987) pointedly investigates the tensions between these two forms of narrating climate change, finding they are all but incompatible. Still other novelists have used the flood to show climate change's impact on cities, animals, and different groups of people. These capacities are most fully realized in Maggie Gee's *The Flood* (2004), which explores the fragility of complex social networks in an era of global warming.

Early Deluge Novels: J. G. Ballard and Richard Cowper

It is no surprise that contemporary novelists have been drawn to flood narratives as a means to think about the ethics of human emissions and the danger to humanity's survival. Narratives about floods stretch back to the beginnings of literature. Both the Bible and the Qu'uran give accounts of a great flood, as do the Greek myth of Deucalion, the Mesopotamian Epic of Gilgamesh and the Hindu myth of Manu. These stories of divine judgment, creation, and destruction suggest humans have used floods to understand the limits of humanity, its ethical boundaries, and our ultimate dependence on the land since the beginnings of civilization. Moreover, the supernatural dimensions of these stories grant a sense of totality that is easily—if imperfectly—matched to a contemporary "global" crisis. Such novels can be grouped as "deluge" narratives as a means of distinguishing them from accounts of floods in specific, local places.

Climate science and its popular articulations provided a useful justification of deluge narratives. As global temperatures have risen and ice in Antarctica has broken up, there have been rather obvious calculations showing that the melting of Antarctic and Greenland glaciers would result in disastrous sea-level rises. The thermal expansion of water has a less appreciated but also significant impact. According to the *IPCC Fourth Assessment Report,* after nearly two thousand years of stasis, sea levels rose about 1.7 millimeters per year in the twentieth century. Since 1993, the rate has increased to 3 millimeters per year, and IPCC studies have projected 4 millimeters per year of rise by 2090. Global sea levels may be between 0.22 and 0.44 meters above 1990 levels by 2100, under some projections.[9] These findings did not take into account changes in ice flows from Greenland and Antarctic ice sheets, which could significantly increase the total. With more flooding, the relative depth of continents would also shift, also increasing apparent sea-level rises. Contrary to popular imagination, the melting of Antarctic and Greenland ice is projected to take several centuries. Even if all of this ice were to melt, the rise in sea levels would not eliminate all land or cover the Himalayas. Nevertheless, a relatively modest increase in sea level can have a catastrophic impact on islands and coastal regions, destroying freshwater stores, eroding coasts, and destroying habitats. Moreover, climate change is expected to produce more cyclones, destroy coastal defenses, create larger waves and storm surges, and alter precipitation and runoff, all of which can be disastrous by themselves and can also contribute to the flooding envisioned by novelists.[10] In the UK, regional flooding has recently been described as the greatest threat posed by climate change, with up to 3.6 million people at risk by the middle of the century.[11] In the United States, the Midwest, Northeast, and parts of the Gulf Coast are expected to be at increased risk of flooding. Striking projections of the threat to other low-lying countries, such as the Netherlands, Bangladesh, and Pacific island countries, have also captured public imagination. While these effects are quite distinct from biblical deluge or the full melting of the ice caps, the public's understanding of climate change has been shaped by reports of Pacific island nations like Tuvulu being washed away, as well as disasters like the 2004 Indian Ocean tsunami that killed over 230,000; New Orleans after Hurricane Katrina in 2005; and the extensive floods in the UK in June and July 2007. Popular nonfiction has also emphasized sea-level rises. The cover of Mark Lynas's popular *Six Degrees: Our Future on a Hotter Planet* shows Big Ben being washed away in a dramatic wave. Al Gore's *An Inconvenient Truth* suggested melting ice could raise sea levels up to twenty feet in the near future; his images of maps redrawn made compelling viewing.

Thus, the literary history, scientific predictions, popular accounts, and recent disasters have overdetermined that the flood would channel literary accounts of climate change. Scores of novels have been written about climate change–induced floods. Climate change flood novels take one of two forms. In the first, which might be described as postflood narratives, the reader is confronted with a broken world after massive sea surges have subsided. In the second variety, the novel directly describes the effects of floods and the transition from a recognizable world to one markedly remade by climate change. Both varieties of flood novels draw on the mythic roots of the Great Deluge for a sense of epic scale, moral judgment, terror, and an end of time. However, these novels are less the result of a philological interest in ancient myth and more the effect of recent conditions.

Through the first half of the twentieth century, "deluge" novels were a recurrent feature of the literary landscape.[12] Deluge novels describe the obliteration of civilization on a massive scale and are distinguished from flood novels by their description of a global, rather than local, catastrophe.[13] Anglophone deluge novels almost always draw on the Genesis flood but also must violate one of its central features—the covenant between God and humans that there would never be another such deluge—erasing the moral structure of the biblical narrative.[14] Although there are a few American examples in this period, most Anglophone novels were the result of a British, Wellsian tradition of scientific romance. For an island nation and a collapsing empire, deluge presented a potent metaphor to explore apocalypse. Deluge seemed apt after the horrors of the First World War and was renewed by Hiroshima and the threat of nuclear annihilation. John Wyndham's *The Kraken Wakes* (1953), John Bowen's *After the Rain* (1958), and J. G. Ballard's *The Drowned World* (1962) use the deluge to explore the decline of the British Empire and symbolize nuclear holocaust. Typically, these deluge novels have been interpreted as a metaphor for "inner," moral meaning, rather than "improbable," literal destruction. By necessity, climate change novels must reverse this critical preference, since an interpretation of climate change as metaphor all but evaporates its ecological significance.

If such deluge novels act as precursors to many climate change novels, they are also indebted to wider trends in post–Second World War fiction. Despite scattered allusions to Genesis, early climate change novels drew on enormously popular postapocalyptic novels from the 1950s and 1960s that dealt directly with nuclear fallout and plagues. In terms of nuclear fallout, Nevil Shute's *On the Beach* (1957) and Pat Frank's *Alas, Babylon* (1959) present vivid accounts of a world decimated by human technology. Walter M. Miller Jr.'s *A Canticle for Leibowitz* (1960) also shows the aftermath of a nuclear war, when Catholic monks have tried to preserve human knowledge for millennia, until humanity is again ready for it. Plague also became popular in the period; George R. Stewart's *Earth Abides* (1949) and

Richard Matheson's *I Am Legend* (1954) are particularly prominent examples. However, M. P. Shiel's *The Purple Cloud* (1901) specifically describes a plague caused by a mysterious cloud, with perhaps a much more direct link between "atmosphere" and a postapocalyptic future than most climate change novels. Stories about human annihilation from nuclear weapons remained popular throughout the 1980s, although the fall of the Berlin Wall and the end of the Cold War diminished the public's concern in the last decade of the twentieth century. More recently, plague narratives have become ubiquitous, with blockbuster films and novels regularly capturing public attention. Allusions to an unspecified plague also appear in a significant proportion of climate change novels.

The development from these fallout and plague novels of the 1950s to anthropogenic deluge novels seems to have taken an important, intermediate step. Years before the first novel about human-induced global warming, J. G. Ballard's *The Drowned World* (1962) provided a strikingly stable archetype for subsequent fiction.[15] Previous interpretations of the novel focused on its mythic dimensions, but the dawn of the Anthropocene encourages a more material interpretation of the novel. Early in the twenty-first century, the novel recounts, a "series of violent and prolonged solar storms" destroys some of the Earth's upper atmosphere, allowing solar radiation to heat the Earth by a few degrees each year (22). Temperatures at the Equator hover at 180 degrees, and continuous rain falls as high as the twentieth parallel. Melting polar ice caps raise the seas, while erosion remakes waterways, completely altering "the shape and contours of the continents" (22). Much of Europe is flooded, and eventually even the wealthiest cities see their sea walls breached (22–23). The United Nations has led the world's survivors, a mere five million people, to Antarctica and the northernmost regions of Canada and Russia (21). The novel's protagonist is Kerans, a biologist and medic on a UN mission to rescue the last refugees and map the shifting lagoons of flooded Europe.

Through Kerans's eyes, Ballard slowly unveils Europe's changed landscape. In every case, the landscape is rendered as a palimpsest, with striking juxtapositions taking the place of detailed description. At the opening of the novel, Kerans has adopted temporary accommodation away from the main expedition's boat, living in a suite at "The Ritz" decorated in black marble and gold plate. Evidence of the previous owner, a Milanese financier, is everywhere, from the photographs of his family dotted around the suite to the initials on the monogrammed silk shirts Kerans has adopted instead of his brown UN uniform (11). But the most striking juxtaposition is between the flat's luxurious interior and the apparatus that maintains its boundaries: air locks, thermostat alarms, and an extraordinary quantity of fuel and spare parts are needed to maintain a bubble of luxury against the flooded lagoon immediately outside its walls (16). From the hotel balcony, Kerans surveys abandoned department stores and dense groves of giant gymnosperms, the sun "[fanning] across the eastern horizon like a colossal fire-ball" (12). Despite Kerans's shell of civilization, primitive elementalism dominates the scene. At times, Ballard's descriptions echo the racialized language for which Conrad has been justly criticized. Nevertheless, the language does something remarkably productive: the emphasis on the co-lossal, relentless, deadening sun, burning the water and air beyond any fantasy of tropical paradise, emphasizes that no quantity of silk and air con-ditioning can bring an exemption from climate. If Kerans is able to fulfill wishes of extraordinary wealth, this is only at the cost of the annihilation of European civilization from climate change. While capitalism gives the appearance that these things rule the world, in the novel's future, luxury is a tiny cubicle surrounded and overwhelmed by the sea.

In *The Drowned World*, climate change also reorganizes humans' evo-lutionary history. The climate itself is figured as a new Triassic age, with lagoons infested with iguanas and alligators from the equator. Members of the expedition are remade by this renewed Triassic: Kerans finds himself responding to "the powerful mesmeric pull of the baying reptiles," and the heat makes the waters "[seem] an extension of his own bloodstream" (71). According to a colleague of Kerans, the climate creates a kind of biologi-cal reversion. This is not an argument for evolutionary reversion, of *Homo sapiens* becoming Sinanthropus, but rather that the human neurological system encodes an "archaeopsychic past," since "each one of us is as old as the entire biological kingdom" (44). Landscape is the trigger for this trans-formation: "the landscapes of each epoch," with "a distinct geological ter-rain, its own unique flora and fauna," cause older modes of consciousness to be expressed in the characters. Viewing climate change, even the human mind is absorbed into it. In the prehistoric climate, Kerans is gradually submerged, "marooned millions of years away" in this archaeopsychic past (121). Finally, Kerans abandons his colleagues and equipment in a death march southward toward the sun. Even so, it would be a mistake to accord Kerans's gesture with evolutionary credit. Instead, the gesture is only meaningful within the web of civilization it purports to reject.

In a pattern that has extended through many more deluge novels, *The Drowned World* interrelates the layers of consciousness and landscape. Two-thirds of the novel accustoms the reader to a new climatic reality of flooded lagoons and unbearable heat. Suddenly, however, the waters begin to sink, exposing "an immense intact Atlantis" beneath the lagoon (121). Kerans wanders a web of streets, a flâneur walking idly by "empty display windows of the old department stores," watching "the black slime oozing down the escalators below the office blocks into sluggish pools across the street," as though the city has been "resurrected from its own sewers" (126). Only at this point is it revealed that the entire novel has been taking place above London's Leicester Square and Piccadilly (125). However, for Kerans, "London" is itself meaningless, and the exposing of the urban mesh of meaning is unbearable, a "total inversion of his normal world" (121). Kerans experiences the mirror image of the reader's discomfort: a lagoon over the wreck of a nameless city is bearable, but the precise juxtaposition of a familiar London, emptied and besmirched, reconnects emotional attachments to an otherwise alien landscape. The effect is horrific, bringing the reader into sudden contact with the mortality of not just the individual but also the entire material edifice of the modern world that we call reality.

Superficially, the novel encourages a horror of the primitive, but its real aversion is to the economy. Early on, Kerans experiences a palpable distaste for his boss and colleagues. The antipathy spreads to the novel's love interest; both find the labor of sex (and the possibility of creating future workers) distasteful. The force responsible for this shift is the climate, which creates "a new zone, where the usual obligations and allegiances ceased to operate" (81). In this way, Kerans's investment in the Triassic landscape is a kind of hygienic action, a cleansing of the land from humans' ever-deepening interference with it. When Kerans confronts Strangman, an overlord dressed in a white suit who inspires supernatural fear in his crew of cannibalistic, idiotic "Negros," Kerans is horrified by the uncovering of the London market and the colonial logic of labor. Acting as the hero, Kerans tries to cover up the view of the present, blowing a hole in the dike and resubmerging the past. His real goal is to conserve a future, alien landscape, purifying it of the reader's present and concealing what has been lost through climate change. In doing so, Kerans explicitly suppresses what most climate change novels have left submerged: the subterranean economy of the Anthropocene. In the final chapter, we will reexamine the consequences of this obstruction.

In *The Drowned World*, Kerans's search for a purified landscape is intimately connected to the novel's literary allusions. The novel repeatedly references Genesis—the lagoons are called "walled gardens in an insane Eden" (53). Instead of returning with his colleagues to the northern outpost, Kerans plans to be left behind without the benefit of his crew's supplies, seeking a kind of "inverted Crusoeism" (47). As we have seen, Kerans's aversion to both his present and the reader's is bound up with a "horror" directly imported from Conrad. When he confronts Strangman, Kerans might have mustered an aversion to *The Heart of Darkness*'s colonial logic and its importation into a future utterly cleansed of its political and geographical reference points. Instead, the allusion deploys historical racism to heighten Kerans's interior need for purification. T. S. Eliot's *The Waste Land* also recurs, not just through direct quotation (116) but also in Kerans's desire for a "curiously potent image," full of "dormant magic and mesmeric power . . . some spectral grail" (46). When Kerans finally goes south, "a second Adam searching for the forgotten paradises of the reborn sun" (175), the biblical past replaces the technical labor that has followed all human activity since the fall. Thus, Genesis acts as a master narrative for the rise and fall of humanity. The novel might have attempted a systematic view of the English landscape after the temperatures had risen and the ways geographical features, plants, animals, and humans would have been forced to adapt. Instead, literary allusion serves as a surrogate for concrete description, turning landscape into a mirror for character. The sun's inescapable gravity serves as a metaphor for evolutionary and literary history, inescapably drawing humans back to destruction. If *The Drowned World* is taken as a novel about nuclear anxiety, as most critics agree, its most striking feature is the elision of humans' material interaction with landscape and moral responsibility for that interaction. Sunspots do it, not the fission of an atom bomb. This has proved to be a perilous metanarrative for anthropogenic climate change.

Surprisingly, it is the novel's weaknesses that have made it an attractive template for subsequent flood narratives. First, the flood acts as a terrific form of compression, homogenizing a whole world of ecological and climatic variation into a single, distorted disaster. Second, the flood eliminates the diversity of human experience, making one antiheroic figure the archetype for postapocalyptic man. Third, the flood eliminates the complexity of humans' material engagement with the world, suggesting the only economy is in the past. As a result, the new material practices of a climate-changed future are all but eliminated. Finally, the surface of the flood reflects a literary history, turning climate change into a historiographical experience. When floods have come before the onset of a novel, these features recur to a surprising extent.

As soon as anthropogenic climate change appeared as a subject for fiction, the deluge presented itself as an obvious structure for global warming narratives. The first of many, Richard Cowper's *The Road to Corlay* uses global warming as a device to create a new medieval age.[16] This would prove to be a remarkably durable way of imagining a postdisaster future. *The Road to Corlay* is set just after the turn of the third millennium. By 1985, "the global climate had been modified to the point where polar ice caps were affected" (42). Through the next several decades, five billion people are killed, and the survivors are knocked back to a new Dark Ages, an event subsequently known as the Drowning. One thousand years later, England has become an archipelago of seven island kingdoms. The most powerful political and military force is the Church Militant, which violently persecutes theological challenges to protect its hierarchical rule. At the outset of the novel, Tom—a boy with a split tongue and a magical flute—travels the archipelago, his music inspiring the masses with a new vision of collective, spiritual kinship. When he is martyred in York by a representative of the church in the year 3000, a populist cult of "The White Bird of Kinship" spreads through the seven kingdoms; the novel's protagonists travel on quests to preserve relics of the young piper, avoid inquisition and murder by representatives of the church, escape to Corlay on the Brittany coast, and protect the unborn child ordained to lead the Kinship movement. Thus, the Drowning is a millennial event directly analogous to the piper's martyrdom one thousand years later. As in other postapocalyptic narratives, anthropogenic climate change acts as an eschatological device, but its specific operation depends on the discursive and material features of the flood.

The effect of the Drowning is to create a historical break with the present, initiating a new era of medievalist fantasy. The novel is framed as an apocryphal text, with RJC of St. Malcolm's College, Oxford, commenting on its provenance and composition from June 3798 (3). In *The Road to Corlay*, not just technology but the entire architecture of society has returned to a blurry middle ages. This is a world of travelling "tale-spinners," church towns, and peasants. Dialogue has reverted to stilted, hackneyed figures: "Sweet God in Heaven! . . . Welcome back, old rogue! I'd given you over for worms' meat years ago" (11). There is a real delight in anachronism: characters move between homesteads, taverns, and castles, riding on horseback or in carts, and they dress in archaic garments such as woolen robes and hooded leather tippets. These anachronisms are suggestive of a wider fantasy that things will return to how they once were, doubling the present back on itself. The only significant trace of modernity is magic: Tom's "magic flute" is apparently the result of contemporary advances in neuroscience, and Peter the tale spinner tells "magical" sagas of television, "glittering carts drawn by invisible horses," and "metal birds" (35). The elimination of machines, arbitrarily and totally, shows the novel's medievalism to be an ideological fantasy: windmills, steel parts, coal-fired engines, and animal-powered machines could be manufactured in England even with an end to global trade. Despite awareness of the "physical causes" of melting icecaps, the church and the rebel Fellowship agree to view it as a "Final Warning" and "Divine Judgment" on materialists (42, 100). Thus, anthropogenic global warming is turned from a physical event that kills five billion people into the sign of an omnipotent God. Besides killing the vast majority of the world's population, the novel's deluge also drowns technological modernity, clearing the way for an immaterial universalism.

In effect, the Drowning is a literary effect to compress geography and homogenize society. Characters' travel is fundamentally a device to indicate history, not place: characters encounter ruins and sail over long-drowned boroughs "beneath [a] thousand year old quilting of red silt" (63). Although the novel is obsessed with journeys, these are only between the homogenous "kingdoms" within Britain. Neither Ireland nor the territories of France have exerted any influence over the archipelago, nor have the kingdoms drifted much from each other in terms of culture. Moreover, the novel carefully excludes any knowledge of the world beyond the Seven Kingdoms or the fate of people beyond Europe after the Drowning. The novel's medievalism is hardly an excuse for these exclusions—there are no signs of the lively trade networks that once operated throughout Europe and Asia. All trace of immigrants, in the case of foreign names, words, or physical features, have disappeared. Instead, the novel's geographical simplification authorizes a new form of social homogenization. This purification sets up the operation of magic. The novel's hero, a young piper, creates a mystical connection with his audience, a "bridge" between all listeners (34), "a master-key" his audience experiences as a vision of "The White Bird" (34). The White Bird "reveals" the brotherhood of all humanity, but one that curiously depends on a "world" of just Britain. Conversion is described as a violent yet blissful submission to cliché: explosions of whiteness, appalling and crazy, lightness and invisible wings, hosannas and surrender, the becoming of a tiny infant and a joining with the sun (32). There is a direct line of influence from Christian mysticism (particularly of the Holy Spirit), to the secular brotherhood of the Romantics, to the environmentalist universalism glimpsed here. Troublingly, though, the novel's account of kinship depends on a Drowning that eliminates all social difference.

Despite the power of this homogenization, *The Road to Corlay*'s fantasy of the future is authorized by contemporary, scientific realism. In the novel, the archaic texture of the third millennium is intercut with scenes from the late 1970s: scientists at the Livermore Foundation in Somerset witness the post-Drowning future through out-of-body experiences and improbable machinery (the "Encephalo-Visual Converter"). More surprising is the shift to realist description, spending a page to describe a dark blue Volkswagen's progress on the M5 motorway, through "the sodden pastures of Sedgemore," traffic slowed by rolling low gray waves of rain, and the cars "dragging clouds of spray behind them like trailers of smoke (72). Such descriptions are far more evocative than the tankards and hearthstones of the third millennium, not least because the banal rainstorm presages the decades of flooding the stalled drivers cannot yet imagine. The narration also enables the precise documentation of place—the car is on the junction before Taunton, the village of North of Petherton, and then the Quantock Hills. This precision finally enables the scientists to match the landscape outside the hospital windows, early experiments on the melting of the ice caps, and the protruding Quantock and Blackdown hills glimpsed in the out-of-body experiences (153–55). Despite the medievalism of the future, its fantasy ultimately depends on the narrative realism and scientific apparatus of the present.

In *The Road to Corlay*, global warming becomes comprehensible in the tension between a fantastic future and a scientific present, between a quotidian experience of weather and a model of future climate, between prophetic vision and verifiable landscape. The Drowning is used to authorize a fantasy of organic unity, but it eliminates the very real, material problems that face human beings. Similarly, Ballard's *Drowned World* deploys the deluge to simplify humans' complex, diverse relationships to geography and labor. For this complexity, both novels substitute a literary historiography, prehistoric or medieval, to cover the future. Nevertheless, landscape reemerges from the fantasy as something more durable than either the technological society of the present or the anachronism of the future: a foundation for both science and fiction.

Surveying the Deluge: Will Self's *The Book of Dave*

The theme of regression has been a recurrent trope in British fiction since the early twentieth century. Conrad's *Heart of Darkness,* Ballard's climatic retelling, and Cowper's neomedievalism sit within a wider cultural anxiety about cultural decline. So often, the language of decline has been taken by novelists to mean reversion, a movement back to medieval or "primitive" order. There have been numerous novels that have followed this template, with more or less derivative results.

Two examples indicate the tip of the iceberg. In Marcus Sedgwick's *Floodland* (2009), a girl is one of the last inhabitants of Norwich, now a small island disappearing into the sea. After Zoe is left behind by the rescue boats, she is plunged into a world of technological decline characterized by allotments and the rotting remains of cars.[17] Zoe finally escapes a maddened mob in a rowboat, only to be stranded on a smaller island controlled by a hierarchical, violent band of children living in a cathedral. After enduring predictable torment from the stunted, sadistic children, Zoe finally escapes to a shantytown where her parents have been waiting for her. Thus, *The Road to Corlay*'s gothic medievalism is paired with Ballard's primitivism, with a clear debt to William Golding's *Lord of the Flies.* In Julie Bertagna's *Exodus* (2002), a similar girl lives on a stranded spit of land, its community also eking out a living through subsistence farming in the shadow of a cathedral, as the seas continue to rise.[18] Separated from her parents at the boats, once again, the girl encounters distinct communities: refugees stranded outside city walls, an underclass of gentle tree people, and a wealthy city-state of Internet traders who live on virtual reality and roller skates, ignorant of the slave labor that sustains them. The narrative turns Mosaic when the heroine leads a slave revolt, saving the survivors of her home and the tree people, sailing for the promised land of Greenland. Bertagna's world is more imaginative than Sedgwick's, but both depend on the same hackneyed structure of regression. There are many more novels that use a fantasy history to paper over the problem of depicting a climate-changed future.[19]

In this literary context, when warnings of being knocked back to the Iron or Stone Age have become all too familiar, a need has grown to re-animate the underlying threat of the Anthropocene. So many deluge novels display an earnest humanism, assuming that historical regression can lay the ground for a happier time, renewing familial and communal intimacies while fostering an ecological way of life. Even in Ballard's savage vision, re-gression opens man to a new freedom, recovering the real meaning of his genetic inheritance. Superficially, such deluge novels warn of the horrors of unabated emissions, but read more closely, they display an unaccount-able faith that climate change will restore humanity's organic inheritance. Will Self's *The Book of Dave* directly confronts these assumptions, satirizing both the blind emissions culture of the present and the easy idealization of our Anthropocene future.

Like *The Road to Corlay*, *The Book of Dave* is set in two time periods, a time roughly correlating to the present and a distant, postapocalyptic fu-ture.[20] The narrative that spans 1987–2003 describes the working life and private descent of Dave Rudman, a London taxi driver. Alternating chapters describe events from 509 to 524 "AD"—that is, "After Dave," when Rud-man's angry, deluded writings have become the basis for a whole religious and political culture. Also like *The Road to Corlay*, *The Book of Dave* does not narrate the sea's surge or the mechanics of transition. However, both time periods relentlessly reflect on the unrepresented deluge that destroys modern civilization, floods Britain to approximately one hundred meters, and pushes the archipelago into a new Dark Ages.

The Book of Dave draws heavily on British dystopian forebears. J. G. Bal-lard was a friend and influence to Self. Self also acknowledges Russell Ho-ban's postapocalyptic novel *Riddley Walker* (1980): both books are set in a future Iron Age, depend on "an entirely constructed dialect," and question the delusions of history and progress.[21]

In *The Road to Corlay*, the church is frightening and sinister, led by an ominous archbishop obsessed with orthodoxy and enforced by mysterious henchmen whose appearance sends townspeople into hiding. Self, by contrast, was influenced by the idea that religion "is a necessary function of state formation and that the content of this or that 'holy book' is more or less irrelevant to what people make of it."[22] That Dave's mad but wholly un-spectacular, undistinguished, and stereotypically middle-class rants should form the basis of a future religion works to ridicule both contemporary val-ues and the future idealism those values conjure. Far from a pastoral uto-pia, the future kingdom is overseen by "drivers," "dävine" priests one part cabbie, one part slaver. However, the villains' dignity (so important for the fantasy genre) is undercut by narrative descriptions: they dress in a cassock called "jeans and T-shirt," crowned with a ridiculous mirror so they can follow Dave's injunction to know what is behind oneself. At another point, the narrator declares, "The Drivers were queers—men who had no desire to father children."[23] The PCO ("Public Carriage Office") rules the king-dom with relentless torture, mutilation, and executions borrowed from "ac-counts of what happened at Tyburn in Elizabethan London."[24] The PCO's doctrine combines bibliophilia—"I come to bring you the Book!"; sexual and moral censure—"daddies and mummies consorting in grotesque pro-pinquity"; sacrificial redemption—"Dave forsook the Lost Boy for your own miserable fares"; misogyny—"sullied by rag and blob—whorish, licentious creatures!"; and revelation—"See the Wheel! Read the metre! Know that the final tariff is at hand!" (176). Such preaching, made ridiculous with the combination of Latinate dogma and taxi-driver slang, can never be taken as seriously as the church's Black Bird in *The Road to Corlay*.

Self's novel also resists Corlay's fantasy that environmental democracies are a simple next step. In Ham, the traditional, democratic council of men is in terminal decline, and the local Driver easily subverts it. An evangelical "Geezer" may occasionally try to preach direct communion with Dave and egalitarian local fellowship, but such an upstart is tortured, broken, and his tongue torn out (80–81). Nor are local traditions benign: children are anointed in rituals that often kill them, girls are sexually exploited and then ostracized (71), and older women are routinely beaten and raped (309). The violence, ignorance, and prejudice of the local community hardly bode well for a local democracy.

Hamsters are not particularly interested in celebrating natural land-scapes. Certainly, they have a complex knowledge and belief system that depends on local place, but they wholly lack the purifying category of "na-ture." Their world is divided into things that are "reel" and "toyist" ("fake, unreal, or taboo" [495]). The assignations of these categories, however, are surprisingly inverted: "As it was written in the Book, plastic was only the vital clay from which the world had been moulded" (75). Thus, the Dävine orthodoxy ironically privileges the vestiges of twentieth-century London as natural and the rest as artificial, inverting our own sense of plastic as non-biodegradable rubbish. Amusingly enough, "MadeinChina" is the demotic term for creation (490), and Inglanders prize plastic charms that "[bear] the phonics M-A-D-E, H-O-N-G, or .-C-O-M" (75). Thus, the future religion celebrates anthropogenic creation over what moderns might term the natural, much as Christian dogma privileges divine creation for its imprint of a higher intelligence. The Hamsters have an intimate, spiritual relationship with the landscape that has nothing to do with a belief in or interaction with nature.

Neomedieval climate change novels often simplify or suppress human economy, playing into the fantasy of a return to local villages in harmony with nature. *The Book of Dave* relentlessly exposes the problems with such a regression. In 523 After Dave, mining, hunting, farming, and husbandry are all intertwined with older technology. They dig up "London Brick" thinking it is from creation; kill whole flocks of blackwings nesting in skyscrapers; harvest "wheatie"—a branded cereal signaling the attenuation of grain; and herd "motos"—genetically modified, semi-intelligent pigs used for meat, oil, companionship, and sex (243, 491). Just as important, the island's local products are thoroughly shaped by a larger, feudal economy, whereby the exploited periphery harvests goods for the center, New London. In short, the king and the PCO build enormous vanity products replicating the London of the Book of Dave. Understood systematically, Ing's feudal economy is entirely ordered to justify power relations between peripheral communities and the center of New London. Small, local communities are not ecologically self-sufficient, so much as artifacts that enable economic and environmental exploitation.

Although *The Book of Dave* ruthlessly satirizes utopian localism, the novel counteroffers a remarkably meticulous account of England's landscape as it has been transformed by deluge. In setting *The Book of Dave* at least five hundred years in the future, Self was able to draw on IPCC calculations that "the present Greenland and Antarctic ice sheets contain enough water to raise sea level by almost 70m," leaving enough time for the entire ice sheets to melt.[25] In Self's novel, the physical terrain is rather precisely drawn according to a new, much deeper sea level.[26] The local island of Ham's features corresponds directly to the physical and cultural geography of Hampstead Heath. The shape of the coastline, ponds, woods, and fields is determined by the current elevation and features of the famous park and neighborhood. Similarly, the names of the paths, homes, and other places are closely derived from existing roads, golf courses, historic homes, and landmarks in Hampstead Heath, with a new layer added by future events and Dave's personal history. Beyond London, the Ing Archipelago is constructed with similar care. The main place names correspond to shortened names of cities and geological areas.[27] Geographical features continue to determine settlement patterns, and the motorways of the twentieth century continue to determine travel in the archipelago. The "Emwun" (M1) has become a "great trading route," as an embanked road paved with now-"pulverized crete" (240–41). As the novel's glossary attests, Hamsters have a detailed vernacular knowledge of local species, but a wider knowledge of different species is lost with science. When Carl travels beyond Ham, he is surprised to see "alien species of tree and shrub that jostled the shoreline," with "dwarfish smoothbarks, silverbarks and crinkleleafts, familiar from Ham . . . interspersed with larger trees with deeply grooved, ash-grey trunks and others that were like glossier, greener versions of the pines at Wallötop" (239). Far from offering a glimpse of purified nature, the geography of Ing is a tangled mesh of modern industrial works, peasant knowledge and technology, and the geological and biological features that persist after the flood. The detailed sense of future landscape found in the novel is a product of this entanglement.

The Book of Dave's successful satire of a *post*diluvian future is also predicated on a far more exhaustive grounding in the material practices of the *contemporary* world. As an author, Will Self has positioned himself among other British "psychogeographers," particularly Iain Sinclair, Peter Ackroyd, and Pat Barker, who explore space as simultaneously produced by physical geography and the projections of the mind.[28] For Self, psychogeography avoids the picturesque city and bucolic countryside and the English Romantic tradition that authorizes these views, exposing the "shit" "where people live and breathe and think and emote."[29] Thus, psychogeography suggests a renewed engagement with actual, rather than idealized, space and an environmental awareness predicated on material reality instead of perfected nature. *The Book of Dave*'s antihero allows Self to account for both the physical geography of London and the psychic experience of moving in the city. Like all London black cab drivers, Dave Rudman has completed the Knowledge, a famous test comprising "every single street within a six-mile radius of Charing Cross, together with all the principal buildings." As Self has described it, the cab driver, far more than the mayor, queen, or prime minister, would be able to memorialize the metropolis if it were flooded as a result of environmental catastrophe.[30] Neuroscience experiments have indicated that this act of memorization actually increases drivers' posterior hippocampus; Dave Rudman is materially shaped by his knowledge of the city.[31] But Dave's experience of that city is also critically important. Self has described Debord's psychogeographic theory as a marvelous, implausible vision of freedom, that drifting drunk through Paris could magically disintegrate capitalist society.[32] The young Dave of the late twentieth century understands cab driving much like Debord, leapfrogging from fare to fare, away from "the supervisory eyes [of] adult working life" (392), "the bliss of driving" (101), and a deep knowledge of the city and its people, so that everyone—cops, bartenders, fellow cabbies, and fares—"knew and respected him" (160). This free fellowship presents a powerful, political alternative to hierarchical capital, predicated on a psychogeographic engagement with urban reality. And yet, Dave's original freedom breaks down under the material experience of antediluvian London.

Poised between psychogeographic liberation and corporate control, Dave adheres to a neoliberal system of freedom while speeding its collapse. In an earlier story by Self, Timothy Clark has argued, traffic is used as a "a kind of environmental criticism that does not rest on an anachronistic appeal to some supposedly lost relation to 'nature' but which traces the structures of the auto-interruption, auto-paralysis or auto-immunity of the heritage of consumerist liberalism."[33] In *The Book of Dave*, the "auto-interruption, auto-paralysis or auto-immunity" of London's system of transportation emerges as an ironic force within the novel. Dave experiences the Knowledge as a form of governance imprinted on his mind, conditioning all movement in the city. He is further obsessed with surveillance, speed restrictions, and the PCO (392). (No wonder the regime proves so adaptable to the future medieval.) The scrutiny is imprinted on his body, leading to the indignity of piles, forming cabbies into "arseholes" (51). But while Dave experiences himself as an ellipsis, one of any number of "exes," he emerges as "an emblematic figure," "a kind of everyman . . . of contemporary London," "a representative man of his time."[34] Dave's contempt comes from his recognition of being a part of a system he cannot condone, the perpetrator and victim of its autoimmune response.

The work of this autoimmune response becomes etched on Dave's consciousness, dictating the flow of his inner monologue. Dave once hoped driving a cab would enable him to move through London in fellowship with every class of person, a psychogeographic omniscience. Instead, Dave finds himself forced to act as though he cares about football (which he detests) and to speak "mockney"—a fake cockney accent: both confirm the stereotypical identity of the cabby by "evoking a happier age of honest amity and sturdy deference" (106).[35] Internally, Dave begins to rage at "racist cunts," "spinnies" and "lezzers," "young slappers and old boilers," "fucking coons and fucking Yids." The narrator suggests judgment is endemic to the brief, stereotyped conversation between the fare and the driver, with prejudice forming "the deepest, darkest, most atavistic stream of cabbie consciousness" (161). This violent inner monologue is not opposed to the internalized order of the PCO; it is part of an interiority that depends on the bureaucratic simplification of people and places. Even during sex, Rudman's approach to a woman is conditioned by the PCO's language: "[Dave] approached Michelle as he would call over a run: *leave on left tit, comply throat, comply mouth, left shoulder, right hip, forward cunt*. . . . The junctions of her body were well signed, and his Knowledge was sufficient to hold her" (112). The PCO's methods of structuring space are literally imprinted on the body. Similarly, Dave's experience of nature replaces nonhuman entities with artificial, self-referential terms: rain becomes screenwash, the moon a headlight, the Milky Way the dashboard, and the day is divided into "tariffs" (140). In short, Dave's inner monologue traces the London's circuit of power.

The Book of Dave describes the capitalism of London in the late twentieth century as a confused system, but no less totalizing for that. For Self, Rudman's complex class position is indicative of "what has happened in English society . . . in the last twenty to twenty-five years." Dave is not purely plebeian, with his mother a teacher and his father "a small and slightly shady businessman."[36] Complicating the picture, his ex-wife is a "fashion victor" who uses computer courses and conference organizing to vault herself into a new class position with Cal Devenish, a wealthy television producer. As a young taxi driver during the recession of 1992, Dave learns that

London is determined by finance capital, with the collapse of BCCI, heavy losses by Lloyd's bank, and calamitous declines on the stock market affecting the operation and mood of the entire city (202). These entities shape a large economic climate, but other entities dispense economic "reality" to London's citizens. Not much later, Dave begins to learn the connections among finance companies, skip tracers, and loan sharks (225–26). Even earlier, Dave had learned to fear an arbitrary PCO that would "ruthlessly [fail] black cabs for their annual test, picking up on such tiny infractions as underinflated tyres and 'lacklustre' bodywork," with the real cause being a driver's failure to pay a kickback (108). Corrupt financial interests motivate the city's transportation network.[37]

The parameters of London's financial interests also shape awareness of climate change. In the novel, Dave never becomes fully conscious of how his own behavior or London's transportation system might exacerbate global warming. Instead, proleptic visions of the destruction of London appear within the received channels of communication. Driving from Soho to the Thames Barrier, a fare tells Dave he's a runner for a film about the flooding of the river (263). Not long after, Dave sees a vision of London's destruction:

> Finally, he peered up through the windscreen of the Fairway at the huge electronic signboards covering the buildings of Piccadilly Circus. One showed the Circus itself—the teeming crowds, the enmeshed traffic. Then, without warning, water began to flood between the buildings, a tidal bore that came surging along the rivers of light. Dave was shocked—what could this apocalyptic vision be selling? The flooded concourse wavered, fragmented and was replaced by a slogan: DASANI MINERAL WATER, A NEW WAVE IS COMING. (291)

In Piccadilly Circus, the deluge is broadcast as an advertisement. In such a spectacle, Dave finds himself enmeshed in a reality that rivals his own subjective experience, shocking Dave that "the Circus itself" is destroyed, even as his cab stands within it. The irony is doubled over as Dave realizes Dasani has created the vision, first to advertise itself but also as a product that exemplifies the proliferation of greenhouse gases with little benefit to humans. In such moments, Dave's taxi becomes one link in the circulation of desires, images, and capital, all conducted with fossil fuels. Through such spectacles, disaster itself is circumscribed, its potential to rupture reality never extending beyond the screen.

Dave's Book acts as an interpretive device for the recent past and distant future, ironically reflecting both times in light of climate change. Dave's prophecy, "a comprehensive blueprint for a society in which, once the old world had been swept away by a MIGHTY WAVE, EVERYTHING WOULD BE SPLIT DOWN THE MIDDLE" (349), ironically reflects a recent past when apocalyptic deluges are so banal as to advertise filtered water and a future so changed by global warming that Dave has no hope of envisioning it. By having the book bound in metal and burying it in the backyard of Beech House, his son's home, Dave sets in motion the political and social vision that shapes the postapocalyptic world. Rudman models the book on the Koran (just after the World Trade Center attacks) (209), the Kaddish read at his father's funeral (229), and the golden tablets shown to Joseph Smith and starting the Mormon religion (233), although he personally dismisses religion (233). Nor could a sane Rudman accept the book's bitter misogyny, its silent censorship of the Knowledge's "shitty points" (346), or the repressive society it inaugurates: objections that compel Dave to write and bury a corrective second book (477). This belated vision of tolerance finds much less traction in future Ing, bringing repression down on the Hamsters who advocate its message. Dave's first Book, on the other hand, shows the effects of power, capital, and emissions as usual, ironically advocating nothing less. Indeed, the force of the novel comes from the recognition that a cartoonish, thoroughly unreal recent past could well lead to a postapocalyptic future, without any individual's endorsement. The deluge is the narrative mechanism for representing this transformation, and the Book is the structure for giving it meaning.

The Book of Dave is a remarkable book in a number of respects. It incisively interrogates both the dominant cultural values of the recent past and the supposedly environmental values of a neoprimitive future. It invents not just a dialect but a whole future worldview out of the misshapen geographical, urban, economic, and cultural climate of the recent past. More subtly, it never affords too much dignity to either ideology. In *The Book of Dave*, contemporary modernity and postdiluvian medievalism are scandalous constructions rather than historical inevitabilities.

All the same, the novel's use of the deluge as a postapocalyptic device obscures important aspects of climate change. Chief among these is the parochialism of Rudman's London and future Ing. Clark has described how, in Self's writing, London "emerges as an illusory physical and psychic space that has blocked off anything external to its own functioning."[38] In *The Book of Dave*, the focus on the Knowledge obscures a wide world beyond: even after the Deluge drowns London's late-twentieth-century ideology, future Ing has received no new input from a wider world, much of it far drier than the new archipelago. Similarly, Liorah Anne Golumb has observed that "the hows and whys that set [Self's stories] in motion are not only unimportant, they are virtually beside the point."[39] Like all of the deluge novels examined in this chapter, *The Book of Dave* takes a startlingly distant approach to the unfolding of a global catastrophe, eliding direct description, scientific mechanism, and any sense of real humans, animals, and landscapes as they are transformed by climate change. The novel never gives much sense that the worst effects of climate change could be averted or that real people suffer from anything other than human oppression. In *The Book of Dave*, climate change is a local, causeless, and inevitable catastrophe. If even satirical treatments fall into this trap, the deluge, as a literary form, would inevitably seem to elide political accountability and responsible organization. However, a variation on the deluge novel begins to redress these shortcomings.

Floods

In the 1980s, novelists began to draw on a different tradition of flood narratives. The defining feature of the deluge novels described thus far is their temporal setting: they imagine the effects of climate change in the far distant future, after the ice caps have melted. The relatively slow geological process of melting polar sheets matches the enormous social transformations of these novels, altering the coastlines of the Earth and the boundaries of human society in the long sweep of history. By contrast, a recurrent trope of the contemporary novel is the flood-as-duration. In these narratives, a quotidian, recognizable setting is transformed by a local flood, providing the means to illuminate, rupture, and challenge the boundaries of the social order. George Eliot's *The Mill on the Floss*, Emile Zola's *The Deluge*, D. H. Lawrence's *The Rainbow*, Zora Neale Hurston's *Their Eyes Were Watching God*, and William Faulkner's *As I Lay Dying* are all examples of Victorian and Modernist texts that use a flood in this way. All of these novels invoke the deluge of Genesis but focus on the plurality of the people in the present, rather than recovering the privileged viewpoint of the exceptional Noah. As in many ballads from Mississippi blues, the focus is on loss, not salvation.

This version of flood narrative received a second, important infusion with the rise of photography and contemporary disaster media.[40] The documentation of catastrophic floods, the submerging of homes and familiar landmarks, and the images of grief-stricken victims have, over the last century, become a recognizable cultural product. At the same time, the spiraling effects of perilous urban development, a crescendo of record-breaking storms, and a twenty-four-hour news cycle have intensified the sense that floods are not merely a longstanding historical possibility but rather a distinctly *contemporary* disaster. In the 1980s and 1990s, prominent floods would seem to have provided inspiration for a series of important climate change novels. Since the turn of the century, floods in Malaysia, Bangladesh, the UK, Australia, and throughout the United States have made the threat omnipresent. Particularly in 2005, disastrous floods in Calgary, Canada, Cumbria, England, Mumbai, India, Eastern Europe, and New Orleans set records for deaths and damages, challenging assumptions that human societies could easily adapt to outlier weather. There is a strong indication that Hurricane Katrina and the subsequent flooding of New Orleans altered the American public's opinion of the Republican Party. More recently, President Obama's handling of Superstorm Sandy days before the 2012 election seemed to give his candidacy a boost. Politically and scientifically, it has been a challenge to tie these storms to climate change. The novel has had no such difficulty, using the flood as a productive means of structuring our immediate experience of climate change. Despite their shared imagery and sources, such flood narratives are necessarily contemporary, where apocalyptic deluge narratives offer a continually deferred future.

George Turner's early climate change novel, *The Sea and Summer* (1987), integrates both types of flood narrative. The novel, published in the United States under the title *The Drowning Towers,* was shortlisted for a Nebula Award and won the Arthur C. Clarke award. Although the novel's economic implications will be examined in more detail in the fourth chapter, *The Sea and Summer* is also of interest as a means of distinguishing deluge and flood novels. In a frame story, "The Autumn People," the characters live over a thousand years in the future, long after the ice caps have melted and Australia has been submerged. The skyscrapers of the past have become tourist attractions visited by boats, a trope familiar from Ballard's and Self's deluge novels. In Turner's postdiluvian vision, society is rigidly compartmentalized, population is severely restricted, and people look back on the "greenhouse culture" with disdain. The frame story revolves around an Artist who tries to stage a play about the near future, while a future archaeologist lends factual and imaginative insights, reconstructing attitudes of the period. Ultimately, the Artist finds the poverty and ethics of the society bizarre, concluding the past is unstageable, impenetrable.

The majority of *The Sea and Summer* focuses on a closer period, from 2041 to 2061, when Australian society is stretched to the breaking point by floods. The greenhouse effect has altered the basic parameters of human life: world average temperature has surged by 4.5 degrees since 1990; the ice caps are melting; oceans have risen thirty centimeters.[41] As the Antarctic ice shelf melts, ocean currents, temperature gradients, and wind patterns are altered, "drowning untellable desert in useless water while ancient forests grew brown and bare under a brass-faced sun, giving this year and taking next, turning grassland to tinder while it poured unwanted, polluted water down the rivers" (227). Economic woes brought on by climate change have split society into two groups, the Sweet, a minority made up of employed workers living on high ground, and the Swill, an enormous, unemployed underbelly ghettoized in flood-prone high rises. The novel traces movement between the groups: when the Conway family loses its sole paycheck, the father commits suicide, the mother brings her two sons to a social borderland, and the sons try to claw their way back into Sweet society as a police spy and an agent in fraud. The heroes of the novel are a different pair. Kovacs runs a protection racket in the Fringe but enforces a violent social order in the Towers that ultimately protects the Swill; Captain Nikopoulos, a high-ranking police officer, forges a cadre of indoctrinated brothers dedicated to preserving society, even through the use of covert force. The differences between the two parts of the novel are significant. The distant future of "The Autumn People" encourages condemnation of the entire greenhouse culture, while the nearer flood narrative invites more careful examination of the social mechanisms of the early Anthropocene. Instead of a simple apocalypse, individuals in different positions are faced with the repeated crises of climatic erosion. Many subsequent novels have used floods to investigate the breakdown of civil society as its material parameters are destroyed.

Many excellent novels have used a flood to engage directly with the bio-logical, ecological, political, and economic implications of climate. A num-ber of novels throughout this study might have been discussed in greater detail here. In Saci Lloyd's *Carbon Diaries 2015,* a teenager, Laura Brown, her family, and the London neighborhood she lives in are transformed by a year of carbon rationing and disastrous weather. The climax is a major flood that overwhelms the Thames Barrier, forcing Laura to reevaluate the social structures that hold her world together. Paolo Bacigalupi's *The Windup Girl* describes a future Bangkok overshadowed by tall dykes holding a dark sea at bay. When economic conflict precipitates a civil war, one faction blows up the city's vital pumps, inundating the entire world of the novel. The loss of species and genetic material is explored in T. C. Boyle's *A Friend of the Earth,* as steady rains in California decimate the condos that have replaced natural habitats and wipe away the private menagerie of an aging rock star, indicating the limits of conservation in an era of climate change.

Kim Stanley Robinson's *Forty Signs of Rain,* the first novel in the "Science in the Capital" trilogy, gathers many of the tropes of the flood novel. (Later, we will examine the trilogy's Anthropocene political organization.) In *Forty Signs of Rain,* a flood materializes the abstract idea of climate change by locating it in a familiar place. The geographical details of Washington, DC, make the city susceptible to flooding: the Tidal Basin only ten feet above sea level, the fluctuations of the Potomac River, the "usual correlation of money and elevation."[42] The combination of the tide cycle, the remnants of a tropical storm blocking the Chesapeake Bay, and a commonplace thun-derstorm flood the capital: the National Mall turned into a body of water, Constitution Avenue a river two feet deep, "the city south of Pennsylvania Avenue" turned into "a building-studded lake," the Kennedy Center and Lincoln Memorial surrounded by flood waters, Arlington National ceme-tery inundated, and Reagan Airport completely gone (330). Through this, Washington's familiar monuments are turned into public symbols of cli-mate change.

The media itself is central to the contemporary experience of flooding, its conventions lending familiarity to the singularly disastrous event. Tele-vision meteorologists treat the climate as bad art or unstaged reality TV; friends and colleagues mention the storm in cell phone conversations; cooks and patrons watch the weather on a café television; being engrossed in the Internet lets a character nearly miss the storm's effects; an office television lets everyone learn of the storm, until they realize a live feed is showing the view from their own building. Views are assembled from cameras on buildings, monuments, and bridges; drone cameras on blimps and balloons; and footage from other channels (329). In the presence of such pervasive media, a pure, individual, naturalistic experience of the flood is impossible. But neither is the converse accurate, that the intensive mediation of the flood makes a postmodern event that "never really happened." On the contrary, these different forms of mediation are material features of a material disaster articulated in the novel.

One of the striking features of the flood is its displacement of place, bringing a relatively common disaster into "the capital of the hyperpower" (342). The flood is realized as it alters and erases not just geographical detail but also human connections to place. This is not a single literary effect so much as a rich collection of literary strategies that work to the same end. The final section of *Forty* is a catalog of these strategies. In the opening passage, Charlie awakens from a dream in which he can finally persuade politicians of the need to reduce emissions (314). Charlie's first view of the storm is as a quotidian dream: it seems "glossy and surreal," suggesting "ungraspable meaning" (323). On television, a reporter describes the weather system with an incongruously "happy smile" (328). Charlie can't call his wife because all telephone circuits are busy; the break in "permanent communication" brings terror, dizziness, and a feeling of amputation (329). The familiar landscape of the Capitol appears as Venice (326); the Washington Monument is like "an obelisk in the Nile's flood" (354). Reporters themselves are distanced, as foreign journalists can only get to the edges of the storm, and news helicopters are drafted into rescue operations (342). Unsurprisingly, literary discontinuities emerge, as the National Zoo releases its animals in "a reversal of Noah's flood . . . in which the people mostly survived, but two of every species were drowned" (344). Social boundaries are interrupted by looters and the reimposition of law by the National Guard but also by thousands of spontaneous volunteers helping to sandbag important landmarks (337). Later, a festival mood prevails on the Mall, with people in canoes, kayaks, motorboats, and blue pedalos, dressed in Hawaiian shirts, bathing suits, even carnival masks, creating a Mardi Gras scene (355). Charlie notes a racial shift as well, with "many more black faces than Charlie was used to seeing on the Mall," comparing it to a festival in Trinidad (356). Finally, congressional politics are inverted, as politicians rush to address climate change. Thus, Robinson's novel gathers many of these literary strategies for dis*placing* narrative realism: wish fulfillment, surrealism, affective incongruence, bodily nausea and amputation, foreignness, media failure, ironic allusions, social unrest, racial integration, carnival, and legislative revolution. These pluriform effects would themselves be dizzying and alienating for a reader, except that they all act similarly. By interrupting the sense of rooted specificity, they make climate change knowable as a narrative effect that disrupts place and mediation. Robinson's novel, like so much climate fiction, is neither realism nor fantasy, because both are needed simultaneously to articulate climate disaster.

One of the most sustained and thoughtful engagements with the flood-as-event is Maggie Gee's *The Flood*. As in the other novels discussed in this chapter, *The Flood* uses the catastrophic event to consider the whole of society in a climate-changed era, and like the best of these novels, it uses material disaster to force the reader to think beyond the purely social aspects of environmental politics. More important, Gee brings to the trope an extraordinarily rich account of what contemporary society is, and how those connections might be articulated by the form of the novel. Ultimately, Gee's society novel comments on the limits of individual revelation, humanism, and society itself in the Anthropocene.

Maggie Gee's oeuvre is often described in terms of multiculturalism and feminism, and *The Flood* continues these concerns. Gee's fiction has examined how characters interact with others, social and domestic institutions, and the "social phenomena that metonymically constitute the fabric of England and motivate myths of Englishness."[43] Gee has long been a critically acclaimed author, having been listed in *Granta*'s 1983 "Best of Young British Novelists," but her challenging engagement with race in *The White Family* (2002) led to the loss of her book contract with Harper Collins and further publication difficulties.[44] In *The Flood*, Gee explores the social and domestic institutions that frame individual character and Englishness more generally, without ever treating Englishness as a homogenous category. *The Flood* concentrates Gee's longer exploration of how individuals engage with the social and domestic institutions that constitute English character by drawing characters from Gee's previous novels, "metonymically [constituting] the fabric of England" in a tighter weave than would otherwise be possible in a three-hundred-page novel.[45]

The novel's characters are grouped around families, with other social and business connections complicating the picture. The portrait is intricate, but a summary of its interconnections suggests the deeper structure of the novel. The White family is central to *The Flood*. May, the mother of three grown children, reads Tennyson, babysits her grandchildren, and pines for her dead husband; Alfred was a racist and rather brutal father, but also fiercely committed to a working-class ethic and his family. The eldest son, Darren, is relatively absent, a "radical" but feted journalist invited to the climactic gala. May's daughter, Shirley, is taking a course on "accessing culture"; is married to a black hospital administrator, Elroy Edwards; and has twin sons, Franklin and Winston. Dirk, May's younger son, has recently been released from prison for killing Elroy's gay brother and has found a home in the racist One Way cult. Love and violence connect the White family to the Edwards family. Besides the murdered Winston and the philandering Elroy, the Edwards sister Viola is a swimming instructor tied by business and love to Zoe, while Delorice dates Davey Lucas and has become a famous but racially pigeonholed publisher at Headstone. The third family, the Lucases, is dominated by Lottie, a high bourgeois woman in her forties taking the Accessing Culture class with Shirley. She is married to Harold, who has spent the better part of twenty years writing a single book, *Living in Time*. Davey, Lottie's child, is a television presenter of an astronomy program (lightweight enough to be confused with astrology by viewers), while Lola is a teenage daughter interested in conspicuous consumption and protest. (Lola's friend and partner-in-crime, Gracie, has a journalist mother acquainted with Darren White.) Several other families are also significant. The Ships are dominated by Angela "Lamb," while her parents, Henry and Lorna, have become domestics and caretakers of Gerda, Angela's daughter. Mohammed and Rhuksanna Habib are an Anglo-Muslim family: Mohammed leads another "ethnic" list at Headstone, and Rhuksanna is the teacher of Winston, Franklin, and Gerda; Mohammed's sister in "Loya" (a near-equivalent of Iraq) is killed during the novel. Other characters (including Dirk White) are bound together by the cultish One Way group, led by the sociopathic Father Bruno. Moira Penny renounces her academic career as a scholar and biographer of Lamb and joins the One Way group. Milly and Samuel are a mixed-race couple in the group, with Milly also employed as a janitor at Viola and Zoe's pool. Susie is in the group and is also the brother of a gay art dealer, Isaac, who is friends with the painter, Ian. Faith and Kilda are also significant: Faith is Lottie's housekeeper and also watches

Winston and Elroy for Shirley; her daughter, Kilda, seems to have the power of foresight and also is a member of One Way. These thirty-odd characters thus represent a complex mesh of affiliations, a social fabric crisscrossed by gender, race, class, age, celebrity, culture, and belief.

This network is rather different from the matrix often used to suggest a social totality. Frequently, novels about society attempt to blanket all possible characters by bringing representatives into a coordinated grid of identity, with axes of race, sexuality, and class. Instead of following this logic, *The Flood* builds up social relationships through families, developing a society that is interconnected, diverse, and patterned by individual agency. As an origin of family, sexual relationships are the most obvious aspect of Gee's approach, creating household "units," whether heterosexual or lesbian, religious or secular. At the same time, the novel attends to the more complex affiliations created by sex, tracing connections based in the imagination, flirtation, repressed desire, infidelity, casual affairs, and obstructed sexuality. Such connections are marked by patriarchy and sexual norms, but they are not representative of a truth of heterosexuality, queerness, or spinsterhood. The power dynamics of these interactions are not straightforward, either. Strong men exert control over their wives but are influenced by sisters or white women. Other women, Viola and Angela Lamb, control lovers and parents, and Lottie dominates her husband with patronizing dismissals and is in turn manipulated by her spoiled daughter. Finally, Father Bruno's leadership of One Way is predicated on symbolic patriarchy that violently polices women like Kilda and Moira but does not rely on sex. For all of these characters, sexuality shapes their world, but ideology works with the desire, will, and meaning-making of individual characters, rather than being solely a force of repression in a grid of identity.

This tension between individual will and shared ideology suggests a complex model of economic, social, and cultural power. Different characters have vastly different levels of access to cultural authority, from "inside" academics to access-course students. Conversely, Moira, the academic, finds herself disempowered, while Lottie's private collection of artists discussed by the class suggests both authority and its limits, as she finds herself unable to discuss her paintings in the public space (96). In *The Flood*, authority and critique are interdependent: a painter sells his caricatures to museums by excluding himself from the culture industry (292); a journalist accuses the president of fraud, even as he hopes to win "an honour" (242–43); editors of ethnic "lists" at a major publisher can't influence its direction or even save its flooded masterpieces. The most pointed tension between individual power and collective ideology is President Bliss, a caricature of Tony Blair at the time of the invasion of Iraq.[46] Invading "Loya" is a way of keeping the Hesperican empire—a double for the United States—"onside" and of uniting "the people [who] are restless around the Towers" (38). When skepticism overwhelms the invasion and a child declares Bliss is "the Emperor with No Clothes" (255), Bliss's lack of personal agency is exposed. In short, Bliss can only advocate a war to keep burning oil. The structure of the job permits neither social inclusion nor a meaningful response to climate change.

In *The Flood*, power is a function of exclusion, but Gee never loses sight of how such exclusion is always predicated on continued relationship. At either end of the scale are the Lucases, who live in luxury, "safe behind walls and windows, in nice green neighbourhoods" (90), and the families who live in the Towers—socialized housing designating the pariahs of the social order. But rather than enforcing an absolute separation between classes, "the walls had become as thin as paper" (90). Housekeepers, children, religious devotees, burglars, and family members continually pass between. Sears argues Gee's novels "are acts of inclusion" that try to represent a social totality by describing the interdependence between privilege and "a social structure which demands disadvantage and poverty of some of its members."[47] In *The Flood*, the operation of this social totality is laid bare at the Gala, a climactic party toward the end of the novel. Those who walk the red carpet are at the top of society: political leaders, stars from every media, and those "real people . . . who have climbed to the top of something worthy" (235). This celebrity economy is underpinned by the machinery of power: journalists, PR people, protesters, and a military-industrial complex of generals and arms manufacturers (242–43). Others are invisible: waiters, caterers, prostitutes, guards, and children. And yet the narrator never falls under the Gala's spell, observing, "Actually, most of the world isn't here": laborers, rat catchers, door-to-door vendors, plumbers, bus conductors, lice inspectors, primary school teachers, midwives, babies, bin men, illegal immigrants, mini-cab drivers, cleaners, young offenders, and has-beens (246–47). These people's appearance, beyond the margins of the Gala, reveals but does not accept the force of exclusion.

Just as important, *The Flood* repeatedly directs attention to the nonhuman participants in this hierarchy. Early on, the narrator describes the city as "designed for humans" but also as supporting pets, billions of microbes, worms, birds, and urban foxes (7–8). At the Gala, rats are just beneath the surface, in sewage pipes and bins, "sniffing and whiffling" at the "wonderful plenty" of endangered species fed to the guests (245). In the flood, rats, mice, and "bright mats of microbes" thrive (165). By including these animals, The Flood traces a network of life beyond the margins of human society, undermining its privileged position. Thus, the novel indicates a network of the included, those who underwrite and protest privilege, the excluded, and the beings that prey upon and are sacrificed to its operation. At all points, individual, distinct consciousness is balanced with an ecosystemic view of a city desperately in need of rebalancing. This method creates a sense of totality, without ever losing sight of distinct beings worth caring about, worth conserving.

This view of living beings might be taken as an entirety, but The Flood emphasizes that it is underpinned by a material reality. Before The Flood's publication, Sears argued Gee's oeuvre was characterized by "the persistence of history, the material effects of abstract ideological assertions, and the prevalence of the social as the horizon of individual experience."[48] The cast of characters is utterly preoccupied with their social concerns. Beyond these concerns, the material effects of climate change act as a historical force, first insidiously, then cataclysmically, flooding her characters with a "'real' rather than a symbolic social world."[49] The first chapter opens by stating, "After months of rain, the sun broke through" (11). It is only in the break from a relentless cloud cover that consciousness and narrative are able to emerge. The rain both blocks thought and enables beauty: "Water on roads, walls, bridges, washed the lights into long slurs of colour, peacock-eyed where traffic lights stared. Trapped motorists listened to their radios" (81). In such passages, beauty is shared in many motorists' gaze, even as they sigh, stalled in traffic, at reports of further rain. And despite repeated official pronouncements that flood waters are going down, the narrator reports how "people say" that "the flood-waters have hardly receded," that they are even "rising again" (284). If even the "President" has "loads of stinking black sludge" in his garage (286), the floods give a collective ground of experience in the capital. The "real" includes both society and its material apparatus for creating social distinctions, bank accounts, architecture, parties, and television. But just as important, The Flood shows the persistence of a climate that acts without the permission or intellection of the city's inhabitants.

Despite a shared ground, social stratification distributes effluvia unevenly. Wealthy areas have both higher elevation and better services (14) and largely escape the flood's effects. Drivers can sigh and switch off their radios when they hear reports of "demonstrations in the south and east, where the populace claimed they were being neglected, their basements left flooded, their drains left blocked" (81). Beyond these neighborhoods, however, the base of the Towers stands in water, people wait hours for water buses, water supplies are contaminated, and public services, gardens, and swimming pools are closed. Dirk has been driven to rage by the smell of stinking drains in a small cell (23), and the rhetoric of the One Way cult is dominated by images of biblical apocalypse in the guise of floods. It is a major turning point in the novel when Harold realizes that the wealthy inhabitants of riverside homes (likely a double for Chelsea) have also fled: in the Towers "people expected things to break down," but he's surprised that "even politicians couldn't protect themselves" (106). The real cause of Harold's surprise is that he, like most of the characters in *The Flood,* expects surging water to be diverted by *social* barriers.

The disproportionate effect of the floods on the poor could be seen as accidental, a "natural" disaster, but this doesn't account for the active force needed to keep the poor and the floods in the periphery. Lottie, the wealthy matron, has her SUV diverted through a council estate. Afraid of the "rabble," a "mob of thieves," she mows through a One Way protest. The SUV enacts environmental and social violence simultaneously, disproportionately causing climate change as it crushes the protestors of its more dangerous world. This is of a piece with the government's climate change policy. Bliss distracts attention from global warming and the flooded capital by beating the war drum in a foreign land. Finally forced to confront the floods, he claims they are the result of "sabotage," a striking lie that continues to divert attention from the flood's real cause and the government's responsibility. This is an obvious satire of Prime Minister Blair's prioritization of Iraq, but it also breathtakingly anticipates the Bush administration's failure to protect the poor and black citizens of New Orleans after Hurricane Katrina. Perhaps the most important achievement of *The Flood* is the way it shows society's too quick acceptance of the standing water. People complain but take water buses, follow diversions, ignore localized riots, and generally turn an extraordinarily dangerous situation into something entirely peripheral. By the time the real disaster comes, the government and its citizens have wasted weeks and months avoiding the problem, displaying a denial that is all the more terrifying for having been shown to be accurate. The flood is not a singular event, but an agent that insistently demands recognition.

When the climactic moment does arrive, it takes the form of thousands of failed epiphanies rather than a single, omniscient revelation. *The Flood* could be interpreted as a Judeo-Christian apocalypse, drawing on Genesis and the book of Revelation, if refusing its forebears' final judgment.[50] However, *The Flood* thoroughly critiques the narrative form of revelation. In revelation, the climactic moment exposes a single, divine truth. Yet the novel's seer, Kilda, tells the One Way group that there is not a single revelation coming: "I do see it, now, I see a big wall of water. I do see, like, the end of the world, the thing you're always going on about. What you don't get is there's lots of different endings" (302). Instead of tying the dozens of narratives into a single conclusion, *The Flood*'s climax describes a series of concurrent "endings": innocent, compelling characters die from flood sickness, riots, suicide attacks, and a tidal surge. Each crisis overlaps the others, undermining any sense of a divine Event. Just as important, the ends of the world don't result in epiphany: the media interrupts flood warnings to run a fashion piece on waterproof boots (266); the president makes useless pronouncements to avoid being upstaged (257); and the public, oversaturated with disaster threats, ignore the warnings. This collective failure to recognize disaster proves deadly.

The Flood creates the expectation that salvation will be unevenly distributed, but the wall of water is, finally, indiscriminate. When at last the wealthy do try to leave the city, believing "they can always leave, that money will always get them away," they find most phones busy, taxis gone, helicopters already hovering over the sky (303). Instead of participating in the rapture of the rich, Lottie, Harold, and Lola's helicopter is overloaded by jewelry, shoes, art, and "other people who paid so much they could not be left behind" (312). Finally the helicopter "finds a blind silver wall, a final valley" (312). The poor, by contrast, "believe they can never leave" and drown just the same (303). Sarah Dillon interprets the novel's afterword ("After"), when the characters gather happily in a more familiar Kew Gardens, as proof that sinners and saved alike survive the flood (388), a kind of universalist afterlife. Nevertheless, the novel is rather more materialist than otherworldly: "City suspended over the darkness. Above the waters that have covered the earth, stained waters, bloody waters, water heaving with wreck and horror, pulling down papers, pictures, people; a patch of red satin, a starving crow, the last flash of a fox's brush" (325). The passage creates a pointed ambiguity about the relationship between the city suspended over the darkness and the waters below, but what is clear is that the reader is denied the comforting amnesia of the characters in the park. Climate disaster kills the elegant woman, the scavenging bird, and the fox, and it destroys truth, beauty, and humanism in a single, crashing wave. This is not purification, but a stained, bloody, horrific disaster. Rich and poor, black and white and brown, men and women, humans and animals live in a shared, interdependent world, but it takes an extraordinary narrative force to bring them to the same end. By emphasizing the bloody, indiscriminate wreckage, the novel denies the revelatory function of the apocalyptic narrative, as well as its escapism, returning the reader to a sense of real loss.

This refusal of revelation raises a central problem for narrative, not to mention the trajectory of the Anthropocene novel. Since Modernism, the novel has been seen as a form that can transcend time and difference, crystallizing points of view and granting vision to the reader. In *The Flood*, Harold articulates a new physics that owes much to Virginia Woolf's celebrations of consciousness: an immanent heaven with "no past or future, only a single infinite structure. A hall of time from which the moments opened, a mansion of many sunlit rooms" (91). This "mansion of many sunlit rooms" is reminiscent of *Mrs. Dalloway,* in which characters find moments of revelation in the quotidian activities of looking at light, shopping, and hosting a party. In the first chapter of *The Flood,* Lottie has a similar experience:

> Lottie loved light, and the day was alight. The morning poured in, glorious, between the curtains she never closed. Lottie heard birds, though she didn't know which ones—if only Harold were awake, she could ask him—and she lifted her head and glimpsed the blossom outside, bobbing blossom in February, Japanese something, Harold had said, scarlet flowers with golden centres, Japanese Quince, for the whole world was connected, red cups blazing on black leafless branches, glorious against the blue. Lottie let her head fall back again. She never stirred till her tea was brought up. (15)

Environmentalists and novelists have long hoped immanent experience would unlock progressive politics and conscientious stewardship of nature. And yet, Lottie's environmental revelation depends on her privilege to lie in, the subservience of a husband turned waiter, the cleaners who change her bed linens twice a week. While Lottie fancies her gaze transcends all creation, she is ignorant of the birds singing, the flowers she owns, and the boundaries of her own walled garden. The garden itself depends on a global trade in genetic material and a radically altered climate. Unreconstructed epiphany proves a weak light in the striated society of the Anthropocene.

For nearly fifty years, authors have struggled to locate the Anthropocene. If the novel draws climate change closer to its readers, allowing them a surge of immediate experience, its mediations have also dissolved the economic and social connections of contemporary reality, letting any sense of urgency drift away. In Ballard's and Cowper's early novels, the deluge substitutes humans' complex relationships to geography and labor, leaving behind a simplified sense of local place. Will Self's *The Book of Dave* satirizes these fantasies, but it passes over their dangerous fatalism, placing the reader on an island already destined to sink. By attending more closely to the unfolding of climatic disaster, flood novels address some of these shortcomings.

The Sea and Summer investigates the breakdown of civil society as its ecology and economy are eroded. In its place, Turner envisions a coercive, militant state, run by slumlords and secret police joined by a new chivalry. Robinson addresses another problem of the deluge novel, restoring immediacy to the fantasy of the Anthropocene future. Instead of renewing transparent realism, Robinson reveals a world obsessed with mediations of the weather, but *more* real for it. Gee develops the account of contemporary climate change by dwelling on the interconnected society of the immediate Anthropocene. If Turner cannot imagine an order beyond the breakdown of capitalism and patriarchy, Gee describes how the breakdown of civil society leaves behind its constituents—families, lovers, and vulnerable individuals—who are all too vulnerable to postnatural disasters. Gee also addresses the tension between realism and fantasy, describing a flooded world with political, social, and environmental features that are all too familiar.

In the final pages of *The Flood*, this tension among dystopia, arcadia, and the real is brought to a crisis. Throughout the novel, characters have dwelled in familiar doubles of this world's places. After the flood, however, all the novel's characters play together in London's Kew Gardens, animosities forgotten, glorious along the rose beds, "safe in the grass," happy in the sun (324). Certainly there are elements that raise comparison to a Christian afterlife, but this world is not a "paradisiacal spatial and temporal space."[51] Instead, the narrator describes a fictional world drawn closer, bearing the novel's characters into *our* place. If the novel's characters were relocated to paradise, this would suggest that climate change is of little consequence, since heaven is found beyond the changing world, in individual moments of peace and revelation. On the contrary, *The Flood* suggests that peace and human connection are wholly dependent on material place, that climate change has decimated the characters with whom the reader has identified, and that it also threatens to kill real people we love in *this* world. Even the paradisiacal scene discloses a quiet threat. "The heat is terrific: soon they will rest, lie down easily among the others" (324). In this world, where global warming is real, bodies lie down all too easily. Ultimately, the reader is placed in the uncertain ground between fictional reverie and climatic nightmare.

Unlike earlier deluge novels, *The Flood* reworks Judeo-Christian, individual judgment for the Anthropocene. Where Genesis imagines divine rage at moral sins, in the Anthropocene humanity condemns itself by miniscule trespasses on the atmosphere, accumulated over decades and centuries. *The Flood's* final tsunami is both a punishment and an opportunity for humans to resume animality. In verse, the narrator swells to omniscience:

> three thousand generations of humans
> stiff and damp from their spell underground
> pushing up alive from the flood-washed catacombs
> pulling themselves to their feet like apes (320)

Of course, the passage is highly reminiscent of the first section of *The Waste Land,* where the renewal brought by spring rains is figured as a painful reincarnation. While Genesis imagines the cleansing as joyous release, both *The Waste Land* and *The Flood* are more ambivalent about humanity's renewal on Earth. While Ballard and his inheritors imagine the deluge as the cause of catastrophic devolution, here humans are risen by a resumed kinship with apes, but it is a painful awakening. By describing the moral landscape of a world vulnerable to deluge, *The Flood* reroutes climate change's most enduring narrative. Like a shipwrecked sailor, however, Gee's reader is left with no means of interpreting the new country she finds ashore.

Locating the Anthropocene turns out to be surprisingly difficult. Hypothetically, the novel should be able to incorporate any describable disaster, but the archive of climate fiction suggests that narrating climate change is highly dependent on existing cultural narratives, particularly polar tales and deluge stories. These narratives are often inadequate for the new conditions of the Anthropocene. Climate change novels articulate a world that is contiguous with our own, but drawing these connections presents fundamental problems. The familiarity of realist fiction is often broken down by climatic transformations. On the other hand, apocalyptic writing typically describes horrors that are unmoored from the real causes and conditions of the Anthropocene. Satire, as in Will Self's *The Book of Dave,* may allow the inherent limitations of the deluge narrative to be challenged, critiquing the supposed sanity of the recent past and the idealized vision of a pure, communal future.

Instead of relying on ancient narratives, other authors have begun to develop new forms that can articulate contemporary challenges. Kim Stanley Robinson's *Forty Signs of Rain* deploys new modes of mediation to make weather more real. It seems likely that future novelists will learn to narrate genuinely new disasters, such as ocean acidification or the sudden release of Arctic methane, using similar devices. Maggie Gee's *The Flood* is similarly innovative, challenging the twentieth-century novel's dependence on epiphanies and social omniscience. *The Flood* shares a common preoccupation with class, gender, and social construction, but it also describes climate change's effects on animals, places, and infrastructure. This breadth allows Gee to trace the troubling connections between poverty and disaster, while undermining any sense that the wealthy can simply transcend their climate. Ultimately, *The Flood* finds new ways to narrate the breadth of climate change's effects, while accounting for the limits of knowing the Anthropocene. It seems likely that subsequent novels will continue to develop ways to locate a global, enduring disaster.

THREE

POLITICS
Opposition, Bureaucracy, and Agency

Despite constant calls for a depoliticized climate science, climate change inexorably provokes politics. In the last decade of the twentieth century and the first of the twenty-first, the basic science surrounding greenhouse gases was heavily politicized, particularly in the United States. Conservative groups notoriously adopted claims of scientific uncertainty and outright denial, while liberals' proposals were made to seem unreasonably partisan. Plans for dealing with climate change have almost always been political as well, betraying preferences for international cooperation or unilateralism, preserving the influence of wealthy countries or permitting development of poorer ones. Even nongovernmental proposals involve choosing winners and losers: distinct parts of society are rewarded and punished by private mitigation schemes, environmental regulation, and direct carbon and fuel taxes on consumers. And all such proposals demand state leadership, public consensus, and some degree of international agreement. While there is an enormous literature examining the policy implications of global warming, these details have little to do with the ways in which fiction has engaged with climate change.

To be sure, nearly all climate change fiction is political, in one sense or another. Political theorists describe the policy inertia on climate change as the result of underestimations of the profoundly negative impacts of climate change and assumptions that future generations will be richer and more able to deal with its effects.[1] Arguments for urgent action, then, rest on an awareness that the damage is likely to be great, perhaps unpredictably so, and that future generations "will not be so well placed to offset the environmental damage with their greater man-made capital." Persuading people of the ethical need to act on climate change involves shifting "the perceived trade-off between damage and cost."[2] Predictions about future climate raise ethical issues as well, demanding we balance the cost of reducing emissions in the present against the harm done by climate change to humans both in the present and in the future.[3] Almost universally, it is these questions that are dealt with in climate change novels, even when they fail to represent the formal politics of global warming.

The most common strategy of climate change novels is to describe contemporary inertia as a catastrophic miscalculation of climate change's costs. The disasters described in the previous chapter are all directed at the reader's sense of the future costs of present emissions. In novels like Octavia Butler's *Parable of the Sower* (1993), Margaret Atwood's *Oryx and Crake* (2003) and *The Year of the Flood* (2009), Cormac McCarthy's *The Road* (2006), and Will Self's *The Book of Dave* (2006), humans have wholly failed to respond to the threat of anthropogenic climate change.[4] In *The Road*, the total collapse of the state and civilization more generally has led to a nightmarish fantasy of scavenging for basic food and avoiding cannibals. In *Oryx and Crake*, unchecked corporations have neglected the environment, leading to a major extinction, while individuals use engineered viruses to check further ecological violence. In *The Parable of the Sower*, small, armed bands of religious devotees fight off water thieves and drug-crazed rapists after California has become a failed desert state. In *The Book of Dave*, the stupidity and self-absorption of the present, allegorized by the taxi-driving protagonist, have directly led to a benighted, repressive, medieval state in the archipelago of what was once the island of Great Britain. Such dystopias precisely foreground the inability of future generations to adapt to climate change, suggesting not just that it will be more expensive and society will be poorer, but that its impacts may be more disastrous than might otherwise be assumed. In this sense, climate dystopias attempt to shift the political and ethical calculus between present and future, indicating the necessity of immediate action. By the same token, such dystopias trace the failure of politics to craft an effective response to climate change and a subsequent disintegration of the political sphere as a result. The consequences of political failure implicitly ask to be contemplated by fictional scenarios, when humans find themselves in a violent environment beyond the structure of a state. In practice, however, climate dystopias gloss the present moment, effacing both the political opportunities and the shortcomings confronted by the contemporary reader. In an important sense, then, such dystopias fail to represent the politics of climate change, while covertly willing a new political climate.

In contrast to such climate dystopias, novels that directly investigate the politics of climate change are generally structured by conflict between two parties. One common strategy, particularly in thrillers and science fiction, is to narrate a central conflict between states to explore the geopolitical dimensions of climate change. The first section of this chapter will examine novels like Michael Glass's *Ultimatum* (2009) and Paul McAuley's *The Quiet War* (2008), whose plots are based on struggles between states that would address environmental collapse.[5] *Ultimatum* tries to expose international obstacles to reaching an international consensus on emissions cuts, by building a thriller on the high-stakes negotiations between the United States and China as climate change threatens to become abrupt and catastrophic. Glass's novel deals with the international landscape much as it is today. In contrast, *The Quiet War,* along with other science fiction novels like Paolo Bacigalupi's *The Windup Girl* (2009) and Bruce Sterling's *The Caryatids* (2009), explores political conflicts of the more distant future, after climate change has provoked severe ecological consequences as well as serious political responses.[6] A relatively short reading of *The Quiet War* suggests the ways in which novels set in the further future can shed light on the ideological conflicts in contemporary environmental discourse, though they rarely lend insight into how to avoid catastrophe in the first place.

Another group of novels uses a similar structural conflict between radical environmentalist groups and a capitalist establishment bent on ignoring climate change. Ecocriticism, and literary criticism more generally, has often assumed that political progress will be the result of activist modes of critique. Environmental rhetoric often opposes environmental activists working outside the system to the forces of capitalism: corporations, energy companies, car manufacturers, and states that are controlled by these interests. A number of novels have been written using this opposition for its basic structure, but the results are rather surprising. Of the novels I have read, only one has been able to envision wholesale environmental transformation as a result of political activism: George Marshall's *The Earth Party: Love and Revolution at a Time of Climate Change* (2008).[7] However, Marshall's novel is something of a test case, because of the extraordinary transformations it must make to the Earth Party's political organization and environmental aims in order to make it a viable power. T. C. Boyle's *A Friend of the Earth* (2000) takes a very different tack, following a committed, radical environmentalist from failed protests in the 1990s to the ecological collapse of California in the 2030s.[8] Although fiction might be expected to imagine how public outrage could lead to action on emissions, these two novels suggest there may be limits to politicizing global warming in this way.

The final section addresses a very different group of novels that articulate the politics of climate change without depending on a structural conflict between political entities. Thrillers often imagine that a crack team of experts, gathered by a bureaucratic agency, will respond to a crisis and save the world. Arthur Herzog's *Heat,* written in 1977 and one of the first novels about anthropogenic global warming, follows this pattern. A scientist in an imaginary federal agency of the United States recognizes the threat of abrupt climate change, uses his bureaucratic power to gather together other scientists, and transforms the world's social organization and means of generating energy in the nick of time. The plotline is equally familiar and implausible, but it reveals important things about the ways political agency can be imagined in climate change discourse. More recent thrillers, such as Clive Cussler's *Arctic Drift* (2005), employ the same plot device, with little enough variation not to need amplification here.[9] However, Kim Stanley Robinson's climate change trilogy, "Science in the Capital" (2004, 2005, and 2007), uses the trope of the bureaucratic agency to provide a new mode of utopian action in the face of climate change.[10] These novels certainly have human antagonists who would block political action, but their theorization of political power is very different from the international and activist novels described earlier in the chapter. Most pointedly, such novels imagine the creation of a composite political entity with sufficient agency to redress climate change.

The argument of this chapter is not so much that one literary strategy has yielded the perfect climate change novel, either representing the utter truth of the political moment or impelling all readers to action, but that these approaches deserve interpretation on their own terms, as experimental investigations of social structures responding to climate change. If the political issues of climate change are too big to be dominated by a single academic discipline, they are also too capacious to be contained in a single novel.

Oppositional Politics: International Relations and Environmental Activism

Since the late 1980s, the prevailing assumption of policymakers and politicians has been that effective action on climate change must take the form of international accords leading to the decrease of greenhouse gas emissions. The creation of the International Panel on Climate Change and the Rio Earth Summit of 1992 gave rise to the United Nations Framework Convention on Climate Change (UNFCCC) and led to the drafting of the Kyoto Protocol in 1997 (which, however, did not come into force until 2005). A multilateral agreement is generally deemed necessary because nonemitting fuels have been relatively expensive: countries outside a climate agreement would operate at an economic advantage to signatory nations, (unfairly) bolstering their economies and creating price incentives for more production to flow to the emitting country. However, the Kyoto Protocol has largely been judged a failure. The United States never signed it, and ratification was blocked for many years. Further, many emissions targets will not be met; even if they were, there is significant doubt whether the reductions would effectively reduce global warming. At the time of writing, efforts to produce a successor agreement have ended in failure, and influential policy analysts have argued that the basic approach is flawed. For success, a multilateral accord would require "universal participation, binding emissions targets, integrated emissions trading and compensation to poorer countries to get their cooperation," but these elements may be politically impossible to negotiate under Kyoto-style architecture.[11] Dieter Helm suggests a number of other obstacles to effective climate change policy: global warming enables new sources of oil and gas to be exploited; there is enough coal for another century; and a massive shift *toward* coal-fired power plants, particularly in China and India, will determine emission levels through 2030. According to Helm, "both energy demand and carbon emissions are rising faster than population growth." Moreover, any meaningful deal would seriously impact standards of living, challenging its political viability.[12] Helm concludes that the basic conditions for agreement, compliance, and enforcement of a multilateral solution "are largely absent."[13] Anthony Giddens is even more certain that an effective response to climate change must be multilateral but argues that the institutions, mechanisms, and international relationships to deliver climate change goals are absent. Put rather dramatically, we lack a geopolitics of climate change.[14] The novels and criticism to address this shortcoming are only just beginning to emerge.

Recent environmental criticism has begun a reorientation, enabling it to engage with these international political currents. As Ursula Heise has shown, ecocritics have typically been interested in literary forms that focus on individuals, families, and nations, but climate change art necessarily considers connections and disjunctures between "local, regional, and global forms of inhabitation."[15] Timothy Clark has expanded these arguments, suggesting that ecocriticism that advances a "bioregionalist idea" and literature devoted to "communicating the particular" may be taking place on the wrong scale, since climate change is a global problem and will require international solutions. Similarly, the political goal of "acting only locally" is superseded by the political need to move beyond "mere individual behavior and consumer choice" and engage with "those national and global structures of economics and forms of government that are ultimately more responsible" for climate change.[16] This shift in ecocritical attention has enabled a more sophisticated engagement with the politics of climate change.

One important strategy for expanding the bioregional agenda has been to bring ecocritical concerns together with postcolonialism's engagement with developing countries, international exploitation, and non-European subjectivities. Summarizing this emergent field, Clark observes that "the boundaries between conservation colonialism and the depredations of international capitalism may often be uncomfortably blurred and uncertain" but also notes that a recent alliance has emerged "between first-world environmentalists and fourth-world people fighting to defend their indigenous way of life."[17] Unfortunately, very few climate change novels have displayed a substantial engagement with developing countries. In Maggie Gee's *The Ice People* (1999) and Saci Lloyd's *Carbon Diaries 2017* (2008), global warming has led to a refugee crisis between Europe and northern Africa, but both novels keep the focus resolutely on British characters. Mike Resnick's *Kirinyaga: A Fable of Utopia* (1998) is also concerned with African development and environmental devastation. The protagonist leads a community of future Kenyans to create a tribal utopia on an artificial planetoid, controlling its climate as the storytelling medicine man. However, no postcolonial critic could endorse the novel's nostalgia for repressive tribalism and its conclusion that neither traditional values nor environmental protection can resist the universal desire for modernization. Ian McDonald's *Cyberabad Days* (2009) describes the fragmentation of future India, driven in part by monsoon failure and water shortages. While it frequently alludes to the impoverished and left behind, the narrative is focused on imagining the powerful players of an Indian cyber-revolution. Perhaps the most interesting novel in this vein is Bacigalupi's *The Windup Girl,* set in a future Thailand struggling to balance environmental protectionism and business development. Climate change and patented, sterile GM crops have brought the country to the brink of collapse, while an aggressive environmental agency blocks imports, burns diseased crops, and terrorizes peasants (discussed in more detail in chapter 4). Despite their limitations, such novels may signal an expansion beyond the irremediably Anglo-European focus of most climate change fiction to engage with global, postcolonial eco-justice.

The sheer complexity of international climate negotiations has made both multilateral accords and international climate change novels very difficult to construct. Given the inertia around multilateral, Kyoto-style agreements, policy analysts have begun to wonder if a bilateral accord might not be more viable, particularly between the United States and China. Although the United States is not the largest emitter per capita, its size makes it one of the most consequential, with average emissions more than double that of EU15 countries and continuing to rise. China has only recently replaced the United States as the world's largest polluter, although its emissions per head are only about one-fifth of those of America.[18] China is expected to build one thousand gigawatts of coal-fired electricity plants and add half a billion cars with conventional engines, "an order of magnitude more important to climate change than virtually any other trend." By 2030, China's total energy generation is likely to be equivalent to current levels of the United States and Europe combined.[19] The United States and China contribute a major proportion of the world's greenhouse gas emissions, compete for energy supplies, and have actively worked to scupper multilateral agreements. China has argued that developed countries had the opportunity to use fossil fuels; that greenhouse gases currently in the atmosphere were mostly put there by those countries; that its per capita emissions are still comparatively low; and that it only produces high levels of emissions on behalf of American and European consumers, who should pay for the emissions. The United States refused to ratify Kyoto, in part, because of a lack of binding targets for China and is unlikely to make payments to China for lower-carbon industrialization.[20] It is little wonder that a bilateral agreement between the United States and China, settling these differences, looks to some to offer a firmer foundation for an international emissions deal.

Given this diplomatic complexity, many novelists have made the politics of climate negotiation comprehensible by staging a conflict between two main entities. Cussler's *Arctic Drift* traces a pressurized standoff between Canada (in the pocket of a dirty energy corporation) and the energy-poor but hero-rich United States, with predictable results. In Robinson's "Science in the Capital" trilogy, a sophisticated examination of American politics is paired with a simplistic, last-minute emissions deal with China: environmental crisis makes Chinese leaders see the error of their ways, and the United States provides remarkable amounts of capital and technology to set its rival on the good path. An account of bipartisan negotiations need not be simplistic or chauvinistic, however.

Ultimatum is a political thriller dramatizing climate negotiations between the United States and China. Literary reviews of the novel were divided, but the novel garnered the most enthusiasm from those most familiar with climate change policy. Robin McKie, the *Observer*'s reviewer, complained that the novel was too concerned with "the minutiae of political process . . . speeches, cabinet wrangling and political arguments," rather than "human frailties."[21] However, this could be interpreted as the novel's strength, developing suspense within the real shortcomings of climate negotiations rather than as the result of a specious notion of character as the determinant of all human events. An anonymous reviewer for the *Economist* recognized in Glass a deep familiarity with "the corridors and committee-rooms of power . . . how policy gets made" and praised his portrait of "diplomatic brinkmanship and political in-fighting."[22] Even higher praise came from David G. Victor, a professor at the University of California, San Diego, specializing in climate change policy, who described the novel as "the most insightful look at how [the relationship between the US and China] might unfold," trumping all existing nonfiction.[23]

The plot of *Ultimatum* allows for this diplomatic detail, while glossing over other aspects of climate policy. An American senator, Joe Benton, has just been elected president after three terms of Republican avoidance of climate change issues and decades of ineffectual, Kyoto-style accords. Benton has won the election on a domestic policy agenda, including a limited relocation program for the areas in the Gulf Coast made uninhabitable by floods and storms, but during the transition, he learns that climate change threatens the survival of the country. Secret findings by the (fictional) Environmental Surveillance Unit demonstrate, beyond any reasonable doubt, that global warming is accelerating exponentially; if massive emissions cuts are not made immediately, entire countries and substantial sections of the United States will be decimated by flooding, and tens of millions of people will become climate refugees. This setup eliminates the uncertainty and gradualism of scientific predictions, issues that have proved deeply problematic in generating popular support for emissions reductions. The emergency is made immediate, tangible, and relevant to Americans, creating a do-or-die suspense atmosphere for the newly elected president while solving one aspect of political intransigence.

From this point, the novel offers an incredibly sophisticated account of the domestic and international obstacles to creating a climate deal. As Victor has observed, *Ultimatum* authentically dramatizes the difficulties of achieving geopolitical cooperation. President Benton has been elected based on his support for the Kyoto process, and EU leaders also support the regime, while the UN secretary-general tries to maintain a "monopoly on global-warming diplomacy."[24] Given the state of emergency, Benton quickly realizes the complex negotiating framework is plagued by too many actors and too little pressure to meet targets, leading him to continue his Republican predecessor's strategy of secret, bilateral talks with China, even as he publicly pays lip service to the Kyoto framework. The secret talks also allow Benton to operate beyond public scrutiny, rescuing the president (and the novel) from the obligation to represent or account for public opinion. Benton's new goal is a final, binding resolution for massive emissions reductions, which China and the United States will cooperatively impose on the rest of the world. (The novel also traces the compelling reasons why any real political deal may follow this path.) As Victor has observed, Benton's neglect of Europe and the United Nations produces further diplomatic problems and undermines American credibility with Chinese negotiators. Victor nicely describes the dilemma: "Neither hypermultilateralism nor pure bilateralism can save the day."[25] One of Glass's signal achievements is that these decisions grow from plausible backroom arguments; the continual tightening of diplomatic tension appears to be the inevitable result of structural and ideological political positions. At the same time, science, the international community, and the public are all but eliminated from consideration, radically simplifying the political task the novel sets for itself.

This frees *Ultimatum* to pursue a detailed account of presidential pressures: cabinet rivalries; political appointments; legislative momentum; election cycles; the tension between misleading and inspiring the public; leaks and investigations in the media; and the ideological disagreements among party strategists, State Department experts, and generals. All of these pressures are organized to heighten the suspense in a series of escalating negotiations between Benton's team and the internally divided leadership of China's Communist Party, whose interests are both misunderstood and opposed to Benton's team. Similarly, the dreadful economic consequences of radically curbing emissions and conducting mass relocations ratchet up tension, heightening the stakes of the negotiations, which escalate exponentially. The negotiators are cool, then subtle, then belligerent; agreements are reneged; walkouts build pressure; sanctions are imposed; Taiwan is invaded; military exercises lead to enemy engagement; nuclear strikes bring both countries to the brink of mutual destruction; Benton finally stands down to his Chinese counterparts as both sides declare victory. In all of this, the suspense is masterfully developed, but the suspense is the byproduct of relentlessly referring complications back to the central diplomatic conflict. Characters repeatedly invoke the Cold War and the Cuban Missile Crisis, an apt comparison because *Ultimatum* uses an oppositional structure to transform climate change from an ecological, global, and public crisis into a binary conflict between the two superpowers. At a remove, the novel is deeply nihilistic: a few powerful men must resolve climate change for the world; there are almost insurmountable economic and political obstacles preventing them from acting; and only the rhetorical force of nuclear war is sufficient to overthrow their inertia. This leads to a page-turner but completely eliminates very real dilemmas of political representation, social justice, and conservation. While environmental refugees are described as an alarming statistic, there is no direct account of them. The question of nonhuman extinction is also avoided. The main sense of loss in the novel comes from the death of Benton's daughter in a nuclear strike, displacing emotion from climate change itself to the diplomatic crisis and its resolution. Overall, international diplomacy is presented as the legitimate means to mitigating climate change, even as the regime is shown to be remote and catastrophically ineffectual.

Other novels are similarly nihilistic about the likelihood of climate action in the United States and China but shift attention to other, more viable nations. In *The Quiet War,* the refusal of both superpowers to adopt sustainable environmental practices has led to their disintegration, but other states have successfully paired environmental and political sustainability. Early in the twenty-first century, anthropogenic global warming caused dead zones in the oceans; flooded the coasts of every continent; and turned much of the Amazonian basin, Africa, and North America into desert. Even worse, rising temperatures led to the "Overturn," "when runaway global warming driven by vast surges of methane released from Antarctic clathrates had threatened to cause mass extinction on a global scale" (10–11). As hard science fiction, the book describes these crises in some scientific detail.

The genre also gives the novel access to speculative technologies, like space ships, computer networks, genetic and neurological enhancement of humans, and new, engineered ecosystems. During the Overturn, some humans escaped to Mars and the moons of Jupiter and Saturn, while billions died on Earth. Aggressive engineering solutions, such as forests of synthetic trees with sails pulling massive amounts of carbon dioxide from the atmosphere and enormous satellite mirrors keeping the sunlight from reaching the Earth's surface, have allowed some human civilizations to survive. Even so, the damage to Earth's ecosystems is irreparable, and it is expected to take several centuries to return the atmosphere to preindustrial levels. The ever-present awareness of humans' capacity for destruction on a planetary scale forms the backdrop for an investigation of environmental politics.

In the future envisaged by *The Quiet War,* societies on Earth and in the Outer Systems have developed in very different directions. On Earth, the United States and the "Democratic Republic of China" are long gone, and the surviving Earth nations are characterized by a radical, green conservatism. An unbreakable political consensus dictates that humans live in self-sustaining cities, "urban islands isolated like pockets of plague from the regenerated and reconstructed wildernesses that surrounded them" (256). Brazil has thrived and expanded as a result of its farsighted de-emphasis on oil, pioneering use of biofuels, and extensive hydroelectric program since the 1970s.[26] *The Quiet War* imagines the ideology of "Greater Brazil" as a conflation of social hierarchy, Catholicism, and a deeply conservative form of environmentalism. A hybrid religion of Catholicism and "the nature of

Gaia" teaches that the evils of technology and humanity's original sin can be overcome by "cultivating their faith, praising God, and tending his creation" (6). "Green saints," who use science to begin to restore the environment, are gurus, masters, and political celebrities. However, the real political power on Earth is held in royal families through an extensive network of consanguinity, and freedoms of expression, movement, and allegiance have been abandoned.

This political conservatism is in sharp contrast to the open society of the Outers, characterized by "posthuman utopianism" and a "burgeoning frontier spirit" (108). Outer society has preserved democratic traditions "long vanished on Earth" (48), such as the custom of public candor, open access to data, and public positions decided by popularity contests, realizing much of the dream promised by social media networks. These ideals also shape the Outer System's economy, "a barter and social ranking system based on the value of volunteer work and exchange of scientific, cultural and technological ideas and information" (108). New colonies continue to pop up farther from the sun, as the young seize new moons to start afresh. Moreover, Outers have embraced genetic engineering, radically adapting their bodies to suit alien environments and for the sake of personal expression. The conflict between the political centralization needed to solve environmental problems and the democratic impulse of technology, represented by the two groups, structures the novel.

The plot of the novel builds tension between Greater Brazil and several Outer city-states, tracing the path to a destructive war. There is an extensive backstory to the animosity, involving the Outers' escape from Earth and their refusal to return to help in its reconstruction and an earlier war that nearly killed all life on Earth and eliminated it on Mars. And, as in much science fiction, there is a rather predictable buildup of terrifying forces, unleashed at the novel's climax. What distinguishes *The Quiet War*, however, is that the characters are never reducible to their ideological positions. Macy Minnot, an unprivileged biome engineer, finds herself caught in the middle of a diplomatic crisis but emerges as a quiet antihero when she refuses to save herself by denouncing either side. Dave Number Eight, one of several dozen clones designed and trained to be saboteurs, arranges the downfall of a whole city with an utter lack of self-awareness but also becomes infatuated with a mentally ill woman in the city and exerts free agency to try to possess her. Professor Sri Hong-Owen, a brilliant genetic engineer for Greater Brazil, finds herself breaking with the green saints' "holy mission of returning the planet to a prelapsarian paradise" (257), dreaming of "a thousand Earths, all different," and believing "nothing was unnatural because nature was not limited to the variations on a few themes that evolution had so far realized" (161). Sri makes for a remarkable antagonist, her loyalty to her own genes and scientific ambition leading her to attempt to broker peace and scientific collaboration and then to unleash a clone army on the enemy, kill colleagues and her mentor, and attempt to enslave the Outers' most important green saint. Her ambition leads her simultaneously to crave academic hierarchies and intellectual freedom, enormous restoration projects and new forms of life; she vacillates between dreams of a plague that would "winnow humanity to a sustainable level" (257) and an ambition to spread her biological inventions far beyond the solar system. Such characters significantly complicate the opposition between green conservatism and posthuman utopianism. Both philosophies seem to be unrealizable in a climate-changed world.

At the same time, *The Quiet War* refuses the easy dismissal of either conservation or experimentation. Sri's cold-blooded ambition is balanced by her rival and foil, Avernus. Avernus is "the Outer System's most notorious gene wizard" (27), the Outers' green saint, "their Darwin, their Einstein, an enigmatic genius shrouded in legend and rumor, a major inspiration for their own radicalism" (110). Over two hundred years old, Avernus created countless new life forms that allowed humans to live beyond Mars. One example, the "people tree," has sugary sap, protein-rich nodules, nutritious leaves, spices and an antibiotic in its bark, fibers that can make a paper cloth, and seed pods that can be crushed to make biofuel (258). Other organisms are designed to grow in the dark vacuum of the moons, and she also created gardens of more than fifty different photosynthetic species that float in the thick atmosphere of Saturn for art and beauty. Unlike Sri, she works for peace, valuing the Earth people's united work "to heal the great wounds inflicted by the Overturn, climate change, and two centuries of unchecked capitalism" and the Outers' "societies founded on principles of tolerance, mutualism, scientific rationalism, and attempts at true democracy" (433). Figures like Avernus and Macy Minnot also carry out a radical revaluation of science fiction technology: the physics that enables space ships and advanced weapon systems is comparatively uninteresting (and cursorily described), but the biotechnology that allows the restoration and creation of life is shown to be both powerful and beautiful, if not a guarantee of the political good. Although Avernus evades capture by Sri, the more principled scientist fails to prevent war, and her bitter retreat to meditate on human nature's failings is a terrible irony for one of the original advocates of the posthuman. By the end of the novel, these failings seem inescapable: unchecked exploration leads to political disorganization and vulnerability to invasion; strong social constraint and scarcity lead to personal ambition that tears the social fabric and exceeds the limits of ecological sustainability. Thus, *The Quiet War* uses a geopolitical opposition to raise difficult questions about the political philosophies that would inform any state's response to climate change, now or in the distant future.

Characters in *The Quiet War* quietly refuse to exist for mere political ideology, but they also struggle to carve out an existence beyond it. Other novelists deploy a different structural opposition, pitching climate activists against a political establishment that resists substantial emissions reductions. Of course, grassroots environmentalists and environmental NGOs have played an important role in raising public awareness of climate change, shaping media reporting, lobbying governments, and engaging in direct action against governments and corporations judged complicit in climate change. However, the connection between climate change and the social and political movement of environmentalism is not as straightforward as conservative talk-show hosts might assume. Michael Crichton's *State of Fear* is hardly neutral, but when it portrays the head of the National Environmental Resource Fund calling global warming a disaster for his organization, it does approach the difficulties of turning the complex problem into a focused grassroots movement.[27] Perhaps more trustworthy is the semiautobiographical *Carbon Dreams,* by Susan M. Gaines, which traces the historical emergence of a scientific consensus about global warming in the 1980s and the tremendous difficulties in allying this with the environmental movement's focus on natural living, organic food, and industrial pollution in that period.

Environmental activist novels would seem to be of particular interest for ecocritics. As Lawrence Buell has argued, ecocriticism was founded not on a unified methodological program, but rather on an "issue-driven ... commitment to environmentality" or "environmental praxis."[28] This commitment is similar to "prior critical insurgencies" such as "feminist, ethnic, and gay revisionism," which aim to rehabilitate "that which has been effectively marginalized by mainstream societal assumptions."[29] Dana Phillips has criticized claims of ecocritical radicalism, and Richard Kerridge has also usefully noted that environmentalism struggles to adopt the "politics of personal liberation or social mobility" that have been so productive to feminist criticism.[30] Clark has taken this point further, arguing that too much "twenty-first-century ecocriticism . . . map[s] out the cultural politics of some issue or concern, usually from an implicitly liberal/progressive viewpoint," rather than recognizing the substantial incompatibility between the Enlightenment goals of universal individual freedom and prosperity and environmentalism's insistence of real ecological limits.[31] In Clark's account, environmentalism struggles between mainstream campaigns and political radicalism: "In order to be heard at all, campaigners must speak in terms accepted within existing structures of governance and economics, the very things they may consider ultimately responsible for environmental degradation in the first place."[32] These difficulties lead Clark to question whether mainstream attempts at, say, fuel efficiency might not be less responsible than the statement that "the only defensible relationship to have with any car is with a well-aimed brick."[33] Whether addressing campaigners or environmental anarchists, Clark understands environmentalism as a protest movement firmly opposed to the political establishment.

Of course, the role of environmental activism in responding to climate change is widely contested. The terms of this debate have been expansive but can be simplified into two schools of thought. On the one hand, advocates of environmental activism have argued that the scientific framing of the issue alienates the communities in which people live and the public spheres in which they exert their citizenship, necessitating the radical involvement of citizens. Moreover, the emissions cuts prescribed by scientists "amount to civilization change," making them impossible to implement without popular, collective efforts to establish "more sustainable societies and to rethink democracy at the same time." In this account, the nonspecialist public has the power to judge luxury consumption, resource depletion, extinction, global inequalities, and chemical pollution and also the capacity to interrogate the rationalizations of realpolitik and the market.[34] On the other hand, establishment commentators have argued that the green movement's "origins in hostile emotions" and opposition to orthodox politics are unhelpful to the task of integrating climate change policy "into our established political institutions."[35] Nor, in this account, does the threat of global warming necessitate a shift toward political reaction: combating global warming has nothing to do with a conservationist "return to nature," and authoritarian governments "have generally had poor or disastrous environmental records."[36] Accordingly, climate change is best addressed with existing democratic institutions creating aggressive reductions in greenhouse gases, rather than through entrenched environmental protest. In this account, environmental pressure groups and NGOs have a role to play in encouraging action, but only within the overall structure of existing democratic states. Many climate change novels have engaged with this debate, testing the capacity of activism to resist the effects of global warming.

In particular, there are quite a number of climate change dystopias structured around the conflict between a resistance group and a hegemonic state or collection of corporations. In *The Declaration* (2007), by Gemma Malley, climate change and antiaging drugs have led to a totalitarian state obsessed with controlling birth rates, while an underground collection of parents with multiple children resist.[37] In *Sharp North* (2004), by Patrick Cave, a girl escapes from a remote Scottish community to discover that she is an illegal clone for a member of a ruling family, one of several owning the corporations that exert authoritarian rule over Britain.[38] In *The Carhullan Army* (2008), by Sarah Hall, the contraction of the global economy and shortages of material supplies have led to Britain's population being concentrated in repressive dormitory towns, where women are violently fitted with birth control devices, and adults are conscripted in hierarchical work teams making useless weapons.[39] The narrator, Sister, escapes in order to join a self-sustaining community of radical feminists who eventually become militarized and lead a revolutionary assault on the local town. These novels, and many more like them, take climate change as a starting point for a radical consolidation of hegemonic powers, either in the state or in corporations that have replaced the state. In practice, these novels are a continuation of a twentieth-century trope of antitotalitarian dystopias. However, meaningful action on climate change is almost certain to involve the state, with its domestic power to regulate and encourage sustainable industry and its diplomatic ability to forge and implement international agreements.[40] Even if the drastic devolution called for by radical environmentalists were achieved, the new local states would still require collaborative agreements about emissions. As a result, the antitotalitarian novel of the twentieth century proves to be deeply limited as a response to global warming.[41]

Related to this class of dystopia, but with a significant difference, are novels featuring an opposition between climate activists and the resistant parties of the state and corporations. A handful of novels have been able to imagine how activism could lead to limited governmental concessions. For instance, Lloyd's *Carbon Diaries 2017* deserves mention here, following a group of teenagers involved in political campaigns and demonstrations demanding action, aid efforts to regions struck by environmental catastrophe, and a garage band that features protest songs expressing anger about carbon emissions and governmental entrenchment. However, the concessions they win are limited, and the novel is more preoccupied with imagining a youth protest movement in a country that has already adopted extreme measures to restrict carbon emissions. On the strength of evidence, fiction seems to have great difficulty in imagining how radical environmental politics could lead to a fundamental shift in our culture's dependence on fossil fuels.

Marshall's *The Earth Party* is one of the only climate change novels to describe an environmental activist group that forces political transformation. The vast majority of climate change novels assume environmental politics will fail to avert climate change, but *The Earth Party* shows, from a different angle, the extreme difficulty of imagining a green revolution that would successfully address climate change. *The Earth Party* takes place in an unspecified near future, when green consumer choices have already made some progress. Bicycles have largely replaced cars due to soaring fuel costs, fewer people are flying, and consumption is down, but not enough has been done to prevent an accelerating climatic crisis. Britain becomes as warm as Kenya; the sea inundates much of Cambridgeshire; London's flood defenses are overwhelmed; and flooded oil refineries and nuclear reactors create an energy emergency. Parliament responds by forming a coalition government of the three main parties, declaring a state of emergency, and deploying the territorial army and regular army to protect the population and enforce a police state. The emergency also transforms the Earth Party. Until this time, the party has been a fringe group with a devolved, democratic structure, primarily encouraging individual actions such as riding a bicycle, installing solar panels and insulation, and growing food on an allotment. But in a matter of days, the party is infiltrated by "the hard left or the extreme right," led by "an army officer involved in counter-terrorist activities," and snap votes are called to transform it "into a centrally controlled organisation . . . capable of quickly mobilising its forces" and able to "enforce environmental action" (25–26). The coalition government declares the Earth Party a terrorist organization, triggering a revolution in which the renamed Peoples Earth Party (PEP) seizes control.

The ensuing program of the Peoples Earth Party is questionable, to say the least. The new state is organized along the lines of the (long-gone) Soviet Union, with the deep ecology movement shaping the party's policies. (Later, it is revealed the PEP's policies are based on a computer model to optimize responses to climate catastrophe.) Cities are evacuated, and the country is divided up into self-sufficient, agrarian "Earth Cells" (61). Movement is restricted, families are split, women are forced to accept contraceptive injections, individuals are renamed, and members of the "Earth Guard" police the party line. Overall, the Peoples Earth Party is undemocratic, misogynistic, violent, and repressive, blending Soviet authoritarianism, medieval reaction, and the inhuman rationalism of a computer program.

The failures of the Peoples Earth Party raise questions as to how to interpret the novel. At times, the novel seems to be a dystopian warning about the dangers of contemporary environmentalism, but it takes global warming seriously and also emphasizes the deep gulf between the green movement's emphasis on democracy and the authoritarianism of the PEP. The organization of the new regime apparently originates with a computer model but never addresses the social catastrophe of neofeudalism. Within the regime, characters almost universally bolster the system, despite their misgivings. Gorse fights for limited reforms but pushes himself up the hierarchy; a love rival unleashes brutal violence to protect the regime; Betony, the woman in the love triangle, plays the men off each other and pays little attention to where she can best serve her fellows. More broadly, the revolutionary regime proves unsustainable without engineered fuel and food shortages; eventually the state is forced to transition back toward the privileges of consumer capitalism. At an ecological level, the regime (and novel) seems unaware that if "every square metre of land" were to be converted to food production, the biodiversity and ecosystem collapses would be devastating (94). Also, the novel acknowledges that climatic unpredictability is likely to make crop outputs quite unpredictable but elides the necessary conclusion that international trade in food will be more critical. Finally, the party hopes the decline in greenhouse gas output will "lead to a stabilisation of the climate" (289), though it will take centuries for human emissions to leave the atmosphere, giving the lie to any hope for a quick fix.[42] Ultimately, the green revolution proposed by *The Earth Party* fails to offer solutions to the political and ecological problems of the Anthropocene.

It would be easy to take *The Earth Party* as merely a bad novel, confused about its political allegiances and the basic goals of environmental activism. However, Boyle's *A Friend of the Earth* also explores the basic affective structures of activism in an era of climate change and finds them deeply wanting. The novel follows its protagonist, Ty Tierwater, in two time periods. In the first-person accounts of the period from 2025 to 2026, Tierwater describes his work as an "animal man," managing a rock star's private menagerie, as the environment and economy around Santa Barbara collapse due to climate change. This frames the third-person narration of the period from 1989 to 1993, when Tierwater became a radical, violent, and angry environmental activist associated with Earth Forever!, loosely based on the real organization Earth First![43] Early readers of the novel criticized it as a nihilistic, carnivalesque dismissal of the environmental movement[44] or as a self-absorbed satire of "the aging white male."[45] However, the specific historical framework of *A Friend of the Earth* allows it to examine the radical environmentalism of the recent past in light of climate change.

By 2025, California's temperate climate has been transformed by global warming, described not as an apocalyptic event but rather as an ongoing misery. Tierwater recalls that in the 1990s, people debated whether global warming was real and wondered if it might not be a pleasant change. In fact, climate change is experienced as a sort of mundane, quotidian torture: "It's like leaving your car in the parking lot in the sun all day with the windows rolled up and then climbing in and discovering they've been sealed shut—and the doors too" (186). The degeneration is, literally, domestic: Tierwater's 1990s guesthouse once featured "all the modern conveniences" (9), but winds have torn off most of the shingles; pots and paint cans catch some of the rain, but "everything is wet, always—molding and wet—books falling apart on the shelves, slugs climbing out of the teapot, the very chairs turning green under our hind ends and sprouting again" (38). Global warming has affected domestic climate control: "the fireplace is bricked up, as per state law," and air-conditioning has all but become extinct, "what with electrical restrictions and the sheer killing price per kilowatt hour" (9). In the new dry season, temperatures reach 130 degrees Fahrenheit, and people are forced to wear goggles and a gauze mask because "the air is just another kind of dirt" (13). In the wet season, it storms for weeks straight, first breaking the windows and tearing the roofing from Tierwater's guesthouse, then making him sandbag the front porch, and finally sweeping his home and the neighboring condos into a river "all roiling muscle and deep-brown ribs" (105). Even the flood is experienced, not as a catastrophic climax, but as a sign of a failed economy: "Nobody's insured for weather anymore and any and all lawsuits are automatically thrown out of court" (2). Health insurance and Social Security have also long since been bankrupted. In *A Friend of the Earth,* climate change has led to the collapse of middle-class comforts that insulate Americans from the world.

As a former eco-activist, Tierwater is also acutely aware of how climate change has transformed local ecosystems. What was open country at the turn of the century has been replaced with "gray wet canyons" of condos; "bobcat, mule deer, rabbit, quail, fox" have been "poached and encroached out of existence" (7). The wine country of Napa-Sonoma has been converted to rice paddies; domed fields are needed to grow arugula. Humans' diet has changed as well: eggs and bacon seem "historical" (8), and an affordable meal out is rice wine and catfish sushi, an invasive species that now dominates the area. Most ocean life is extinct: millionaires eat long-frozen "tuna garni or twenty-year-old monkfish at three thousand dollars a plate" (191). Toward the end of the novel, Tierwater revisits a mountain forest but finds it completely fallen: "trees bent at the elbows, snapped at the base, uprooted and flung a hundred yards by the violence of the winds" (266). Just thirty years before, environmentalists like Tierwater had tried to protect individual species, individual forests, but in the era of climate change, a whole forest can be destroyed by the winds and floods, with no human awareness at all.

The collapse of economies and ecosystems dictates Tierwater's employment. He has convinced his rock-star boss, Maclovio Pulchris, to save the animals "nobody else wants," Mac boasting in Ty's words that it's "selfless and cool and brave" (11). Even so, Mac views the "groovy" animals as just another collection, alongside music-themed rooms, a twenty-car garage including a vintage Dodge Viper (fuel efficiency of twelve miles per gallon, city), a frozen meat locker full of extinct delicacies, and an extensive collection of his own memorabilia. Tierwater's motivations are more complex. Tierwater is desperate to keep a job in California's collapsed economy, and the animals often act as a vehicle for his own self-aggrandizement. At the same time, Tierwater views the pangolins, spectacled bears, giant anteaters, warthogs, peccaries, jackals, and hyenas as a "vital reservoir for zoo-cloning and the distribution of what's left of the major mammalian species" (1), hoping they will adapt once humans are gone and the planet's sixth great extinction has passed. Underlying the rhetoric of conservation is a fundamental belief in the animals' intrinsic importance, beyond the cuteness factor of zoo favorites. Lily, the brown hyena, has a head shaped like an anvil and an ungainly rear unlikely to spawn many stuffed animals. Perhaps Tierwater sees something of his own violent past in the hyena when he calls her an "eating machine": "No codes, no ethics. See it, kill it, eat it—that's the motto of the family Hyaenidae" (145). While feeding her, cleaning her cage, and moving her, Tierwater is never unaware that the hyena would kill him with as little thought as she snaps through chicken backs. This untamable otherness differentiates Tierwater's ethic from the self-interested preservation of picturesque nature, despite any apparent identification. Ironically, the wholly other animals only exist with human care. During a flood, Mac lets Tierwater move the animals into his twelve-thousand-square-foot basement. This seems shamefully incongruous—lions sleeping in piles of shredded rock memorabilia, their hair and teeth falling out; a spectacled bear dying after it breaks into the garage and laps up a gallon of antifreeze—but Tierwater observes there is no such thing as "natural" habitat anymore, "just something we created out of a witches' brew of fossil-fuel emissions and deforestation" (81). After a lion kills Mac, a SWAT team mows down the entire menagerie with machine guns, "furred and feathered meat, extinction in a wheelbarrow" (219). For the SWAT team, the animals are beyond use value, leading to a logic of extinction; Tierwater would save them for the same reason. However, Tierwater's love does not furnish him with the resources to let the animals live in dignity. Tierwater only manages to harbor a Patagonian fox by leashing it and treating it as a badly behaved dog. Neither the natural ecosystems nor the financial resources can be found to do better. In the end, climate change intensifies Tierwater's feelings for the animals but makes an ethic of care impossible.

This collapse of California's favorable climate, economy, and ecosystems in the first quarter of the twenty-first century frames an examination of environmental activism in the late 1980s and early 1990s. During this period, Tierwater and his environmental friends are absolutely correct in their assessment of the dire threat to humanity and the biosphere, and yet they absolutely fail to avert the disaster. Kerridge has argued that this framing device "emphasizes [the] powerlessness of environmentalists," creating a "carnivalesque irresponsibility" by denying that "a pragmatic, incremental environmentalism . . . might begin to turn the tide."[46] However, Boyle's critique is more pointed and incisive. In *A Friend of the Earth*, environmentalists are not just powerless or irresponsible; the environmentalism of the 1990s is both implicated in climate change and structurally incapable of proposing solutions.

The novel describes environmentalism of the period as fundamentally divided between theories of passive resistance and militant radicalism. Tierwater is radicalized by Earth Forever!, an environmental organization that bears a marked resemblance to the real Earth First! group, with shared icons and tactics. Tierwater also regularly invokes Thoreau, Muir, Leopold, Arne Næss, Edward Abbey, and Bill McKibben, authors who had a major influence on the first wave of ecocriticism. On the one hand, E.F.! seems to support a philosophy of "passive resistance," from Gandhi, Rosa Parks, and James Meredith, as a means of resistance that respects "all the elements of a given environment" (51). Tierwater also fantasizes about the Eskimos, who "had no jails or laws and lived within the bounds of nature" (170). This vision of social harmony is related to another fantasy "burned in the atavistic heart of every environmentalist," to return "to the evolutionary beginnings of the first hominids" (175). While on the run from the FBI, Tierwater and his wife, Andrea, a more experienced E.F.! activist, go to live in the wilderness for a month, naked and without any tools. They burn in the sun, fight, nearly starve, and curse the animals that refuse to be trapped. Most damningly, they enviously hover around the well-equipped campsite of their jolly photographer. Although they resolutely fail to live beyond civilization, their naked image on the cover of *Outside* magazine turns them into environmentalist celebrities. Apparently, Deep Ecology's vision of radical, edenic harmony can only be experienced from the outside, a longing that amounts to suffering if realized.

On the other hand, E.F.! evokes militant action. The group borrows energy from radical socialism and the American Black Power movement, dressing in red berets and "T-shirts imprinted with the raised red fist of the E.F.!." Tierwater is inspired by anonymous ecotage figures "who'd struck back, done something, mattered" (126), suggesting a thread of self-expression, even vanity in Tierwater's activism. Philosophically, Tierwater would like to preserve the environment "for its own sake, because the whole world is a living organism and we are but a humble part of it," but disbelieves in the efficacy of this philosophy: "Try telling that to the Axxam Corporation when they're clear-cutting thousands of acres of old growth to pay down the junk-bond debt accrued in their hostile takeover of Coast Lumber. . . . They're going to cut, and Earth Forever! is going to stop them, any way they can" (153). Both groups seek annihilation of the other, with no harmony possible. On campaigns against the lumber companies, Tierwater is repeatedly struck by the violence that precedes him. Clear-cutting is described as "a scar, a gash, an open wound in the body corporal of the forest" (19). Later, he faces a site where a power company "had sheared off the top of a hill . . . and run a dead zone back into the mountains," high-tension wires held aloft by a chain of steel towers "as far as you could see" (244). These landscapes convince Tierwater he is in the midst of a cultural conflict, opposed to "bosses, underbosses, heavy machine operators, CEOs, power-lunchers, police, accountants." Timber workers are "terminally misguided" and "born angry"; Tierwater imagines that they view his friends as "eco-freaks and fossil-lovers" (188), "that all members of the Sierra Club are 'Green Niggers' and that Earth Forever! is a front for Bolshevik terrorists with homosexual tendencies" (30–31). This cultural opposition all too frequently results in violence, when Tierwater attacks police during a protest and is beaten unconscious; when representatives of Coast Lumber threaten to rape and kill his tree-sitting daughter; and then in Tierwater's escalating cycle of ecotage, as he destroys heavy machinery, vandalizes a judge's car, and eventually tries to fell an electrical tower. In a motto that has increasing meaning as Tierwater's story unfolds, he declares, "To be a friend of the earth, you have to be an enemy of the people" (44). This violent cultural conflict between defenders and users of the environment locates E.F.! squarely within a twentieth-century logic of *social* protest.

In *A Friend of the Earth*, the deepest satire emerges from environmentalists' implication in the systems they would oppose. Tierwater's own rage precedes any interest in saving species or preventing climate change. His father is described as "an angry man," an MP during the war, violent toward his family. Teaching Ty a reverence for science that would shape his sense of ecology, his father combines a spirit of empiricism and skepticism with "debate and outright derision" (73): an emotional pattern that produces both truth and human conflict. His father also leaves Ty a small empire of tract homes and shopping centers, the direct causes of the urban sprawl Tierwater will later protest. Tierwater describes himself as a criminal, "just like you": "I lived in the suburbs in a three-thousand-square-foot house with redwood siding and oak floors and an oil burner the size of Texas, drove a classic 1966 Mustang for sport and a Jeep Laredo (red, black leather interior) to take me up to the Adirondacks so I could heft my three-hundred-twenty-dollar Eddie Bauer backpack and commune with the squirrels, muskrats and fishers" (42). Tierwater's actions are deeply contradictory: he enjoys acres of woods and irreplaceable timber; the house burns oil at a prodigious rate, but he wears a sweater indoors; he drives fast, accumulates things, and litters but buys outdoor equipment to bring him into closer contact with nature. After Tierwater becomes associated with E.F.!, the incoherence of his position leads him to a cycle of violence motivated by anger and revenge, of "[wanting] to strike back at the sons of bitches and make them wince, make them hurt the way you did" (209). An ever-escalating campaign of ecotage and resultant arrest leads him to burn construction equipment, start a forest fire in a monoculture forest that spreads to thirty-five thousand acres, try to topple a chain of electrical towers, and even plot to poison Santa Barbara's water supply, ultimately resulting in E.F.!'s disavowal of ecotage. In each of these cases, Tierwater's rage overwhelms the apparent aims of the action and the balance of justice, even by his own standards. In a moment of self-reflection, Tierwater realizes that he has stopped caring "about the press or the organization or the trees or anything else: all he cared about now was destruction" (134–35). Somehow, Tierwater remains a sympathetic character: Boyle writes movingly of his care for his daughter, a wife who betrayed him, the mountains, his mute assistant on Mac's ranch, and the animals in his care.[47] But the sources of Tierwater's violence and the incoherence of its outcomes undermine the credibility of radical environmental action.

On the other hand, working within the system proves to be even more incoherent. Tierwater's wife, Andrea, turns from direct action to media spectacles and fundraising: "Her forte was travelling the enviro circuit, making contacts over the cocktails and hors d'oeuvres, showing the slides, giving the peroration and passing the hat" (127). Before long, Andrea is "knocking down eighty-five thousand dollars a year as a member of E.F.!'s board of directors" (235); at a rally she wears "three-hundred-dollar cowboy boots" and drinks Evian (254); she buys a sleek, black BMW so that the radical environmentalists will have "something with a little class for pulling up at the curb when they've got the cameras going, you know?" (251). As E.F.! becomes a media organization, Andrea's lifestyle is transformed into something indefensible. The "posterboy . . . the big fundraiser," Teo, started by protesting fur by suturing a calf liver to his shaved head, but renounces personal participation in order to lead "camps" for college students in direct action (137). Tierwater's daughter, Sierra, goes directly from Teo's camp to sit in a redwood tree, before falling to her death. Together, Andrea and Teo court major donors like Philip Ratchiss: once a big-game hunter, Ratchiss maintains a mountain cabin stuffed with exotic woods and animal pelts and eventually tries "to go down in history as the agent of extinction" (228) of the California condor. Despite their unethical complicity, Andrea and Teo's tactics seem to work: they sell remarkable quantities of E.F.! berets, t-shirts, and coffee mugs and run off hundreds of flyers in their suburban office. Andrea completely disowns the violence of "eco-nuts": "Seventy-three percent of California voters say they're for the environment. All we need to do is to get them to vote—and we are" (238). Superficially, it seems that environmental politics are finally becoming the mainstream consensus needed for political action. But from the longer perspective of 2025, Andrea's misjudgment is clear. Andrea herself chooses the suburban ranch house, the BMW, the California wine that means the loss of natural habitats and a substantial carbon footprint. And after the deprivation of prison, Tierwater too relishes the fast car, the kitchen appliances, the long hot shower. The California electorate proves even less willing to inflict self-sacrifice.[48] Mainstream politics are mainstream precisely because they do not threaten a lifestyle that inexorably leads to climate change.

Paradoxically, Tierwater's radical action is wholly unsuccessful, but it allows him to glimpse the magnitude of the problem. In a commonplace moment, Tierwater fumes at a traffic jam he has helped create: "cars as far as he could see in either direction . . . each of them pumping its own weight in carbon into the atmosphere each year, every year, forever" (239). If a dramatic media demonstration—living naked in the woods for a month—fails to prevent species loss, new roads being built, trees being felled, this is not the greatest shortcoming. Rather, it is that the tactics to preserve individual species and places are miscalibrated to the challenge of climate change. As Giddens has argued, global warming is qualitatively different from more traditional forms of industrial pollution; key green values like conservation and "staying close to nature" have "no direct relevance to climate change" (55). Tierwater would have opposed nuclear power stations and wind farms in the countryside, though they might have helped avert what was to come. After California's climate has shifted, no pinpointed conservation is possible: a forest is destroyed in a single storm, and whole ecosystems collapse as temperatures shift. When a former logging investigator demands what all of Tierwater's activism accomplished, he is consumed with bitterness: "'Nothing,' I say. 'Absolutely nothing'" (270). Thirty years later, people are behaving much in the same way: "They are infinite, I am thinking, all these hungry, grasping people chasing after the new and the improved, the super and the imperishable, and I stand alone against them—but that's the kind of thinking that led me astray all those years ago. Better not to think. Better not to act. Just wave the futilitarian banner and bury your nose in a glass of *sake*" (260). Tierwater's position of critique, standing alone against the infinite masses, lets him see the fantasies of infinite progress, invention, extraordinariness, and permanence for what they are, the objects of hunger and greed that rule the American establishment.[49] After too many acts he cannot justify to himself, after multiple sentences in prison, Tierwater ultimately accepts the futility of radicalism, justified with ends even he cannot envision.

The problem glimpsed by Tierwater repeats itself in countless climate change novels. Radical environmentalism creates an excellent vantage point, outside the system of contemporary capitalism, to understand how difficult it ultimately is to oppose climate change. But the promise of the environmentalist, to use critique to create a new harmony between humans and nature, is not realized in any climate change novel. This is a striking failure of imagination and suggests a deeper crisis in ecocriticism and environmental activism's ability to respond to global warming. Even so, the politics of climate change fiction is provisional. It is just as likely *A Friend of the Earth* will be remembered as a turning point in environmental activism, when the localism of the 1990s was complicated by a truly global challenge. Similarly, the novels of this section, taken in aggregate, suggest a spreading realization that the familiar structure of human conflict—national, social, and political—cannot wholly imagine our future climate.

Inventing Agencies

In the last several years, something of a consensus has emerged among mainstream political parties in Europe and the United States, that climate change is both real and necessitates some kind of action.[50] Despite this, cohesive action has not been forthcoming, suggesting a deeper uncertainty over the best path of action. One of the most significant difficulties is that the scientific establishment, the public, and national governments do not yet have a coherent organization for collective action. Cameron Hepburn and Nicholas Stern have argued, "Formulating appropriate policy in the face of scientific complexity, an ambivalent general public, and a major international prisoner's dilemma, is exceptionally challenging."[51] Such incoherence threatens the accountability and legitimacy of governments, and it also exposes society and the environment to new risks, suggesting the urgent need to address the "lack of adequate institutions on the interface between science and politics."[52] In the face of these challenges, it seems necessary to enhance the political institutions and democratic processes that already exist, finding ways to embed climate change "in our institutions and in the everyday concerns of citizens." Some of this work involves facilitating the convergence of political and economic goals, like improving public transport, technological innovation, lifestyle politics and the downside of affluence, energy use and competitive advantages, and energy security and energy planning.[53] However, the state will itself need to develop, assuming responsibility for ensuring that public goals are realized.[54] Giddens argues that what is needed is not so much a new era of top-down government, but rather "multilayered governance, stretching upwards into the international arena and downwards to regions, cities and localities." Although states retain most of the powers needed to address global warming, they will need to partner with civil society, other nations, and international bodies like the United Nations to be effective.[55] (A competing vision would see the reduction of national sovereignty and the formation of a new international body, perhaps within the United Nations.)[56] Moreover, climate change necessitates "a cross-party framework" to ensure the "long-term stability of climate change response."[57] Taken together, these demands represent a new vision of political assembly, assembled from existing entities to create the power to respond to climate change.

An important body of fiction imagines how humans might come together in collective action to address the problem. These novels respond to the basic disconnection between different kinds of agents working on climate change: scientists, universities, private companies, government agencies, politicians, and citizens. Climate change demands a collective response among different, heterogeneous groups, creating a new organization in the polis. The novels of this section are a response to that situation, imagining the ways different kinds of groups might unite to produce the needed action. The idea of the "agency" usefully ties together two levels on which such fiction operates: first, as a group of different people assembled within the state to perform a certain category of task or function; second, as an entity defined by the power to act in a particular way, producing a specific type of work. By definition, novels imagining new political agency are neither realist nor utopian. Imagining a new kind of political organization exceeds not just the terms but also the structural possibilities of a political moment, while a realist novel develops its narrative within these terms. At the same time, the novels in question need not have the ideological permanence and separation that commonly characterizes a utopia. Instead, agency novels develop existing institutions in response to a crisis like climate change, rather than as means to achieve an ideal state.

Novels about bureaucratic agency might seem implicitly boring, but the fictional invention of agencies is a common trope in thrillers. The reason for this is that taking action on a major problem involves substantial risks and opportunities, both for the entities that take action and for the wider public and environment. In this sense, imagining agency is diametrically opposed to the environmentalist doctrines of the precautionary principle and sustainable development. The precautionary principle itself may have limited use: recent critics have argued that it can justify opposite courses of action and paralyze any response, and others have suggested that climate change demands forward-looking, progressive, risky action, possibly including geoengineering.[58] Similarly, discussions of sustainable development tend to imagine a stasis that is unhelpful for describing either collective political action or the instability of climate itself, as Marshall's *The Earth Party* suggests. By contrast, many of the best novels about the politics of climate change are science fiction, imagining the social innovations emerging from the technology of climate change, or thrillers, which pointedly weigh risks to governments, bureaucratic agencies, corporations, and the public. For example, Cussler's *Arctic Drift* gathers together a team of scientists-cum-adventurers from an invented US federal agency, the National Underwater and Marine Agency (NUMA), American political figures, and an American scientist who has discovered a means of breaking down atmospheric carbon dioxide, against an embezzling Canadian energy tycoon and the parts of the Canadian government he has bribed, with fairly predictable outcomes. Cussler's novel offers a sophisticated account of some of the technological and political difficulties of mitigating climate change, as well as a series of conflicts likely to emerge between the United States and Canada as oil supplies become scarce and Canada exports more petroleum from bitumen, and international waters become unfrozen due to global warming. On the other hand, the novel is deeply naive about the scientific hurdles needed to mitigate climate change (turning carbon dioxide reduction into a quick-fix solution discovered by a single scientist). This problem is the result of *Arctic Drift*'s dependence on a geopolitical crisis that can be quickly begun and concluded or, more generally, its use of a geopolitical opposition between the two countries, with NUMA agents as the American "good guys." However, from the very first novels about climate change, there have been attempts to frame bureaucratic novels that stage the response to climate change not in terms of a corny opposition, but rather as a process of combining powers into a body that tackles an unprecedented issue.

Written almost a quarter of a century before climate change became a popular topic for fiction, Herzog's *Heat* is often crude in its plot devices and understanding of the problem, but it also anticipates one of the main narrative strategies for responding to global warming. Following a standard plot of scientific thrillers, a scientist and governmental bureaucrat, Dr. Daniel Pick, realizes the threat of global warming and draws together a team to respond. Pick's team struggles to win over the powers that be, while the weather turns catastrophic. In the nick of time, an improbable invention to supply the Earth with energy saves humanity. In an important sense, all of the work of the novel is devoted to imagining the *agency* that could respond to catastrophic global warming. In one sense, this makes *Heat* a novel devoted to speculative bureaucracy, imagining the collection of individuals and institutions needed. In a second, related sense, *Heat* captures the agency of anthropogenic climate change, expressing its agency as the mirror image of all the kinds of individual human will and power it enlists in response. Both senses of agency work together to produce the novel's narrative.

At the center of the novel is an invented institution, CRISES. The Crisis Research Investigation and Systems Evaluation Service was formed when politicians recognized that "catastrophes seemed to have become a permanent part of life" (21) and is tasked with identifying, studying, and warning of potential environmental hazards, including natural calamities, unidentified diseases, atmospheric inversions, and calculating the costs of avoiding and recovering from disasters. This task list is purposely broad, encompassing every kind of threat; indeed, the agency would seem to anticipate the more recent preoccupation with global risk, as described by Beck and Heise. In the lobby of the agency's offices, a projector presents "a 2000 year chronicle of natural disasters" (21–22), including earthquakes, plagues, famines, typhoons, and cyclones, charting millions of deaths, and the agency's motto declares, "The Future Is Our Responsibility" (23). The fictional agency is rather banal in its enormous remit, though this is proved necessary to approach the overarching threat of global warming.

To perform this role, the agency ties together the scientific community and the US government. The agency receives daily bulletins of ecological, biological, and geophysical threats, including oil spills; an early clue is a report that Icelandic pack ice is suddenly retreating. CRISES also acts "as a clearinghouse for advanced scientific information of every sort" (39); Pick is first alerted of the danger when Dr. Bertram Kline, a respected chemist, sends an airmail letter warning of the possibility of climate change. Kline is himself an orchestrator of "big science," having organized "the largest single experiment in science until that time" (29–30), a study of the role of the Atlantic tropics in the global atmosphere, involving forty research ships gathering data together. CRISES also has institutional affiliations with a host of other laboratories, and through the narrative, Pick makes contact with the Geophysical Fluid Dynamics Laboratory, a National Oceanic Atmospheric Administration (NOAA) facility that "specialized in modeling climate" (59), the National Hurricane Center, the National Disaster Warning Program, the National Center for Atmospheric Research, the NOAA Environmental Research Laboratory, the Environmental Studies Program at Dartmouth, and numerous other groups. Even more important, CRISES has a megacomputer in a secret, underground facility. ILLIAC VII monitors "possible ecological modification, inadvertent or hostile," answers question by printout or in "a breathy, staccato female voice," and eavesdrops on major computers in the United States, providing the agency "with environmental information that might not have been disseminated, because of secrecy, caution, ignorance or ineptitude" (46–49). This technology positions CRISES at the center of a vast web of environmental knowledge.

When Pick begins to recognize the threat of global warming, he assembles a new group, creating a subagency capable of grasping global warming. As in so many thrillers, Pick gathers a crack team of "experts" (97): each member is urgently requested to come to Washington; airline tickets, ground transportation, hotel accommodation, and all expenses are provided, along with a daily consultant fee of $145; and short-term leave is prearranged. Pick himself heads the team, and his resume boasts extraordinary affiliations: a double master's in engineering and environmental science from Harvard; a PhD in engineering from MIT, where he had become a full professor before he was thirty; prestigious positions at NASA and the Department of Defense; and expertise in the fields of ecology, space travel, energy technology, computers, and advanced engineering. Dr. Harold Anderson, "a thirty-five-year-old climatologist and computer-modeling expert, one of the best, Pick knew" (59), and Dr. Finley, the director of the National Hurricane Center, are to analyze meteorological data collected by the military. Kline, the chemist, and Baxter, a meteorologist and expert on ILLIAC VII, "model weather futures based on data already on hand" (113). Pick theorizes energy production and consumption levels. Finally, Dr. Rita Havu, a disaster sociologist at the University of Southern California, "explore[s] the shaping of public attitudes" (and doubles as Pick's love interest) (113). The crack team work night and day in the secret, underground bunker, building an early computer model of the global climate that accounts for atmosphere, the ocean surface layer, deep oceans, winds, albedo, changes in carbon dioxide input, human energy use, and so on. The model is mirrored by a (now long outdated) physical model of the Earth, a ball "over forty feet in diameter . . . a perfect replica of the planet as it existed at that very moment" (52), including sunlight, layers of plastic for the atmosphere, simulated clouds, and moveable panels to represent population growth, resource availability, food supplies, and weather. The team and the models, together, are the only force in the world sufficient to produce an interpretation of the rapidly increasing global temperature. The group's reports, collections of compact phrases and capital letters, describe an accelerating cycle of released greenhouse gases, relentless heating, the melting of polar ice, galloping desertification, the abandonment of coastal areas including Holland and Bangladesh, and eventually "Condition Venus," when greenhouse warming makes all life on Earth come to an end (124–27). Within the novel, this assemblage of people and data is necessary for humans to meet anthropogenic global warming, somewhat anticipating the teams of thousands of climate scientists who would collaborate on building global climate models in the following three decades. The team works together, forming an unprecedented intellectual technology, made necessary by the threat of Condition Venus. In the broadest sense, such an assemblage is political, bringing together the chiefs of various tribes of scientists, forming a collective power by assembling bureaucratic and scientific authority.

Moreover, Pick's team of bureaucratic heads and authorities is intended to operate between science and the state. CRISES itself is secretly a hybrid scientific-military operation, justified by the Soviet threat. CRISES's computer, ILLIAC VII, is fed with exclusive military data and uses espionage techniques. But CRISES is also meant to act as a pivot between the scientific establishment and the executive branch of the government. (Similarly, bodies like the Environmental Protection Agency evaluate scientific findings and enforce laws as part of the executive function of government.) The director of CRISES, Edmunston, is meant to be a liaison between the crack team and "the powers that be" (107), but he has a cautionary stance, partly to "disguise a lack of knowledge" and partly as "a cloak to protect himself against old age" (19). The director of science and technology is also in an extremely powerful situation, because the political staff is not competent enough in science matters to screen him from the president. However, the director also finds reasons to postpone telling the president about anthropogenic climate change, rationalizing his delay in the name of public order and the president's reelection. Eventually, the director's delay leads them to try to eliminate Pick and his uncomfortable message, rather than endanger their careers. Weather events make it inevitable the president will speak with Pick, transforming politics. The narrator explains that "neither the President nor his inner circle were any better equipped to understand the complicated problem before them than the ordinary citizen" (223). "Keen instincts" (236) apparently let the president recognize that Pick's proposals to reverse global warming are the world's only hope; the same keen instincts seem to be in play when he calls for a colossal public effort on television, delays the presidential election, and finances the massive effort through E for Energy Bonds, with wage and price controls to keep down inflation. Although Pick is treated as a hero, his proven scientific authority lends the president a tool to extend his own power beyond constitutional limits, creating a "special" political situation. This power, in the name of climate change, allows the crack team and the president to dictate a reorganization of the state.

Indeed, *Heat* traces a social revolution in response to climate change. Like many novels that followed it, *Heat* gathers a sense of the public through the omniscient narration of natural disasters. Early on, an unseasonal hurricane destroys a neighborhood in Virginia. The storm is narrated with scientific language: descriptions of satellite photos, atmospheric conditions allowing it to form, and the forward speed in miles per hour. But it is also perceived through the eyes of a host of characters, including Rick Stewart, "a thirty-five-year-old proprietor of a drugstore"; Cheryl Conner, "a housewife in her twenties"; Tuffy Beccero, "a trained nurse whose skills were vital during the emergency"; Andy Braden, the local disc jockey; and Tinker Wheeler, a farmer of hothouse tomatoes (32–37). Other characters see their family members being sucked into the storm or dismembered by debris. Taken together, these characters form a public, perceiving the weather beside science. Further disasters follow, including a hurricane and tsunami in New York City that leaves twelve thousand dead and a heat wave that leads to riots, office workers hurling furniture through skyscraper windows, softened roads, energy blackouts, deranged animals, freed prisoners, and finally the prostration of a whole city. In the immediate aftermath, the public joins together in mutual aid, but this proves to be a short-lived effect.[59] More important, the disasters, and their narration, emphasize that humanity is collectively subject to the climate.

Interestingly, *Heat*'s hero is also made subject to the double threats of global warming and public irrationality. Early on, Pick reveals that his interest in climate stems from a more popular sense of climate: brought up on a farm in northeastern Pennsylvania, he learned that weather was "an all-important part of life" (17). He also grew up going to church and considered becoming a Presbyterian minister. While he is unable to square his faith and science, he admits to an apocalyptic streak and "a sort of save-the-world complex" (75). Thus, the thriller acknowledges the attraction of apocalypse as a means of narrating climate change, even as it rejects the validity of its more religious versions. An FBI file he happens across describes him as potentially "alarmist" and with a personality prone to views of the "world in peril" (96). Faced with the extent of the climate crisis, Pick struggles not to be overwhelmed with panic about "the future running backward," stemming the line of thought with macho self-possession: "*Jesus Christ, stop,* he told himself" (103). When the real heat begins, Pick is just as prostrated as the rest of the population. In the climactic moment, he even plans to shoot himself and Rita to avoid experiencing humanity's downfall. This irrationality makes Pick a member of the public, subject to the climate, even as science reasserts itself over society and nature.

The novel's omniscient view of society is actually enabled by the work of Rita Havu, the disaster sociologist who stands apart from her male colleagues on the team. Before joining Pick, Havu had been investigating "why Californians were failing to respond to a new earthquake-warming system" (40), concluding the problem was a lack of faith in science and scientists—ironic language given scientific claims to rationality. Pick asks her to research how the public might be influenced in light of climate change. Replicating the roving point of view of the disaster narration, Havu conducts focus groups in Virginia, which are reported as transparent monologues (148). Her findings are sobering. Past efforts by the government to conserve energy have always failed, with forced regulation no more successful than voluntary efforts. While there is an increase in altruism and social solidarity *after* disasters, there is very little hope of "social molding and cooperative behavior" (132) *before* the calamity. Even people who had already experienced disaster were unlikely to trust scientific warnings or make a sacrifice for future generations; their standard of living is more valued. Of course, Havu's "results" anticipate many of the fundamental difficulties that have prevented a public response to climate change. Ultimately, scientists' prescriptions for the public lead back to politics. Havu warns, "Forced to cut way back, they'd throw the government out of office, or revolt if that failed" (158). This threat was even more ominous in the Cold War political moment, with revolution the social analogue to Condition Venus. Interestingly, Havu's knowledge of the public is produced just as much by science as is Pick's knowledge of climate.

While it would appear that Havu's public and Pick's climate present insuperable obstacles, the novel's climax welds together a new totality. Faced with the threat of being the last president of the United States, America's political head cedes total power to his new energy czar, Dr. Pick. (The weaker scientists of the crack team have succumbed to stress and intrigue, heightening tension and leading the way for Pick's apotheosis.) In short order, thousands of (nameless) scientists and over a million workers are brought together, building enormous satellites to gather solar energy and beam the power down to Earth.[60] With Pick "too busy" to oversee the reeducation and indoctrination of the American people, Havu works "in a wing of the Executive Office Building, next to the White House" (238). Havu observes that consumerism "has really come to amount to a form of social organization, and is as much a determinant of how people live, think and believe as the class system is in Britain, or village society in Asia" (238); she calls for more community spirit, shared automobiles, and the use of low-energy entertainment, like cards and music. Propaganda touts the end of atomized individuals as commuters and communities are brought closer together. At the same time, sweeping legislation makes the old form of life all but impossible. Inessential domestic items like power tools, lawn equipment, electric blankets and toothbrushes, electric can openers, garage-disposal units, and microwaves are banned, and unnecessary driving is forbidden. Gasoline rations decrease driving further, while bicycles and public transportation are promoted. Almost instantly, cities are transformed, when clotheslines replace washer-dryers, and crowds are dressed "in Arab caftans or burnouses, ponchos made of sheets, bathing suits, underwear, loincloths, jockstraps, or nothing—except on their feet and heads" (245). Virtually overnight, the country that once made up 6 percent of the Earth's population and used half of its energy is reinvented.[61] But these changes are dwarfed by the final success of Pick's technology: an "earth-sun" that beams the world's energy needs to Earth. In the final analysis, the scientific and bureaucratic crack team paves the way for a new superpolitical order, with democracy replaced by a dictatorial First Couple, who shape the intimate details of their subjects' lives and provide a new sun to be worshipped. *Heat* seems to offer this vision without irony, as a utopian climax, but the details of the new order should give pause. If it seems incredible that such an order is built overnight, it should be even more disconcerting that the step from the crack team of bureaucratic scientists to totalitarianism is so short. In the novel's estimation, the combination of the climatic threat, scientific truth, and individual authority is irresistible.

A more recent and more developed examination of bureaucratic agency can be found in Robinson's "Science in the Capital" trilogy, which is one of the most sophisticated attempts to describe the American politics of climate change in fiction. Robinson's trilogy builds on a legacy of science fiction exploring environmental issues. *Pacific Edge* (1988) depicts a dynamic utopian California "of environmental collaboration and caution," fusing "organic" community with radically democratic (post)modernity.[62] His most famous literary effort, the Mars trilogy (1992, 1993, and 1996), represents the process of terraforming the red planet, as well as a series of revolutionary attempts to found Martian utopias.[63] As something of a prequel to the "Science in the Capital" trilogy, *Antarctica* (1997) imagines the founding of a new utopian settlement on the continent, exiling the capitalistic corporations running the continent, and replacing them with a utopian arrangement of workers organized in a cooperative, benign state interests, scientists and scientific institutions (particularly the National Science Foundation, or NSF), and "ferals" living on the continent.[64] Tom Moylan has argued that *Antarctica* represents a shift in dystopian literature from "the state as the locus of dominant power" to a vision of the state as an important agent in limiting the neoliberal market, restructuring society in the interests of its people, and preserving the environment.[65] In the "Science in the Capital" trilogy, Robinson turns his interest to abrupt climate change. The trilogy has already attracted significant critical debate. Heise has praised it for "attempt[ing] to envision less territorially defined forms of inhabitation" but criticized its focus on local and American national perspectives on climate change, without letting other discourses and perspectives shape its solutions.[66] Roger Luckhurst, by contrast, argues that the trilogy is a "suspended utopia" and a resistance to the quietism of the disaster novel, arguing instead that its genre is best understood as "proleptic realism": "a modeling of the present day tilted five minutes into the future." For Luckhurst, the trilogy is realist, rather than utopian, because it imagines a pragmatic response to climate change with "existing elements of the American polity" and scientific mitigations that "sit within the horizon of current research."[67] Gib Prettyman argues that the trilogy modifies genres in a way that mirrors postmodern sciences: warning about the fragility and unpredictability of highly complex systems such as the environment and simultaneously altering genres to model revolutionary change.[68] Like Luckhurst, Prettyman also emphasizes the trilogy's departure from typical utopian literature by giving a realistic account of the break between the present and the utopian state.[69] Building on Prettyman's argument, Adeline Johns-Putra has argued that the trilogy is exemplary of an ecocritical engagement with climate change, renegotiating the conventions of utopian, science fiction, and environmentalist modes of writing, to move toward a progressive, participatory utopianism.[70] Despite arguments over the trilogy's precise classification, then, there is some critical consensus that it blends realism, scientific details, and critical utopianism, to describe practical movement beyond the American political stasis of the early-twenty-first century. What has been underexamined in all this is the trilogy's political method.

By balancing near-future realism with a belief in utopian politics, Robinson's trilogy imagines a transformation of existing processes to create an ideal response to climate change. In a 2007 interview, Robinson claimed that the trilogy was, in part, a utopian manifesto, promoting the idea "that history could be the story of progress in human organization." Denying that utopia means a concrete goal or final state, Robinson defined utopia as "the name for a certain kind of dynamic process in history rather than any set end state."[71] In "Science in the Capital," Robinson explores the dynamic processes of existing human organizations as they might help contribute to a more remote goal of permaculture. In this sense, "Science in the Capital" attempts to supply what has been only partially realized in policy discussions: "a positive model of a low-carbon future," progressing past negative prescriptions for "saving, cutting back, retreating, retrenchment." Giddens has argued for the need for such a realist vision, moving beyond polarizing green rhetoric and unrealizable utopianism. Such a vision would have ideals supplied by "utopian strands," but it would also be "driven by political, social and economic thinking."[72] Ideally, the state would shape the future by blending technocratic and visionary aspects of policy, "asking what changes have to be made in the present in order to arrive at alternative future states."[73] This technocratic, even bureaucratic utopianism differs from the typical means of realizing twentieth-century utopias: social revolution, anarchism, democratic reform, technological advancement, or charismatic leadership. This was an important reversal for Robinson, attendant to a larger historical shift in utopian thinking. Past utopias have often been "anarcho-communist" or "anti-statist," but in more recent interviews, Robinson has suggested climate change necessitates "a renewed trust in centralized authority," with the democratic proviso that

"The state = us."[74] Instead of starting from popular uprising, the trilogy explores how bureaucratic institutions, such as the United States' NSF, might drive progress in environmental sustainability, climate change mitigation, and social justice. Robinson has described the trilogy as "a kind of narrative experiment," to make NSF (rather than a human) the protagonist, "the utopian hero of a science fiction [novel]." In the trilogy, NSF takes action on climate change not, as a human individual might, by serving as a political leader or inventing a technological solution, but instead through boundary work—collaborative negotiation—with other bureaucratic agencies. This idea came to Robinson after significant work with NSF, first as a recipient of funding in the Antarctic Artists and Writers' Program, then on NSF panels evaluating applications for the program. Robinson also visited NSF in Arlington, Virginia, to give talks and chat with various friends and acquaintances, and two good friends were NSF visiting scientists for a year.[75] In the "Science in the Capital" trilogy, NSF is transformed from its current status as a federal institution that tries to stay out of policy debate into an agency that drives the science establishment, federal government, and electoral politics toward a utopian response to climate change.

The first novel of the trilogy, *Forty Signs of Rain,* traces a threefold crisis of an abruptly changing climate, a deadlocked federal government, and an ineffectual scientific establishment. Despite carbon dioxide levels exceeding five hundred parts per million and an elevated global temperature, American industry adds two and a half billion metric tons of CO_2 to the atmosphere every year, over 150 percent of what the Kyoto treaty would have allowed.[76] Major shifts in weather patterns lead to intense hurricanes from the tropics, record-breaking droughts, disastrous erosion in San Diego, and a collapse of the Ross Ice Shelf. An unprecedented storm floods Washington, DC: the Potomac River overflows its banks; Rock Creek Park is filled to the top of its deep ravine; the Mall is covered in several feet of water. Although climate change has been brought right to the edge of the Capital Building, the US government remains highly dysfunctional. Bolstered by an ideologically committed science advisor, the Republican president offers a series of incoherent excuses to block action: claiming scientific uncertainty about global warming's human causes, arguing it would be too costly and disruptive to stop emitting greenhouse gases and that the next generation should solve the problem. As one character paraphrases, "Easier to destroy the world than to change capitalism even one little bit" (*Forty,*

140). The Democratic senator Phil Chase tries to pass a comprehensive environmental bill, including new fuel efficiency standards, appropriations for Detroit to make the transition, new fuel and power sources, carbon-capture and carbon-sink funding, support for emergency weather agencies, and basic research in climatology, but bipartisan deal-making means the bill is dismantled in committee, never even making it to the Senate floor. After Washington is flooded, both sides find perverse political advantages in refusing to appropriate the money needed to rebuild the city (*Fifty*, 2–3). Even in the face of undeniable, catastrophic climate change, the political system makes it all too easy for Washington to avoid meaningful action.

The scientific community also remains ineffectual. Frank Vanderwal, a scientist with specialties in bio-informatics and socio-biology, traces the crossed allegiances that make action so difficult. Some institutions are apparently committed to the public good: Frank is nominally employed by the University of California, San Diego, a university revered for having helped to invent biotechnology and for being "owned by the people, no profit skimmed off" (*Forty*, 152). A public spirit also informs much scientific labor, like editing journals and serving on panels, "an extensive economy of social credit" (19). In reality, Frank spends most of his time, expertise, and social capital trying to help Torrey Pines Generique, a biotech startup that is run for profit, exploits scientists' labor, protects and hides information, begs for venture capital, and perpetuates a broken health care system, while potentially earning millions for a small group of shareholders. Even within the company, scientists chafe at this mode of work: "Sitting on results, doing private science, secret science—it went against the grain. It wasn't science as he understood it, which was a matter of finding out things and publishing them for all to see and test, critique, put to use" (87). Private science's focus on profits rather than collective progress makes it all but unable to address climate change. As the novel begins, Frank is concluding a year's secondment to NSF, a third variety of scientific institution. NSF supports valuable, basic research, awarding grants rather than purchase contracts, deciding things by peer review rather than bureaucratic fiat, hiring skilled scientists for permanent staff, and hiring temporary staff from the expert cutting edges in every field. Congress created the agency after the Second World War, based on claims that basic research had won the war; since then the agency had been embattled by hostile Republican governments, particularly the Nixon presidency, the Gingrich Congress, and the Bush administration. At NSF, Frank evaluates grant proposals and chairs peer review committees. In an important indication of his priorities, Frank finds NSF work boring, concluding that it is mostly "sitting around rooms talking," while the "real action of science took place laboratories, and anywhere else experiments were being conducted" (17). As an envoy to NSF bureaucracy, Frank sends a "fully substantiated, crushing indictment" (231) to the agency's head, Diane Chang, complaining NSF is hamstrung by a relatively meager budget, the ideological pseudoscience of neoclassical economics, a passive funding strategy, and a policy of political neutrality. These difficulties make NSF unlikely to lead anything, particularly a global response to climate change.

However, a series of events enables a drastic shift in the direction of NSF. Melting Arctic ice stalls the North Atlantic's thermohaline circulation, initiating ice age conditions for the eastern seaboard, with temperatures in Washington plunging to fifty degrees below zero, and turning the capital into a disaster area once again.[77] Within NSF, Diane asks Frank to present his ideas to NSF's board: interdisciplinary synergies, an in-house innovation and policy team, the commissioning of research and funding institutes to address key problems, and a massive lobbying effort to direct the scientific community and demand funding from government. Frank describes the changes as a Kuhnian paradigm shift in scientific organization, driving "the whole culture" of public and private science, reorienting disciplines, scientific institutions, the US government, and global society. Frank argues that NSF should "direct the scientific community to attack and solve" the problem of abrupt climate change (288). Politically, NSF should increase the power of science in policy decisions everywhere, organizing a UN of scientific organizations that would "collectively *insist* they be funded, for the sake of the future generations of humanity" (289). The board is excited by Frank's enthusiasm, throwing out more fantastic proposals for expanding NSF's power. To his surprise, Diane asks Frank to stay at NSF and head a committee focusing on the changes, and by the third novel, NSF is indeed leading a global response to climate change. However, it would be deeply erroneous to read Frank as the heroic leader of the revolution.

In the second novel, *Fifty Degrees Below*, a strategy of bureaucratic agency and diplomacy, distinctly gendered female, allows NSF to lead enormous, collective mitigation and adaptation projects. There has been some argument over how Robinson represents science: Ernest Yanarella and Christo-

pher Rice have claimed that Robinson employs a relatively naive Enlightenment view;[78] Prettyman argues the trilogy understands science in terms of
Kuhnian revolution and postmodern truth;[79] and Luckhurst argues that it
is a Latourian manifesto for remapping the sources of power that produce
scientific truth.[80] Curiously, all of these seem to be correct: the trilogy advocates an empirically real yet indeterminate climate system and a scientific
apparatus of heterogeneous powers that might be revolutionized. The incompatibility between these theoretical sources suggests Robinson is doing
something new, moving beyond the problem of the truth of climate science
to think about how science might become part of a utopian political mobilization. This is a turning point for representing not just the mechanics of
social revolution but also the political possibilities of climate change. Diane,
as head of NSF, is a bureaucratic genius, bringing Frank to the board meeting to criticize the agency's limitations, creating an atmosphere of revolutionary possibilities, ensuring the board backs aggressive action, expanding
the agency's remit, and delegating responsibility. Diane also recognizes a
different obstacle to effective climate change action. At the beginning of
Fifty, Frank is eager to embark on a course of aggressive, macho action: "He
wanted to *do* things. . . . He wanted to identify a viable new energy system,
he wanted to sequester billions of tons of carbon, he wanted to minimize
suffering and the loss of other species" (23). Diane, however, recognizes
that ignorance of climate change is not the problem: "The problem is acting on what we know" (69). Neither Frank's scientific action nor Senator
Chase's political efforts, like countless similar initiatives, have led to sufficient agency. She also recognizes that NSF has no hope of making carbon
credits or gas really expensive, since "purely economic or political fixes"
will attract political resistance (109). "Amishization," a "voluntary simplic-
ity movement" started by NSF, will fail just as quickly (112). Thus, Diane's
to-do list is preoccupied with different, more boring tasks: coordinating
federal programs, establishing new institutes, crafting legislation, creating
international partnerships, and evaluating climate mitigation possibilities.
Instead of trying to *do* things herself, Diane wholly identifies with the federal agency, "trying almost by force of will to make NSF a major node in
the network of scientific organizations working on climate" (176). Here the
novel turns to baroque lists of institutional meetings and affiliations: Frank
and Diane are immersed in "bureaucratic swamps" with supportive members of Congress, federal agencies, scientific societies, environmental and

charitable NGOs, carbon emissions trading groups, UN delegates, IPCC representatives, "even the Pentagon" (232–34). Diane lobbies Congress for money to take action on climate change, "in a strictly scientific manner" (107), and creates pilot projects, scientific competitions with prizes, tax incentives for private research, and an unsolicited grants program to drive NSF's agenda (326). Frank himself is exhilarated by the pace of meetings, work he once dreaded as an excuse for science. He also comes to recognize Diane's "true métier, as some kind of international diplomat or technocrat," appreciating her ability to be friendly, warm, and yet relentlessly push for action (251–52). Unlike Frank's desire to "do things," this bureaucratic work is politically neutral, asks little of the public, and is all but unopposable by politicians. At the same time, this boundary work addresses fundamental obstacles to sustainable energy: evaluating new technologies rather than prejudging them, generating subsidies for sustainable energy to overcome the twenty to thirty billion dollars of fossil fuel subsidies in the OECD countries, creating "[models] and econometric studies to assess the likely consequences of investments and controls," and developing already practicable energy technologies that struggle to overcome "technological inertia" of "existing markets and the surrounding structure of supply."[81] It is also socially and politically productive, constructing an enormous institutional web capable of addressing the enormity of abrupt climate change.

Yet there are limitations to understanding this bureaucracy as the heroic work of a single leader. *Fifty Degrees Below* describes how "people thought of agencies in terms of human qualities," so Diane might be interpreted as the embodiment of NSF's power, will, and effectiveness (121). If the personality of NSF can been understood on these terms, its *agency* should not. Recent research in science and technology studies has begun to describe how scientific institutions are assembled through "boundary work." In a seminal paper, Susan Leigh Star and James Griesemer describe how Berkeley's Museum of Vertebrate Zoology was formed through collaboration among financial sponsors, scientific theorists, and amateur collectors: groups with very different intentions acting relatively autonomously.[82] Using "boundary objects"—simultaneously concrete and abstract things like specimens, field notes, museums, and maps—these groups could maintain very different meanings for their work while collaborating on a shared set of objects. The objects themselves appear simple, with a straightforward, transparent value, but also sustain multiple, intersecting social worlds.[83] Following this work, science and technology studies scholars such as Simon Shackley and Brian Wynne, Clark Miller, Myanna Lahsen, and Sheila Jasanoff have been particularly interested in the emergence of new sorts of social organizations: scientists collaborating on global climate models, the Intergovernmental Panel on Climate Change, the UN Subsidiary Body for Scientific and Technological Advice, and the National Science Foundation.[84] These organizations draw together a host of scientists, policy analysts, policymakers, lawyers, industrialists, and environmentalists into unprecedented arrangements, with credibility dynamically balanced between them. Climate models, carbon dioxide projections, error bars, carbon sinks, and carbon credits are similarly concrete and abstract, allowing scientists, policymakers, businesspeople, and politicians to have different but mutually productive relationships with them, without ever demanding a shared worldview. In *Fifty Degrees Below*, abrupt climate change supplies an inexhaustible source of boundary objects between NSF and scientific, governmental, political, and business groups, allowing NSF to become an unprecedentedly powerful scientific organization.

Fifty Degrees Below also tries to find new language to describe boundary work. The collaborations created by NSF are not a case of bureaucratic affability, identification with NSF, support for it as world leader, or even scientific consensus. The novel replaces the language of active revolution and individual force with other models of interaction. At the same time, it challenges the trope that bureaucracy merely wastes time in a deferral of action. One NSF scientist thrills to see "ripples caused by her perturbations, cascading through the global scientific network of institutions, the agencies and companies and academies and labs—the scientific polyarchy, from individual scientists up to labs, institutions, corporations and countries" (461). Such boundary work preserves the diversity of scientific power ("polyarchy"), while linking it in a vast network like a "cat's cradle" (461). In a different way, NSF funding becomes a boundary object to link with the financial world of venture capital, pension funds, investment banks, and the stock markets, when Diane's team uses cascade math "to model ways for distributing money that would perturb other sources of it" (459).[85] But the most interesting aspect of boundary work emerges as NSF confronts its bureaucratic enemies, like the Department of Energy. Republican administrators have staffed the department with nuclear and oil industry people, and the bureau does all it can to obstruct NSF and depose Diane, starting a

"War of the Agencies" (233). Interestingly, Diane does not fight back in the usual way but continues to broaden and link energy innovation programs, until suddenly the Department of Energy is on NSF's side, in pursuit of "a really powerful photovoltaic cell" (463) that would also promote its own brief. In the third novel, Diane becomes a kind of tsar of science, and everyone expects her to amalgamate a massive science agency, but she explains that "turf battles matter in Washington" (*Sixty*, 118) and refuses to change the bureaucracy too much, getting remarkable work done by aligning interests around climate change. Thus, boundary work brings heterogeneous groups—science institutions, global capital, and hostile agencies—into collaboration.

Boundary work's dramatic potential emerges in climate crisis. In *Fifty Degrees Below*, the stalled jet stream and sudden ice age provide a new space for collaboration. NSF scientists are among the first to realize that melting Arctic ice creates a cap of fresh water, blocking warming currents. NSF and NOAA create a model showing that the North Atlantic circulation could be restarted by dumping five hundred million tons of salt. Of course, both agencies lack anything like the operational capacity to conduct the mission. Frank then develops a partnership with General Wracke, the grizzled, impish head of the Army Corps of Engineers, who relishes the logistical challenge: "The Corps has always done things on a big scale. Huge scale. Sometimes with huge blunders. We're still gung-ho to try" (184–85). The general can provide the technical and logistical expertise but is blocked, like NSF, by the Republican-controlled Congress. The turning point is when Diane and Frank meet with "the four biggest re-insurance companies" (331), which are facing a government bailout or bankruptcy from the disastrous winter. The reinsurance companies stump up one hundred billion dollars to avert further insurance claims, reasoning it is "not actually very expensive, compared to some projects we have been contemplating" (333). Suddenly, the congressional block is circumvented. Diplomatic pressure is exerted on oil companies to provide five hundred very large crude oil carriers past due for retirement; the National Maritime Organization is brought in to oversee shipping; the United Nations Environmental Program makes arrangements for the salt. Hundreds of salt-laden tankers converge in the North Atlantic, stretching to the horizon, where Diane meets the secretary-general of the UN, Germany's environmental minister, and the prime minister of Great Britain (483). Thus, boundary work in NSF's board room ties together the scientific expertise of NOAA, the Corps' desire for big projects, the financial interests of the reinsurance companies, the oil companies' need to meet previous legislation, the UN agencies' interest in global governance, and European leaders' defense of the continental climate. These unlikely partners restore a petawatt of thermal energy to the North American and European climate. The project even begins to shape domestic politics, when the Republican president and the Democratic senator Chase try to seize credit. Most of NSF's staff is furious with the president, but Diane is more pleased that "they're all trying to get on our side now. So science is getting some leverage on the situation" (468). Continental weather systems and even presidential candidates can be moved with the lever of boundary work.

Although boundary work is typically understood as an institutional function, "Science in the Capital" also explores its ethical limits in a democratic state. In one subplot, NSF fields a theoretical "science candidate" alongside the Democrat and Republican candidates for president. Its policies are based on ecological theory, systems theory, and economics, with the idea of showing "what science would do if it were in the White House" (215–16). In fact, the hypothetical candidate's policies largely mirror those of the Democrats. Under considerable pressure from the political right, the team in charge of the project holds a conference with "representatives of a hundred and sixty-seven scientific organizations" examining a host of scientific methods. Boundary work allows a joint statement to be produced, withdrawing the science candidate and endorsing the Democratic senator Phil Chase as an "electable first approximation of the scientific candidate" (471–72). NSF risks skewing the Democratic vote and is also accused of "illegally entering into presidential politics" (392) by the Republican Party; Diane is called to congressional hearings and worries she could lose her job. In the end, boundary work allows NSF to frame scientific questions that indicate policy and even electoral preferences, while narrowly remaining within its bureaucratic mandate. Although the intervention might seem questionable, another subplot emphasizes the difference. A black-ops government agency tries to manipulate voting machines, using "various statistical models and decision-tree algorithms" (441), to reverse votes and ensure the Republican president's reelection. When they learn of the plan, Frank and a friend at NSF decide on the fundamental importance of elections and develop other government contacts to avert the manipulation.

These parallel examples suggest that, in the trilogy at least, science may have an obligation to influence democratic politics and may still escape real tampering with the objectivity of elections.

One of the strengths of Robinson's trilogy is that it tries to theorize bureaucratic boundary work as a scientific, social, and philosophical program. Frank's background in sociobiology and game theory provides a theoretical structure to understand social interaction. Frank's sociobiology privileges social consciousness: humans are "social primates" whose "bodies, brains, minds and societies had grown to their current state in east Africa over a period of about two million years, while the climate was shifting in such a way that forest cover was giving way to open savannah" (*Forty*, 13). Climate and evolution, then, shape the totality of human experience, cutting through simplistic models of individualism, free will, or social control. Initially, sociobiology produces a deep nihilism in Frank, as he sees sociability break down in elevators, in the workplace, on highways, and when people hoard food during climate crises. This personal nihilism is tempered as Frank begins to explore Buddhist ideas. Heise has claimed that the Asian climate refugees whom Frank meets function "as rather grotesque stereotypes of Buddhist wisdom and serenity," but the displaced Tibetans are far more complex characters.[86] Acting first as diplomats for the island nation of Khembalung, the Buddhists are most concerned about rising sea levels; Drepung and Rudra become Frank's friends—a roommate and a kayaking partner respectively—rather than stereotypical New Age gurus; Frank never practices meditation. Instead, Frank is influenced by their idea that altruism is the best strategy to help both oneself and the human species: an idea that Frank translates into the idea that game theory's "always generous" (*Sixty*, 311) strategy, apparently a loser in simulations, may be viable in practice. His encounter with Drepung and Rudra also gives him the courage to pursue his own ideas of happiness, largely developed from sociobiology: he lives in a tree house, simulates hunting by throwing a Frisbee, and actively counteracts global warming by shaping the social consensus and climate. More important, characters in the trilogy learn to interact altruistically with very different others, performing a nonbureaucratic variety of boundary work. Living in Rock Creek Park, Frank becomes friends with a group of Viet Nam veterans based on the exchange of beer, pizza, fire, and banter; each of them saves the other in moments of real danger.[87] Frank and a thoughtful Quibbler child track escaped zoo animals, and he exchanges playful conversation and companionship with an aging monk. A much longer analysis could be written of the Quibbler family, who are among Frank's friends: Anna, an NSF scientist, and Charlie, an environmental aide to Senator Chase, rebuild their nuclear family as a response to the science, politics, and personal consumption involved in climate change and become more fulfilled in the process. As these examples are gathered together, they begin to suggest a fundamental human craving for cooperative work, reciprocity, and mutual enjoyment: "We live for this, we crave this" (*Fifty*, 256). In these relationships, boundary work is transformed from a way for heterogeneous groups to construct knowledge into a means of organizing "always generous" collaboration. In short, boundary work becomes the practice of utopia.

In the final novel of the trilogy, *Sixty Days and Counting*, both the utopian potential and the limits of boundary work are explored. After Phil Chase is elected president and Diane Chang becomes an unprecedentedly powerful science advisor, they relentlessly reform the American economy's relationship to the environment. The presidency brings with it the ability to print money, start huge public works programs, and legislate private investment, an "apparatus of power" allowing the president of the United States to rule the world, "both by direct fiat and by setting the agenda that everyone else had to follow or be damned" (41). New partnerships with the navy promise overengineered, failsafe nuclear plants; collaborations with NASA and the air force look to space-based solar power. While a cautionary note is sounded about the limits of mitigating climate change's worst effects, particularly ocean acidification, other enormous terraforming projects begin to take shape. A partnership with England and Holland promises to lower rising sea levels. Quite suddenly, China is brought into collaboration: America provides emergency power generation, subsidies, and technology to replace dirty coal plants, while China agrees to accept an "impressively low" (476) carbon cap and to free Tibet. All of this progress starts in an altruistic program of collaboration.

However, boundary work seems to collapse when it comes to the United States' partisan politics. Certain agencies are deemed intractably Republican, like the Treasury Department and Departments of Interior and Commerce, and are made to toe the line. Through the threat of decapitation, the World Bank and the International Monetary Fund are brought to heel. After Chase survives an assassination attempt, he blames the right-wing media and sends a dream sheet of Democratic reforms through Congress, including raised fuel efficiency standards, a doubled gas tax, a progressive tax system, an end to corporate loopholes, heavy support for international aid, "gun control legislation to give the NRA nightmares" (420), guaranteed health insurance, and full employment. This unnegotiated, totalizing victory eliminates Republican policies in every area. Although few of Robinson's (presumably left-leaning) readers seem to have noticed, "Science in the Capital" woefully underrepresents half of Washington: the first president, his science advisor, and a shadowy black-ops villain are the only Republicans in the whole trilogy, and each only merits a few pages of direct representation. Robinson himself has described the political situation of the first decade of the twentieth century in immoderate terms: as a "feudal regime" and the utopia of the right.[88] In Robinson's trilogy, there is no space to imagine how boundary work might move beyond the structural acrimony of party politics, toward a settlement on climate change issues. Climate change requires action, not just for four-year presidential terms, but over decades and even centuries, and all of the trilogy's boundary work is liable to be upset at the next election. Heise is also right to note that the trilogy is largely "stuck in Washington and American government perspectives"; partnerships with Europe, China, and Khembalung are superficially treated, and the UN climate framework is hardly even mentioned.[89] Yet more political imagination will be required.

A second issue with the trilogy is more difficult to recognize, but it is endemic to the agency novel more generally. Both Herzog's and Robinson's visions fundamentally originate in human agency. In the philosophical sense, the utopias produced are the product of human ingenuity, extended to the limits of plausibility. In the social sense, agencies are a form of social organization that permits the catastrophic limits of anthropogenic climate change to be transcended. In both cases, this leads to a deemphasis of the real, material agency of things. Both novels demonstrate an awareness of ecological limits and pay lip service to finding new ways of curbing consumer demand. In *Heat*, this work is shunted onto Rita Havu, who uses emergency politics and propaganda to achieve an unlikely new consensus. In "Science in the Capital," efforts to curb consumption and emissions are preemptively rejected in favor of terraforming and technological breakthroughs for unlimited clean energy. Both novels are notable for creating detailed accounts of climate and climatology. But Herzog's masculine agency and Robinson's boundary work stand between untamed nature and the victimized public, blocking the emergence of new grassroots responses to the changing material world.

The broad range of novels described here should go some way to suggesting that there can be no single, ideal representation of the politics of climate change. Despite the capaciousness of the form, even a long thriller, like Glass's *Ultimatum,* struggles to capture more than a single facet of the geopolitical networks involved. A trilogy, like Robinson's "Science in the Capital," may go further, representing the scientific establishment, federal government, and popular politics of the United States. Nevertheless, Robinson's trilogy all but excludes Republican politicians, energy lobbyists, corporations, transport concerns, conservative voters, and international political figures, to name but a few groups. But beyond mere concerns over size and complexity, different structural features open certain kinds of consideration, while closing others down.

Novels exploring the geopolitical dimensions of climate change almost universally simplify these relationships into binary oppositions. This strategy can be highly reductive, as in *Ultimatum,* and it can also lead to further complexity, as in *The Quiet War.* Certainly, the power dynamics, rivalries, and alliances between states have been decisive factors in trying to build international climate accords and coordinate global responses. On the other hand, such novels commonly privilege strong characters as embodiments of the states they represent, perhaps including more "common people" stuck in the middle (as in *The Quiet War*). Such a structure tends to falsify the complexities of the modern state, which cannot be wholly reduced to the will of a few men or women; bureaucratic institutions, scientific findings, and economic measures matter more than this would suggest. Lobbying groups exert considerable pressure but are typically unrepresented because they make leaders seem craven, detracting from the drama of the high leader in the hot seat. Similarly, the political willingness of voters to sustain leaders who take a stand on climate change, inflict costly regulation, or participate in emissions-reducing behaviors is of fundamental importance to international political considerations but is rarely broached in geopolitical climate change novels. Even in Robinson's *Sixty Days and Counting,* President Chase is turned into a heroic politician who ignores domestic doubt and sues for peace with China. The analytical errors of turning international policy into characters have proved difficult to overcome; these representational difficulties raise serious questions about the limits of political solutions wholly enacted on a world stage.

In an important sense, novels about climate change activism capture an essential aspect of environmental discourse, particularly in the United States in the first decade of the twenty-first century. After Al Gore's loss to George W. Bush in the 2000 presidential election, climate advocacy was mostly advanced beyond the federal government, by activist groups and subnational politicians.[90] *A Friend of the Earth*, in particular, captures the deep sense of alienation between activists and a Republican White House in this period. Also, activist novels are able to capture an emotionally rich sensibility of everyday people, outside of political office. However, *A Friend of the Earth* raises more serious questions about the limits of environmental activism developed on a civil rights model. Activists are either seduced by media campaigns or drawn into unproductive, private rage, breaking down the productive tension between the activist group and mainstream politics. At the same time, *A Friend of the Earth* questions whether activist politics are likely, themselves, to realize significant action on climate change, with activists both unable to access the global economic and political structures in question and deeply implicated in the lifestyle choices that lead to climate change. These difficulties raise deeper concerns about the usefulness of critique in this era.

Bureaucratic novels about climate change would seem to be far more limited than novels about international relations or radical environmentalism. Such novels have much to overcome, not least the boredom of bureaucratic meetings compared to swashbuckling heroism. On the other hand, the bureaucratic agencies of *Heat* and "Science in the Capital" use science to span the diverse modalities of climate change politics, from the apparently "individual" lifestyle choices of consumers to the electoral calculations of those in the highest office, from scientific studies of climate to enormous engineering projects that bring public and private capital together. These novels also have proved able to begin to engage with the practical steps necessary beyond the social goals of "consensus" or "political action," imagining (in a more or less sophisticated way) the concrete projects and the political affiliations needed to realize them.

The fictional progress between *Heat* and "Science in the Capital" is instructive for another reason. Both novels flirt with a kind of bureaucratic authoritarianism that is more concerned with shaping the public than bringing it into democratic processes. Then again, the thirty years between *Heat* and *Sixty Days and Counting* have seen enormous formal innovation in the representational politics of climate change. While *Heat* can only imagine a supine couple, locked together in sex or feverish exhaustion, *Forty Signs of Rain* describes a postnuclear family making passionate choices to develop the next generation and reduce their carbon footprint. While *Heat* creates an imaginary bureau of emergencies, *Fifty Degrees Below* explores how existing agencies might usefully lead a meaningful, collaborative response. Herzog's fiction elevates a single genius to the position of climate king, while Robinson traces a cooperative political process. Herzog endorses the most improbable of technocratic solutions, electricity beamed from space, while thirty years later Robinson is able to describe a host of energy and transportation technologies all but ready for implementation, given public and political will. At this moment, it seems that the most politically engaged novels are not those that threaten the public with annihilation, but rather those that show the alliances between readers and institutions that might lead to a climate of abrupt action.

FOUR

ECO-NOMICS
Domesticity, Ecology, and
Political Economy

Thinking about climate change, there is always a temptation to reduce it to a discrete, bounded question. Largely, the preceding chapters have explored just such questions: what the science of climate change is; what literary forms enable its expression; what political responses are possible. These are important questions, and many more could be asked. Nevertheless, they tend to compartmentalize climate change into a discrete set of practices. With a momentous threat, there is a tendency to jump to solutions. Faced with an anthropogenic catastrophe, perhaps the most natural responses are either denial or an immediate demand for actions that will "solve" the problem.

In the case of climate change, however, the "problem" cannot be deferred or resolved. While many novels concentrate the disaster into a single tsunami, climate change's real effects are more distributed: desertification, contamination of freshwater, fiercer tornadoes, extinctions, destroyed mangrove barriers, crop failures, and so on. These effects have different time scales, they impact communities differently, and they have different implications for local and distant humans. More important, these effects are already with us. Oddly, one of the rarest occurrences in climate literature is the truly contemporary novel. Even so, there is a discernible (if subjective) difference between two types of literary futures. The first is the threat, or more charitably, the jeremiad: if humans don't get it together, the future will be insufferably bad. The second is wholly different in intent, describing where we are now, based on where we seem to be heading. This future may be heightened, stylized, even horrifying, but it is recognizably of a piece with our own. It sensitizes the reader to what is before us, rather than demanding we turn away in revulsion or "solution."

These latter novels engage with the "eco" at several levels. Following the Greek meaning of "home," the novels in question explore what it means to dwell in the Anthropocene, when climate change already affects the reader here, not in a distant time or place. Predictably, many—though not all—of the novels in question take up the question of contemporary domesticity as such: the fitness of twentieth-century homes, food, family arrangements, work, and shopping in the Anthropocene. After the disaster, whatever it might be, these quotidian activities reassert themselves, although often in very changed circumstances. Second, these novels are more broadly economic, dealing with the material circumstances of human beings. Instead of taking a single disaster (a storm) or a single loss (an extinction), they attempt to describe the systemic transformations of the Anthropocene. Economics, in the present day, is one area of study that examines humans' visceral relationships with environment. As climate change affects scarcity, security, technology, enterprise, energy, trade, production, markets, and consumption, humans' way of living must also adapt. After the adaptation, the resulting system indicates a new mode of Anthropocene living. Third, these novels engage with the ecological. This is not to say that they are themselves part of that science, nor that they promote an ecological "way of thinking." They are not paeans to "nature," either. What these novels do, instead, is to begin to account for the agency of nonhuman things in human affairs. Rather than offering anthropocentric character studies, they capture how geology, geography, and species radically shape human experience. They also examine the *agency* of nonhuman things commonly called artificial, such as technology, vehicles, and capital. Instead of relentlessly purifying action into the result of human character, these novels allow the direct influence of things to shape narrative. More than this, they explore how things are a fundamental part of what it means to dwell on Earth. Domesticity, humans' way of making a living, and the situatedness of this activity in a wider world of things combine to form the ungainly term *eco-nomics*, to which this chapter refers.[1]

The eco-nomics described here has fundamental differences from the Marxian economics and formal politics popular in the humanities. Marxian criticism has played an important role in literary theory, lending a language to analyze class, alienation, labor, and consumption. However, popular Marxian theory has been resolutely anthropocentric. Attempts to bring environmental issues into the framework are intriguing. Even so, literary Marxism has been insufficiently concerned with the operation of real economies, the production and distribution of real things in the contemporary world. Climate change refocuses attention onto questions of where our bread will come from and who will drive it to us, not to mention what species of grains might yet thrive. Similarly, the novels of this chapter are less concerned with the position taking of political criticism. In the third chapter, climate politics are described in terms of political opposition, critique, and bureaucratic organization. All of these strategies are resolutely *human:* grouping and differentiating humans by belief and agency. To a greater or lesser extent, they are also centralized, describing power in terms of formal groups, even in resistance. Change is expected to come by human power. By contrast, the eco-nomic novels here account for the nonhumans and distributed populations of the Anthropocene, treating the political process as but one input into a far more complicated system.

That system might be called the market, although this should not be confused with the idealized construct of the political right. Markets would seem to be a fundamental space for defining the Anthropocene. Critics from the left and right have vociferously attacked the creation of carbon markets that would allow economies to value and restrict emissions across different forms of production. The practical alternative, direct environmental regulation, would also have costs that would eventually be borne by the market—either producers, consumers, or a third party. There are compelling arguments to support the thesis that markets have a central role to play in mitigating climate change, by bringing the environmental costs of emissions into the real costs of goods, instead of letting them be externalized.[2] Many of these novels touch on these issues. Legion economists have also tried to describe the costs of ecosystem collapse, mass flooding, extinction, unpredictable crop yields, severe restrictions on carbon energy, and the reconfiguration of industrial production and middle-class consumption. The novels of this chapter address these issues through specific characters in a scene, but they also try to trace the wider, systemic implications for an economy.

The literary strategies for depicting carbon economies have changed radically over the last thirty years. In the 1980s, there were countless predictions of capitalism's collapse; climate change gradually became an important feature of such predictions, with its ability to disrupt the distributive system on which billions of people have come to depend. George Turner's *The Sea and Summer* (1987) exemplifies this moment, tracing decline from late-twentieth century urban domesticity to a totalitarian, welfare state in peril, caused by the breakdown of the global economy, widespread flooding, and unpredictable rainfall.

Toward the end of the 1980s and into the early 1990s, authors found renewed optimism that capitalism, having triumphed in the Cold War, could also overcome global warming. Ben Bova's *Empire Builders* (1993) exemplifies these hopes, depicting a swashbuckling entrepreneur who takes on states and the entire economy to build a sustainable future. Through the 1990s and the first decade of the 2000s, novelists and critics shared a remarkable agreement on the economic causes of climate change, while growing ever more doubtful that the existing system could adapt. In the last several years, climate novels have become far more complicated in their accounts of Anthropocene life. Instead of predicting systemic failure, as such, authors have begun to articulate more of the subtle economic transformations. These novels span hard science fiction, genre fiction, and, increasingly, adult realist novels. Across these works, the future is not a sustainable utopia or a regressive dystopia. Instead, these novels articulate the unsettling of familiar systems and the reconfiguration of human ecology. Species, weather, social groups, and financial interests act on their own terms and allow the reader to integrate ever more concerns when considering the Anthropocene. The practice implied by these works may prove to be one of the more important critical tasks when confronting global warming.

Threatening the Tower

In the 1980s, climate change was often subsumed under a larger desperation about economic and environmental injustice. When it was recognized as a major problem, climate change was often seen as a symptom of the advance of market-based conservatism under Reagan and Thatcher; the elimination of social protections; and a rapacious capitalism that was also polluting the air and waterways, producing near-permanent nuclear waste, proliferating toxic chemicals, and causing the depletion of the ozone layer. In terms of the economy, the media and arts closely chronicled the breakdown of postwar projects for the urban poor. Many of these projects were founded on a belief in social welfare, the creation of a safety net for the entire public after the galvanizing experience of the Second World War. These projects also bespoke a form of environmental constructivism: the belief that the undesirable aspects of the poor (criminality, idleness, antisocial behavior) could be reformed by placing them in an artificial environment. With the failure of these projects, the dystopias of the period reconsidered their underlying environmental arguments.

From this period onward, the economic dystopia would strongly inform Anthropocene fiction. J. G. Ballard's *High-Rise* (1975) is an important document of the period, crystallizing the environmental implications of the economic dystopia.[3] Instead of focusing on the "irredeemable" poor, *High-Rise* describes the social breakdown of "an apparently homogenous collection of high-income professional people" (53). Soon after completion of the building, the residents seem to rebel against it and the social structure it implies. Elevators are jammed, maintenance and trash removal cease, supermarkets and pools are sacked, barricades of broken furniture appear in the stairwells, raiding parties and violent clashes break out between floors. Chic, high-rise living had promised the invisibility of waste, but the tenants sabotage the trash chutes and garbage trucks. The residents discover an inner compulsion to live with their trash, wallowing in abjection. Repulsed by the building's egalitarian promise, the residents split into three distinct and hostile camps, apparently forming a "proletariat of film technicians, air-hostesses and the like"; a middle class of "docile" doctors, lawyers, and accountants; and an upper class oligarchy of minor tycoons, actresses, and "careerist academics" (53). Eventually residents lose the basis of class distinctions, abandoning careers for the more absorbing tribal living of the building. Local clans, based on floors, dominate identity. Similarly, the discreet delineation of apartment units collapses as raiding parties break down doors, trash chokes whole rooms, and residents form polygamous tribal affiliations. Ballard's yuppie dystopia overstates its case, but the novel provides a framework for future climate dystopias.

Specifically, the transformation of the high-rise is accompanied by multiple layers of meaning that recur in subsequent novels. Paradoxically, the transformation of the building into a "high-priced tenement" (43) indicates a renewed faith in the environmental determinism of the postwar period. Physical infrastructure—not culture, character, or even class—determines how people behave. Although there is little engagement with people beyond the white bourgeois circle here, the novel anticipates the environmental justice movement, drawing attention to the material conditions of social oppression. Early on, the tenants recognize that "their real opponent was not the hierarchy of residents in the heights far above them, but the image of the building in their own minds, the multiplying layers of concrete that anchored them to the floor" (58). This is an implicit exoneration of the failure of working-class tenements. At the same time, the high-rise critiques the idea of human perfectibility. Instead of allowing residents to live in harmonious community, Ballard argues, the modern building allows for "the expression of a truly 'free' psychopathology" (36). Despite threats of hunger and assault, this violent, tribal living leads residents to a contented happiness (154). Ultimately, *High-Rise* narrates how a new environment breaks down late-twentieth-century "ideal" domesticity, clearing the way for postmodern affiliations undergirded by physical environments.

George Turner's *The Sea and Summer* also explores the reconfiguration of domesticity but traces the cause to global climate change and economic transformation. *The Sea and Summer* was already briefly discussed in the second chapter, as a novel that blends together the distant postapocalypticism of the deluge novel and the more immediate consequences of the flood novel. However, the novel is more significant for the ways it reconsiders the urban dystopias of the 1970s and 1980s in the context of climate change, incorporating economic and climatic degeneracy into a vision of "greenhouse culture." As in Ballard's *High-Rise*, the future holds a new, more hierarchical society, glimpsed through a falling family. The Australian economy has been split into two groups, the Sweet, encompassing the entirety of employed workers, and the Swill, the new majority, permanently unemployed and ghettoized in concrete high-rises. This is a significant departure from typical class politics, which divide society between working and owning classes. Instead, merely having a job makes a worker a Sweet. These classes are also geographically determined: most Sweet live in single-family homes on high ground, while the Swill are warehoused in enormous tower blocks in low-lying areas that are subject to flooding. Between the two classes is the Fringe, a buffer zone between Sweet and Swill neighborhoods, made up of families who have lost their income and are slowly sinking into the Swill.

Through the eyes of the Conway family, the usually segregated class structure is evident. Initially, the Sweet family's experience is indistinguishable from that of a middle-class family in the late twentieth century, possessed of a single-family home in a good neighborhood, little luxuries, and a healthy dose of familial pride. But after the father is made redundant, he realizes there is little prospect of him ever finding work again, and he commits suicide. The mother, Alison, uses the family's remaining money to move her two sons into substandard housing in the Fringe. Instead of understanding the move as a social deprivation, her two sons are startled by their new physical environment. They are appalled by the street's broken traffic-light standards, the pot-holed road surface, the lack of a nature strip in the footpath; the house's windows are "narrow and secretive"; everything is "shabby and untidy" (56). As for the house itself, its windows are nailed shut, the lighting fixtures are without elements, and the taps drool rusty water; the rooms have not been swept out, and the kitchen is "decrepit and indefinably wretched" (68). Behind the house, "a small back yard held a square of patchy lawn and some dusty geraniums" (68). These details indicate the absence of a local council, a neighborhood that has "given away pride," and the collapse of the family's material foundation.

More frightening is the family's glimpse of the Enclaves. Soon after arriving, Billy Kovacs visits the family, describes exactly how much money is in Alison's bank account, and demands a large weekly payment to his Protection Racket. Kovacs is smelly, rough tongued, and threatening, pointing out they will have no protection from the louts "who rob and terrorize," since the "coppers look after people with property" (64–65). The furniture left from a Sweet life is now a liability, since the Swill who "live just down the road . . . [will] think how *they* can sell it. Over your knifed guts if need be" (60). The Conways are horrified that their home cannot protect them from Kovacs or the violence of the towers. Soon enough, Alison empties the account that maintained a narrow difference between her home and the Towers, and then she becomes Billy's lover as a payment to maintain her position. All this is motivated by a desperate desire to avoid the Towers, buildings one hundred meters on each side and seventy stories high, each holding seventy thousand people (14). The flats would be tiny for two but swell beyond single families to hold eight to eleven people, most crammed two to a bunk. A "triv" (television), broken furniture, adulterated food, obscene and cartoonish graffiti, and a large helping of body odor complete the picture (21). Both Conway brothers rebel from what they see, doing all they can to escape from the horror of the Enclaves. The elder, Teddy, passes tests that let him enter into state care, to become a Sweet, and Francis has a remarkable talent for mental calculation, making him useful to powerful Sweet trying to fiddle their books. In doing so, Turner's protagonists raise the expectation that individual talent and determination will transcend economic conditions. More generally, *The Sea and Summer* draws on the horror readers in the 1980s felt of the welfare state and, conversely, the terror of middle-class families falling into bottomless poverty.

Turner's novel is different from most dystopias of the 1980s in its recognition that climate change reconfigures the underlying assumptions of modern economies. The late twentieth century is painted as a time of childlike innocence, innocence resonant with the bourgeois ambitions of *High-Rise*'s tenants. The mother, Alison Conway, remembers how the warming first seemed like permanent summer: "Paradisal time of cold drinks and coloured salads, skimpy frocks and games under the garden hose, days at the seaside with sunburn and jellyfish, sand and seaweed and lush wavelets of cuddling water" (35). Turner's dystopia slowly unravels this idyll of the contemporary, making clear that the basic parameters of human life have changed. By the middle of the twenty-first century, world average temperature has surged by 4.5 degrees, the ice caps have begun to thaw, and oceans have risen thirty centimeters (110). As the Antarctic ice shelf melts, ocean currents, temperature gradients, and wind patterns are altered, "drowning untellable desert in useless water while ancient forests grew brown and bare under a brass-faced sun, giving this year and taking next, turning grassland to tinder while it poured unwanted, polluted water down the rivers" (227). The idyll of an endless summer appears hopelessly immature. The old wheat belt is turned into a dust bowl, leaving ghost towns and refugees. As the sea rises, water "advances up the streets from shores and rivers," and "coastal cities face death by drowning" (36). Instead of focusing on the effects of a single disaster, *The Sea and Summer* examines the systemic effects of climate change.

As the relatively stable climate is eroded, the world economy begins to disintegrate. Thinking about class, it can be easy to imagine the wealthy are omnipotent controllers, but doing so mistakenly attributes coherence to a chaotic system. Early in the novel, the Conway brothers glimpse the "City Centre, the grandest of all surroundings." Only in adulthood do they realize that the grand, mysterious palaces "were office blocks and heartless, bustling hives": centers of power, but lacking conscious life at their core (56). From the perspective of an elite character, Nola Parkes, the lack of a central intelligence is yet more obvious. As she describes it, the global financial system collapses under the pressure of soaring population, starvation, and international blackmail: "Earth's resources were sacked to shore up the illusion of an endlessly expanding economy" (97). The distinctions between the West and the Third World break down as well: "The idea of selling to people who bought with money lent by the seller lest the system collapse was more than idiotic; it was the final self-criticism of a system that could exist only by expansion and when expansion ceased for lack of markets must eat its own body" (104). Australia is able to escape the fate of poorer countries, with "shanties and lean-tos, no sewers, no taps, no way to distribute food, only street mud to walk on" (227). Even so, there are jobs for fewer and fewer Australians, forcing most of the population to subsist on paltry government subsidies. Humans have the technological knowledge to hold back rivers and oceans, but there is no governmental money for the massive projects. Farms are ruined by drought and torrential flood, leading to continual crises in food supply: "sudden dearth of cereal . . . vanishing of sugar for a month or so, midsummer rationing of milk, or—most infuriating of all—trial runs of staple-substitutes which neither substituted nor in any way appealed" (210–11). In *The Sea and Summer,* climate change and economic depression are interrelated effects of an unsustainable financial system. The result is not a once-and-for-all apocalyptic fight, but the slow sinking of a society with no pilot at the wheel.

The effects of these changes are distributed unevenly. In a frame narrative that gives the perspective of the distant future, a historian explains that the greenhouse culture's class system was intended for preservation, rather than oppression. The educated, competent Sweet "were necessary to administer the State," while the Swill were "a burden on the economy" (131). Faced with the "collapse of trade and all but essential industry," the government warehouses the unemployed but cannot protect all people. Most Swill seem to accept that the "state-given share is sufficient" (216), but frequent problems with food supply and distribution show this complacent trust in the state is unmerited. Meanwhile, official lies assure the Sweet that new technology can avert storms; that all citizens are guaranteed windows, running water, and adequate sewers; and that regular maintenance is assured by a fixer in every Tower (187, 190–91). Beneath the lies, the political class faces an economy that cannot meet society's most basic demands.

This economic failure undermines many of the twentieth century's most cherished ideals. Faced with the bleak poverty of the Towers, Alison Conway displays pious shock, saying there should be "equal sharing" between poor and rich. Kovacs coarsely dismisses the idea: "Equal arseholes, lady!

There isn't enough of anything to be equal with. Equal shares would mean everybody in equal poverty" (74). In an era of true scarcity, egalitarianism ensures common suffering. Since the novel was written during the Cold War, communism is similarly dismissed: "Communism is only an idea that has never been tried—except perhaps the by Pilgrim Fathers for a very short while, and they were happy to backslide as soon as cash became available" (106). Nor does meritocracy provide an answer. It gradually emerges that Sweet and Swill are anything but fixed "classes": Swill children make up half of each new generation of workers, Sweet workers are regularly superannuated, and undercover Sweet pull the strings behind the tribal governance of the Towers. Their careful meritocracy differentiates society but utterly fails to redress its ills. Most vividly, floods are a filthy eyesore in the Sweet neighborhoods, but in the Fringe, rainwater flattens the gardens and seeps into the houses, leaving wet walls "with a mud line ankle high" (274). For this class, regular floods make respectable domesticity impossible. Although the television dismisses four meters of floodwater as "rain in the hills," two floors of the Towers are swallowed. Such flooding transforms their identities. When Teddy visits them as part of a police sting, he is struck by the stench: "the dense odour of cramped, sweating, filthy humanity and its effluents after a week's imprisonment by flood. Heaven only knew what had happened to their drainage as the tide rose but it is certain that we had swum through raw sewage. I heard behind me the sound of vomit being choked back" (262). Water, sweat, and excrement invade the boundaries of homes, turning them into prisons. Here, the sense of smell also does important work. Teddy's disgust at the stench, his sense of revulsion, complicates his sense of pity, disabling a direct experience of compassion. The destruction of lived environments also undermines humanism, meritocracy, and egalitarianism, leaving visceral antipathy in their place.

Even as *The Sea and Summer* traces the collapse of these ideals, it exposes the injustice of the late "greenhouse culture." The Swill are framed as degenerate criminals, but a social order slowly emerges: elderly and disabled people rely on "floor groups" to pass food and vouchers through the high-rises (287), and the "worst" elements work day and night to save the young and elderly during floods (187). By contrast, the heroism of the Conway brothers is steadily undermined. In the 1980s, Francis and Teddy's individualism, self-possession, and refusal to be pigeonholed by class mark them as likely heroes of the capitalist economy. Teddy views himself as an intellectual and moral superior, but the academy exposes him as a snob with second-rate intelligence. Francis is not selected to be a Sweet but sucks up to whomever he perceives as powerful, passively offering himself as a pawn in more complex systems of exploitation. Eventually, he is exposed as a disloyal, manipulative brute (396), while Teddy achieves limited redemption by rejecting the Sweet's blind managerialism and committing to a utopian, altruistic vision of leadership (296–97). Surprisingly, it is Kovacs who appears as the best of the novel's characters, "the one irreplaceable soul, contorted and wasted but irreplaceable" (396). Although Kovacs keeps order with "ruthless vigilante justice" and secret assistance from the police, he teaches fallen Fringers how to live in the Towers and also personally works himself to exhaustion and risks his life to save the elderly and children during floods. Surprisingly, then, Kovacs is simultaneously a brutal thug, stool pigeon, and neighborhood protector. In the crumbling economy of *The Sea and Summer,* Kovacs's use of violence and chicanery to hold a Tower fiefdom enables the basic distribution of food, protection, and even a kind of morality. Ultimately, the novel refuses the reader a safe haven for identification: all are compromised by global warming.

The Sea and Summer undermines the economic assumptions that underpin most responses to climate change. It is easy to advocate solutions based on the global economy, current food and manufacturing outputs, benevolent management, and a collective human equality. However, climate change is capable of creating new levels of scarcity, impoverishing wealthy countries, threatening the nourishment and shelter of whole populations, undermining systems of social reward, and destroying societies' cohesion. At a more intimate level, the novel suggests people's self-awareness and sense of worth, grounded in the home, workplace, and social class, are highly vulnerable in the Anthropocene. Turner's "greenhouse culture" despairs of collective action, reflecting a moment when neither rampant capitalism nor Soviet authoritarianism seemed likely to provide answers. The questions framed by *The Sea and Summer* have proved to be quite durable, even if their economic context has not.

Heroic Enterprise

The late 1980s and early 1990s were a transformational period for the politics and literature of climate change. Through the 1970s and 1980s, anthropogenic global warming was primarily a matter of concern for scientists. From 1985 to 1988, climate change developed from a scientific area of concern into a political issue demanding solutions. Governments became increasingly involved from 1988 to 1990, and they negotiated the adoption of the United Nations Framework Convention on Climate Change from 1991 to 1995. (The Kyoto Protocol was negotiated and ratified between 1996 and 2001.)[4] Before the late 1980s, literary authors could little imagine a framework for addressing climate change. The few novels that were written treated global warming as an inevitable, apocalyptic event. When this wasn't the case, as in Arthur Herzog's *Heat* (1978, discussed in the previous chapter), authors could only imagine a semidictatorial Manhattan Project that would "make it happen" through American innovation and draconian laws. Many of the real difficulties of addressing global warming—coordinating national programs, negotiating limits of sovereignty, disseminating technology, altering the infrastructure and habits of people, balancing different sources of emissions—were yet unrealized. The project of financing the carbon economy's transformation went unimagined.

From 1988 to 1995, climate change negotiations laid a framework for imagining economic transformations that could avert uncontrolled global warming. Early in the negotiations, developed countries differed as to who should address the problem. In countries such as Canada, the Netherlands, and Germany, the issue was primarily controlled by environmental and foreign ministries, which were relatively eager to negotiate emissions targets and timetables; the US Environmental Protection Agency was similarly inclined. By contrast, the US delegation was controlled by the Department of Energy, the Office of Management and Budget, and the Council of Economic Advisers, "all of whom stressed the uncertainties of climate change and the economic costs of mitigation measures." This mix of institutions complicated negotiations, adding economic forms of consideration to what was primarily an environmental and diplomatic issue.[5] In late 1990, divisions emerged between developed and developing countries. Developing countries pressed for recognition of climate change as a development issue as well as an environmental issue, calling for aid in both the implementation of emissions reductions and the adaptation to climate change. They also successfully pressed for greater representation in climate change negotiations, by placing them under the aegis of the UN General Assembly. (The interests of oil-producing countries, island nations, and manufacturing countries have prevented complete unity.) The convention for climate change was specifically modeled on the Vienna Ozone Convention, which had recently achieved rapid success through a step-by-step process.[6] Of course, climate change would prove to be a much thornier problem, provoking nearly intractable diplomatic differences. What is more difficult to recover is the structuring of climate change that occurred in this period. Starting as a nebulous scientific problem, it became one that would be addressed within national economies, coordinated through a new international bureaucracy, and adjusted based on relative economic power. The program that emerged in this moment was truly audacious, but over time its assumptions have come to seem all but inevitable, even as we have lost faith in national responsibility, the climate regime, and the likelihood of justice between nations. The conclusions of the UNFCC during this period have determined not just the terrain of subsequent climate conventions but also the very horizon for hope in the early Anthropocene.

Perhaps even more difficult to recognize is how the geopolitical events of the early 1990s shaped two decades of climate change fiction. During the Cold War, the poles of American capitalism and Soviet communism provided a structure for an extraordinary range of art, encompassing a defined spectrum of political positions. This structure was changed inexorably after the fall of the Berlin Wall; the same year's revolutions in Poland, Hungary, Bulgaria, Czechoslovakia, and Romania that overthrew one-party rule; the unification of Germany in 1990; the abandonment of communism in Albania and Yugoslavia between 1990 and 1992; the dissolution of the Soviet Union by 1991; the breakup of state monopolies and creation of market economies; and the end of the Cold War. Accompanying these events was a widespread conviction, at least within the Anglophone West, that capitalism was responsible for the defeat of communism, that liberal democracy had triumphed over dictatorship, and that the West possessed the very end and perfection of history.

Ben Bova's *Empire Builders* (1993) was written in the confluence of these two historical trajectories—the rise of international environmental accords and the fall of the Soviet empire. The novel is rather crude on a number of levels. As a particular kind of mainstream science fiction, *Empire Builders* makes use of a strong, white, male protagonist who is smarter and tougher than everyone around him, and there is little doubt he will overcome the villains he confronts. The dialogue is stilted—"double-damned" is a common ejaculation—and the scenes woodenly convey the plot, with frequent show-downs to keep up the action. Bova's novel promotes a crass, reductive view of climate change, international relations, and capitalist economies. And yet, the novel offers an audacious vision of economic transformation in the Anthropocene era, a vision that has been shared by most policy entrepreneurs since. Ironically, it is these weaknesses that foreground the period's biases so clearly, making Bova's novel highly representative of the next two decades of climate fiction.

Although it is set several decades in the future, *Empire Builders* self-consciously locates itself in the contemporary moment. The novel's clear hero is Dan Randolph, an American tycoon who has built one of a handful of corporations that mine the Moon. The result is an economic boom fueled from space, led by European and Japanese companies, with Randolph's corporation an exception to American decadence. The expansion brings energy, raw materials, and manufactured products to Europe and the rest of the world.[7] As the narrator explains, Eastern Europe has only recently begun to recover from "four decades of stagnation and repression" under communism. The novel is dismissive of their capacity: although they had "shouted for democracy and freedom," they really wanted the capitalist societies' "higher standard of living, particularly their 'toys and trinkets.'" Nevertheless, it had taken decades for the "Poles," "Czechs," "Romanians," and "Russians" to "[learn] to work once again" (18). On the other hand, the narrator takes repeated delight in turning Marx against the Cold War countries, claiming, for example, "Slowly, painfully, the peoples of the formerly socialist world learned that it was the capitalists who truly followed Marx's original dictum: 'From each according to his ability; to each according to his work'" (18). Two decades later, Bova's chauvinist predictions have fared poorly: Japan has stagnated; unified Germany quickly became the powerhouse of Europe; and hardworking Eastern Europeans flooded Western labor markets, to the consternation of local workers. Moreover, the novel misses the major movements of the intervening period: globalization, EU consolidation, and Chinese domination of production. Even so, the novel reveals a particular view of economic development: countries find prosperity by producing for the free market, although enterprise will depend on cultural ideas of organization and the character of a nation's people. The architecture of the climate regime has been based on the same assumptions, negotiating action between nation-states, according to each country's state of development and production of greenhouse gases.

Empire Builders poses climate change as a fundamental challenge to free-market capitalism, the novel's central article of faith. Early in the novel, Dan Randolph's private scientists warn him that a greenhouse "cliff" will lead to catastrophic and irreversible climate change, starting sometime in the next ten years. The effects will be legion: "Floods, killer storms, croplands turned to deserts—the whole thing" (16). (Thus, the novel circumvents the scientific uncertainty that has plagued American climate politics.) A series of weather disasters heighten the stakes: after a coalition of "desperate private developers, frantic Florida bankers and frenzied local and state politicians" constructs a seawall to protect Miami Beach, a surge overwhelms the barrier at its opening ceremony, killing Miami's mayor. Another disaster is described with eerie prescience. Politicians in New Orleans refuse to act after environmental officials call for higher levees. After a storm, a wall of water gouges away the levees, the city's pumping stations are overwhelmed, and "a frothing smashing wave of dirty gray water [rushes] through the streets, knocking down poles and highway bridges, collapsing buildings, tossing automobiles and diesel trucks and city buses like flotsam." Afterward, "the water itself was thick with debris and the floating bodies of the dead" (370). These local disasters challenge the self-determination of countries, since the brute force of weather and collective ignorance so easily overwhelm entire cities. If the "greenhouse cliff" is allowed to happen, the visionary tycoon quickly sees, "all the coastal areas on Earth will look like [New Orleans]" (401).

Despite a clear climatic crisis, economic restructuring is problematic. It would have been easy to assume, given Randolph's ideology, that capitalism would bring technological solutions to market to avert the greenhouse cliff. The narrator avers that "the Earth was healing from the wounds inflicted by the Industrial Age"; advances in fusion, solar energy, methane, and population stabilization solve deep environmental problems (18–19). Even so, progress is simply too slow. Randolph values the United Nations as a means of avoiding "the divisive competition of nationalism" and addressing the capacity of small nations to manufacture weapons of mass destruction (10). And yet, he views the UN as "a worldwide bureaucracy that was gradually imposing a dictatorship by committee, levelling everything on Earth to the same flat gray dullness" (10). Ultimately, *Empire Builders* explores the capacity of free markets and supernational institutions to address climate change.

Bova's handling of the conflict is far from evenhanded. The Global Economic Council (GEC) is doubly damned for being allied to environmentalists and bureaucracy. Environmentalists are constantly ridiculed: instead of speaking, they regularly "spout"; when a dozen of the world's leading environmentalists are briefed on the greenhouse cliff, they cannot even agree to help warn the world. But the deeper threat is the GEC's overarching bureaucracy. The GEC obsessively seizes control of private enterprises on the pretext that businesses have exceeded quotas and lowered prices. The effective head of the GEC, Vasily Malik, is a power-hungry, vengeful Russian: a nostalgic villain just after the Cold War. After the GEC seizes Randolph's business, Malik's misguided, villainous plan is to take over the entire economy in order to convert the world to clean energy. In Malik's thinking, every entity from individual drivers to major corporations must immediately accept tremendous sacrifices. The capital to build an entirely new energy infrastructure must be seized (92). Randolph is wholly unwilling to accept such an infringement: "I knew it. . . . The whole frigging world facing disaster and you see it as an opportunity to establish a double-damned dictatorship" (92). When yet more control proves necessary, Malik also tries to seize the world news media (245). In order that the reader should have no uncertainty as to which side is correct, Malik is shown to be controlled by an Italian mafioso with a penchant for coercive sex and a sadistic desire to kill Randolph.

To be sure, Bova's critique overplays its hand, but it also invokes a more real criticism of the climate regime in this period. Far more neutral historians have described how a small group of policy entrepreneurs set the agenda for the climate regime by promoting "what they viewed as global rather than national interests." The meetings they organized were only quasi-official, but their sponsorship by international organizations and sympathetic governments gave nongovernmental actors an unusual degree of control.[8] During this period, FCCC negotiations set a framework; their negotiations "were often more semantic than substantive in character," deferring binding resolutions in favor of formal agreement.[9] To be sure, this period was short-lived, and subsequent negotiations have been dominated by state diplomats. Nevertheless, from the perspective of the early 1990s, the climate change agenda could be accused of being steered by an undemocratic bureaucracy, particularly from the perspective of countries that had strongly defended national sovereignty.

The novel's other critique of the GEC is inherited from Cold War rhetoric. After Randolph's company is taken over by the GEC, it is hopelessly mismanaged. While production falters, micromanaging bureaucrats "put major emphasis on paperwork. . . . Filling out the proper forms had become more important than getting the job done" (239). In place of Randolph's courageous vision, the new managers create plans, committees, subcommittees, and impact statements about plans (240). The condemnation of bureaucrats is all too easy, but twenty years of feeble action later, Randolph's condemnation is not wholly unjust: "At this rate the whole damned world could be underwater and the only way anybody'll be saved is if they stack their double-damned reports on top of one another and climb up to the top of the pile" (240). In the intervening period, science studies research has helped to show the tremendous contributions that can be made by bureaucratic agencies, particularly when they are able to tie together scientific and governmental forms of power.[10] At the same time, state-sponsored bureaucracy has a questionable track record of managing business ventures. Finding a way to bring together private green enterprise and collective emissions reductions has been one of the enduring problems of the early Anthropocene.

The solution proposed by *Empire Builders* is no less symbolic than early climate accords. Early on, the novel gestures toward even-handed critique, describing how governmental ministers can advocate polluting development or environmentalist obstruction based solely on their ministerial briefs (112–13). This paves the way for Randolph (of course) to propose a new era of cooperation: "The whole world has to work together, all of us, government, industry, the corporations, the GEC, everybody on Earth." Randolph once again inveighs against the wrong form of collaboration: Soviet-style collectivism, top-down bureaucracy, "some grand master plan that doesn't allow deviations or creativity or individual initiative" (401). The right way would bring "free men and women" together. Metaphors are alternately militaristic and ironic: climate change demands a battle run by "a good general" who sets goals but allows lieutenants to chose their own strategy; this would "let a thousand flowers blossom," Randolph says, quoting "an old Communist" (401–2). Although Randolph's words seem empty, the audacity of his vision must be recovered. Despite the immediate experience of the fall of the Soviet Union, in 1993 a committed free-market capitalist could see that global warming was a game-changing problem that demanded a grand bargain between economic and political leaders.

In the years following the publication of *Empire Builders*, the climate regime developed an emissions reduction scheme that likely would have satisfied the fictional Randolph. Through the 1990s, negotiators had major differences over the emissions targets for developed countries and whether these targets could be reached flexibly. Ultimately, the Kyoto Protocol avoided a universal emissions target; developed countries agreed to different targets for each country. Additionally, the United States and some industry NGOs successfully argued for the inclusion of emissions-abatement projects, emissions trading, and programs to reduce emissions in developing countries instead of within developed countries, although agreed-upon language also stated that these programs should be "supplemental" to countries' emissions reduction.[11] A charitable interpretation of these agreements would focus on how this preserved the countries' self-determination and acknowledged their different challenges to reducing emissions, allowing emissions to be reduced in the simplest and most cost-effective ways possible. In the intervening time, the results of these negotiations have attracted persistent criticism, focusing on the imbalance of emissions reductions between countries, the insufficiency of the Kyoto Protocol's targets, the United States' failure to ratify the protocol, the difficulty in creating successor agreements, and the questionable results of emissions trading schemes. These shortcomings can mask the extraordinary ambition of the period. Instead of seeking to create a new set of regulations, the protocol calls for a grand collaboration among the climate regime, national governments, and the world economy. Using all the tools of international diplomacy and individual states, a balance was to be struck among the needs of individual factories, enterprises, and consumers, leading to a global reduction in emissions. The outlines of this agreement determined the horizon of imaginable action for two decades.

The results of the Kyoto Protocol and subsequent UN Climate Change Conferences can make it all too easy to condemn the diplomatic and political failures of the last twenty years. However, *Empire Builders* may direct at least part of the blame elsewhere. Unlike most of the political novels discussed in the previous chapter, *Empire Builders* recognizes that the real field for action is economic—accords do little unless they lead to real changes in production and consumption. Nevertheless, Bova's novel attributes far too much agency and goodwill to economic leaders. The novel has little patience for diplomatic proceedings, but it is fascinated by the wealthy, "elegant men and women . . . each multimillionaires, tycoons of commerce and industry, civil leaders who earned their lofty places in their communities the old-fashioned way: by buying in" (304–5). Beauty, character, and civic importance are attributed to capitalists as a matter of course. The magnetism of Dan Randolph is similarly unexamined. Randolph's erstwhile allies are rewarded while his enemies are forced to admire the tycoon's charm and superiority. Even an underclass of unemployed and disabled characters living off the grid is bent to his leadership. Randolph also constantly tests his power on female characters, bedding every beautiful woman around him; less comely women do not merit the narrator's attention. Domination is not a subtext—it is an explicit motive for Randolph. The only woman significant enough for a serious relationship is a former president, who turns into a girl with weak knees in his presence (289). When the GEC promotes another former employee to the head of Randolph's operations, he entertains violent rape fantasies with no comment from the narrator; later she is compelled to admit her attraction to Randolph and then forced to pray to him to save her sister (274, 288). Other female leaders are systematically humiliated: when New Orleans is destroyed, the mayor sobs hysterically instead of coordinating action (370). Ultimately, the novel encourages faithful admiration of the heads of industry and contempt for weaker men, women, and political governance. The subsequent historical record has judged this program. *Empire Builders* simplifies the internal and industry dynamics of major corporations, replacing them with a cult of wealth and personality. Industry groups have been utterly hostile to emissions reductions that impinge on growth, lobbying governments to obstruct emissions legislation and supporting climate denial campaigns to the public, although they have been all too willing to accept governmental largesse to encourage nominal reductions. In practice, the hero of *Empire Builders* has been irresponsible, self-interested, and obstructive, rather than a leader of meaningful responses to the Anthropocene.

The Moment of Capital

Two decades after its publication, a novel like *Empire Builders* seems remarkably naive. Capitalism's heroes have not sufficiently reduced greenhouse gas emissions, and the totalitarian bureaucracy feared by Bova has been all but toothless. Nevertheless, novelists like Bova and the various framers of the UN Framework Convention on Climate Change participated in a moment of tremendous cultural construction, when an audacious mechanism for addressing global emissions was called into being. They envisioned a new climate regime that would mediate between states and world markets, driving down emissions through the structures of sovereignty and capitalism. For two decades, the outlines of this vision would be all but transparent to critics and novelists, determining the horizon of hope in the early Anthropocene. Early critical approaches to climate change deplored economic interventions into climate change, while novelists treated capitalism as the inevitable context of the Anthropocene.

Only relatively recently have literary critics begun to examine the pervasive influence of capital on the politics of climate change. Through the 1990s and early 2000s, much ecocritical theory neglected the role of economic "modes of production" in environmental destruction and climate change. There were many oblique references to the forces of industrial and consumer capitalism during this period, but little in the way of serious analysis. Instead of interrogating political and economic systems, ecocriticism was focused on the individual, whether as a green consumer, nature reader, or backpacker. This reproduced a logic of individual choice that has also been responsible for blocking systematic control of greenhouse gas emissions, letting collective fate stand on the miniscule choices of whether or not to take a flight or turn down the thermostat.[12] This was not a peculiar failing of environmental literary critics; wider campaigns for public awareness, individual action, and green consumerism also deferred political solidarity and economic transformation. Even so, this approach made it nearly impossible to examine the material and systemic causes of climate change.

Starting around 2009, there was a rush to theorize the crisis of global warming. Almost universally, this criticism was underpinned by a Marxist account of capitalism as a hegemonic system that produced emissions, political conditions, ideology, and the climate regime. Critics invoked Foucault, Ulrich Beck, Žižek, Deleuze and Guattari, British socialists like William Morris and E. P. Thompson, Derrida, science studies, phenomenology, postcolonial ecocriticism, and ecophobic prejudice. Despite the apparent diversity, all of these approaches were underpinned by a conviction that critique could reveal the totalizing effects of capital, call its ideological and environmental assumptions into question, and open the possibility of a new order. Thus, an "imaginary" regime controls the subjectivities related to climate change, while the real workings of capital, "futures, derivatives, hedge funds, reinsurance instruments and other financial products," work to secure "a future continuous with the present order of things and people."[13] Sustainability sustains economic liberalism by translating "nature" and "humanity" into economic terms, perpetuating the surplus value extraction endemic to capitalism.[14] The apparent conflicts between "mega-environmental NGOs, philanthropic foundations, corporations and the finance-sector" conspire to essentialize the world as a carbon matrix, consolidating the position of "an imperial ethnic-rich" and perpetuating environmental destruction.[15] Other critics have argued cap-and-trade approaches to emissions reductions are nothing but "a pure market"[16] or have raised the idea of "a Maoist-Leninist *green* state."[17] Even science studies approaches have embraced Marxian dialecticism, calling climate change an externality that could question the "neo-liberal foundations" of "the Western economic paradigm."[18] For these critics, both the problem of climate change and current proposals to address it were the products of a hegemonic system of capital.

This critical moment owes much to a longer tradition of eco-Marxism but blunts much of its nuance. In the early 1990s, pioneering eco-Marxists observed that capital undermined the conditions of its own production, first by creating instability between a shrinking rich elite and a proletarian underclass and second by destroying the nature, infrastructure, and human labor on which capital depends. Thus, the state (or capital operating as the state) is forced to regulate the regeneration of natural and human environments, undermining capital's direct interests.[19] As early as 1991, climate change was recognized as a prime example of capital eliminating the people, places, species, and profits that are its underlying conditions. Such environmental crises necessitated the creation of new national and international bureaucracies to ensure the continued existence of such production conditions, much as the novels examined in the previous chapter began to envision truly new forms of political organization. Paradoxically, socialist thinkers have viewed carbon markets as capitalist conspiracies, while far-right thinkers have attacked the mere fact of climate change as a ruse to justify socialism. Early eco-Marxists were more nuanced, viewing climate change as an indication of the need for "highly social forms of reconstruction of material and social life," making socialism more imaginable, if hardly certain.[20] Ultimately, climate change would seem to be an exigency demanding the reformation of economic relations, but one that is not able to determine a particular future economy.[21]

Recent climate criticism's reflexive Marxism suffers from other, grave shortcomings. By taking capital as the fundamental cause of climate change, it obscures the fact that other economic structures—particularly Russian oligarchy, Chinese communism, and Middle Eastern monarchies—have had abysmal environmental records and produce tremendous quantities of greenhouse gases. The error is compounded when capital is taken to be a malign totality: a plenitude of political, regulatory, manufacturing, and financial organizations are directly involved in climate change. Reducing all such interests to a singular capital catastrophically limits political analysis.[22] An obsessive focus on overthrowing capitalism can also mistakenly replace an intricate atmospheric, economic, and political problem with a purely *social* revolution. Similarly, a critical focus on competing social constructions of climate change, sustainability, and emissions markets can stymie the more serious reexamination of critical methods demanded by the Anthropocene era. Marxian criticism's blame of corporate capitalism's overweening power, or attention to "social constructions" more generally, fails to account for climate's distinct, nonhuman agency.[23] At a philosophical level, a Marxian approach struggles to theorize new modes of living in which humans and nonhumans could both thrive.[24] Although Marxian accounts should be applauded for drawing attention to the economics of the Anthropocene, the critical moment would seem to demand a more sophisticated account of the heterogeneous agency of human organizations, as well as the interdependent agencies of nonhumans.

Novels from the 1990s and the first decade of the 2000s are remarkably consistent in their representation of the economics of climate change. Across genres, capitalism is presented as a timeless certainty, even as it drives the world to inexorable ruin. Naturally, authors from the period differed in how favorably they treated recent capitalism, and these deviations need to be traced in some detail. Despite these differences, novels of the period are nearly unanimous in holding that late, consumer capitalism is the end of history, and its intransigence in the face of climate change merely indicates its more fundamental reality.

To take an early example, in Bruce Sterling's *Heavy Weather* (1994), capital and climate dominate the future.[25] *Heavy Weather* is primarily set in tornado alley, stretching from north Texas into Oklahoma and Kansas, after the region has been made inhabitable by the extinction of the buffalo, the draining of aquifers and the exhaustion of oil wells, and finally by violent, deadly storms. In the terms of contemporary eco-Marxists, the novel imagines a breakdown in capital accumulation: the place has been mined "of everything that could be sold on the market," and then people have given up living there (33). Similar "eco-blunders" have poisoned cropland in China, Egypt, and India, led to the clear-cutting of jungles in Indonesia and Brazil, and hastened the spread of the Sahara (139–40). Despite calls to geoengineer solutions, it proves much cheaper to turn inhabitants into refugees. Governments have also lost control of markets: currency has been privatized due to a global ocean of black-market money, savage runs on most national currencies, and the collapse of stock markets. The collapse of communism is a foregone conclusion, with China having succumbed to irresistible market and environmental pressures (143). "Carnivorous free-market forces" have slipped the fetters of national and democratic control. Ultimately, economies and climates are susceptible to cyberpunk technology: they are chaotic systems that can be "hacked" but are ultimately beyond human control (245).

The world of the 2030s is divided between wealthy spectators of climate disaster and those who are reduced to nothing by it. The novel is set in a ruined landscape, yet the destitute rarely figure in the narrative. The "troupe," a group of weather hackers, is led by Jerry, a brilliant, renegade scientist and charismatic leader who predicts the coming of a raging storm an order of magnitude greater than any the world has seen. Jerry leads the troupe on a relentless search for data and the direct experience of unprecedented storms, a mission that has nothing to do with warning the public or helping the devastated. While Jerry is the leader, the novel is focalized through Alex and Jane Unger, the siblings of a Mexican plutocrat who buy their way into a storm-chasing troupe with exotic, ex-military hardware. Within the troupe, Alex and Jane sit at the top echelon of storm chasers. Beneath them are suicidal types, thrill freaks, storm admirers with little scientific interest, and evacuation freaks addicted to the temporary breakdown of all barriers of class, status, and experience found in refugee camps (236). Little narration is wasted on such refugees or the sufferings of the scenic poor. Instead, the novel chronicles the pleasures of surveying a devastated world as wealthy, amateur scientists. Cameras, sensors, and vehicles open a window to awesome disaster, while models, data, and footage obscure human suffering as an incidental byproduct. Ultimately, the reader participates in the awe, relieved of any sense of moral obligation by assurances that the movements of markets and climates are uncontrollable and inevitable.

Other novels defended the greenhouse culture's social hierarchy. An early and particularly crude example is James Herbert's *Portent* (1997).[26] *Portent*'s protagonist is a hard-drinking, rugged scientist who is led to an upper-class British family living in a country estate. The patriarch of the family, a man of science in the aristocratic tradition, is the only person who "really" understands the import of climate change: Gaia is struggling to rebalance herself after humanity's excesses. The patriarch's beautiful daughter becomes the scientist's love interest, and they all struggle to save the family's beatific, blond twins, ensuring everything meaningful emanates from the narrow circle of power. By contrast, malign humanity is represented by African Americans from New Orleans. A black, obese sorceress leads a voodoo cult bent on destroying humanity, kidnapping white children, channeling storms, and fulfilling every possible racial stereotype along the way. In the meantime, catastrophic "natural" disasters destroy "world" (nonwhite) cities. Finally, Gaia herself steps in, presenting new forms of sustainable energy to conserve the human race in perpetuity, destroying the subversive "black" energy and restoring the social hierarchy. By joining the balancing force of Earth with the British upper class, *Portent* demands that sustainability should also perpetuate the social order.

Many more novels of the period were circumspect about the effects of capitalism but treated it as an inevitable phenomenon. In Susannah Waters's *Cold Comfort* (2006), Tammy, a half-Inupiat teenager in Alaska, hoards news clippings about global warming as firsthand evidence of the changes mount around her.[27] In Fairbanks, Tammy's family home begins to sink and list as the underlying permafrost begins to thaw. Further north, traditional ways of living become impossible for her extended family as sea ice fails to form and hunts have to be abandoned. Tammy falls in love with her cousin George, who tries to preserve his ancestral knowledge by living in a refrigeration truck, artificially reproducing a traditional climate. Both town and village families break down under the pressure of the thaw. Finally, Tammy, George, and some friends try to sabotage the machines of a drilling site and seem to die in the cold after the attack fails. *Cold Comfort* portrays a world of adults too preoccupied to oppose capitalism's inexorable production of climate change and a younger generation out of ideas and powerless to make more than a symbolic protest.

Coming at the end of the decade, Ian McEwan's *Solar* (2010) reveals a collective exhaustion with post–Cold War capitalism, even as it refuses to countenance an alternative future. *Solar*'s world is no less determined by capital than is the life-sized monopoly board created by a minor character for the Tate Modern; parliamentary politics are a reflection of oligarchy (51, 248). Beard, nominally a scientist, positions himself to monopolize academic sinecures and then attempts to become a climate tycoon. In his pursuit of profit, Beard pushes aside academic integrity, political affiliations, and concern for the public. His right-hand man, Toby Hammer, aligns manufacturers, testing laboratories, tax-break lawyers, accountants, grant givers, local and federal government, venture capitalists, billionaires, and presidents (210). In a moment of doubt, Hammer assures Beard, "Sunlight, water and money makes more money! My friend, it's going to *happen*" (214). Despite its satire of Beard's uncontrollable appetites, *Solar* is complicit in the flattery of its First World, wealthy, overindulgent protagonist: no other character figures as a potential source of change. Ultimately, McEwan's novel presents Anglo-American capitalism as the cultural and evolutionary center of the Earth.

John Minichillo's *The Snow Whale* (2011) describes a similar world with yet less reverence.[28] John Jacobs, a suburban salesman of executive novelty toys, takes a DNA test that convinces him he has Inuit ancestry, despite clear physiognomic evidence to the contrary. Insisting on his right to hunt endangered whales, John recruits an African American teenager, Q, to act as his cameraman and joins Akmaaq, an elderly and marginalized chief who also wants to continue the annual hunt. (The rest of the northern villagers are more pragmatic in their search for hard cash, mates, and better-quality whiskey.) Jacobs quickly learns that "crazy weather" has made whale hunting impossible without military hardware; his wife, suburban social codes, and international laws proscribe the hunt. After Jacobs finally kills his whale, he begins selling gear at an outdoor outfitter, employing the same tricks of bourgeois social aspiration to lure other bourgeois "adventurers." Capitalism has stripped Jacobs of any meaningful identity, but it has given him the economic power to pursue an ersatz heritage, even as it further destroys the biological, social, and climatic conditions he craves.

Over two decades, then, depictions of the Anthropocene economy grew more exasperated but continued to foreground the reader as passive consumer of a collapsing economic climate. Time and again, such novels present an interpretive dilemma. *Heavy Weather, Portent, Cold Comfort, Solar,* and *The Snow Whale* vacillate between an indictment of capitalism's environmental and social crimes and a transcendent belief that the market can reconstruct the basis of life on Earth. Other climate change novels of the period directly showed the hegemony of financial interests on a world stage. There are any number of dystopias in which corporations have replaced states as the dominant form of social organization. Patrick Cave's *Sharp North* (2004) starts in a small Scottish village but gradually reveals that a few corporations, headed by powerful families, control the world's resources and manipulate DNA for their own ends. Other novels explore the economies of southern, formerly Third World countries as they confront catastrophic climate change. Mike Resnick's *Kirinyaga* (1998) describes the attempt to recreate African tribal life on an asteroid after Kenya's climate and ecosystems can no longer sustain traditional ways. Finally, the village rebels against the witch doctor who holds the only contact with future Earth, returning to the polluted but technologically advanced cities. Thus, *Kirinyaga* preaches the inevitability of capitalistic "development," even in the face of environmental devastation. In Ian McDonald's *Cyberabad Days* (2009), characters in future India suffer drought, water monopolies, mechanized civil wars, and a postpolitical world of resource moguls. Time and again, the juggernaut of technological capitalism dominates the future, with climate change an unintended and unavoidable consequence.

Other dystopias treat the effects of late capitalism as a historical inevitability, reducing climate change to a secondary effect to condemn twenty-first-century markets. Margaret Atwood's *Oryx and Crake* (2004) received enormous public and critical attention and is featured in many early analyses of climate change literature. Unfortunately, climate change is little more than a footnote to the novel's concerns. Atwood describes a world where hierarchical, corporate capitalism and biotechnologies allow the unprecedented exploitation of human bodies. The world population is decimated by a virus engineered in the center of the corporate machine, and a new race of posthumans is positioned to live more sustainably. *Oryx and Crake* refuses to suggest there could be any ethical or political restraints to corporations, creating an omnipotent bogeyman that is too easy to condemn. Atwood's *Year of the Flood* (2009) follows related characters through the same catastrophe, kindling hope that a gynocentric nature cult could pick up the pieces after catastrophe. If climate change is an ancillary feature of these novels, it is because they are far more invested in bemoaning an economic hegemony they cannot escape.

The Cold War roots of this idea of economies can be seen in still other novels from the period. Many dystopias actively turn away from the Anthropocene, reverting to the black and white alternatives of capitalism's comfortable freedom and planned economies' scarcity and restrictions. Some of these novels are compelling in their own right but lose any grip on the unique moment of global warming. In the near future of Sarah Hall's *Carhullan Army* (2007), climate-induced food shortages and energy scarcity cause the collapse of markets, blackouts, empty supermarkets, and hospital closures. Widespread flooding precipitates insurance scandals, personal cars are banned, and housing is reorganized in cramped, shared dormitories. Britain's failing economy leads to "Civil Reorganization": the Forward Party introduces military police, permanent war with China and Venezuela, deportations, royalism, dependence on the Christian United States, and state energy and armament industries with endemic mismanagement and waste. The topography of this future has everything to do with the Western mythology of the Soviet Union, where chronic personal deprivation, forced housing, militarism, and authoritarianism were constantly compared to a rosy view of the free market. After the state forcibly implants birth control devices in women, "Sister" flees to the mountains, where a self-sustaining, militant, female-led commune presents an alternative to the totalitarian state. Nevertheless, the world apart proves unsustainable, and the women mount a military campaign on the local town, hoping other groups will join in revolution. *Carhullan Army* is noteworthy for the way it shows the climatic conditions on which Britain's markets and political order depend, but its historiography problematically assumes that any alteration from late capitalism must lead to a Soviet-tinged authoritarianism. This historical interpretation is even more problematic, given that late capitalism is blamed for climate change in the first place. The gender-driven guerrilla resistance at the end of the novel ultimately loses sight of the contradictions of climate change, reenacting a battle on the familiar terrain of personal freedom and gender relations.

Many other novels depend on the opposition between current freedoms and Soviet- and Nazi-style totalitarianism. In Gemma Malley's *The Declaration* (2008), an authoritarian government bans human reproduction to ensure the bourgeois lifestyle of existing adults can be extended indefinitely. The novel straddles a comforting veneer of suburban capitalism and a totalitarian state and armed resistance visible mostly to children. In George Marshall's *The Earth Party* (2009) (discussed in more detail in the previous chapter), climate change forces the abandonment of capitalism; a new command forcibly institutes rural communes complete with re-education programs, a secret police, and a centralized party. The only hope *The Earth Party* can offer is a tenuous negotiation between communism's authoritarian organization and capitalism's technological comforts. While these alternatives could seem historically compelling to a readership raised during the Cold War, they dangerously simplify the economic complexity of the Anthropocene. They attempt to warn of the dangers of unchecked global warming, but they misdirect attention from a distributed, systemic, atmospheric problem with economic implications to a simplified political conflict.

Through the 1990s and the first decade of the 2000s, both critics and novelists shared a remarkable consensus about the economics of climate change. Capital was understood as a historically and biologically inevitable system. Its production of climate change was intrinsic to its basic operation, a contradiction that would ultimately ensure its extinction. Critics were tremendously divided about the appropriate theoretical tools to oppose capital, but there was remarkable consensus that dismantling modern markets was the only way to avert environmental and social catastrophe. Novelists were less united in their approach to Anthropocene markets, consumer choice, technological innovation, and shifts in climate. Earlier novels like *Heavy Weather* and *Portent* viewed climate change as an opportunity to reaffirm bourgeois social structures or a new opportunity for spectacular consumption. By the end of the period, novels like *Oryx and Crake, Solar, The Snow Whale,* and *Kirinyaga* tended to affirm the inevitability of capitalism, even as they lamented its contradictions. When novelists imagined climate activism, it was positioned as resistance to the *system* of capitalism: separatist eco-communities, terrorist viruses, or guerrilla warfare. Time and again, capital was treated as a malign totality. Society should mass against the system, as the only hope of deferring an era of catastrophic climate change.

This widespread consensus across criticism and fiction has all the hallmarks of an "episteme." Foucault's pointedly social model of knowledge and power could seem outmoded, but the episteme may usefully indicate redistributions of knowledge that alter the interconnections between scientific disciplines and other knowledge practices.[29] The episteme is not internally consistent, nor is nor is it a *Weltanschauung,* or worldview. Rather, an episteme names a profound shift in the "range of methodologies which a culture draws on as self-evident in order to be able to think about certain subjects."[30] For Anglo-American letters around the turn of the millennium, it seems useful to name an episteme in which climate change could only be thought through capitalism: free markets, individual consumer choice, and global development were responsible for climate change, and climate change could only be addressed on these terms.

Calling this period an episteme could easily be mistaken for an affirmation that climate change is a new form of governmentality, a new name for repression. Persistently, those on the far left have viewed sustainability and economic regulations as reaffirming the premises of advanced corporate capitalism,[31] while the far right has repeatedly called global warming a conspiracy on behalf of big science and big government. It is possible to see environmental discourse as a form of "governmentality": "The ensemble formed by institutions, procedures, analyses and reflections, the calculations and tactics that allow the exercise of this very specific albeit complex form of power, which has as its target population, as its principal form of knowledge political economy, and as its essential technical means apparatuses of security."[32] As seen in the previous chapter, climate change comprises new and existing political, bureaucratic, and scientific institutions. Certainly, addressing climate change involves controlling consumption at the level of the population, transforming political economy to account for energy use and emissions, and acting to secure a (climatic) future like the present.[33] It was a short step, then, for activists on the left and right to declare climate change a ploy of authoritarian repression, for critics to declare a united front against capital's utilization of climate change discourse, and for novelists to warn of the existential dangers of unchecked capitalism, even as they struggled to articulate anything outside that system.

Despite the unanimity, the contradictions of that historical moment seem obvious a few short years later. Systemic thinking about the economics of climate change compelled artists and critics to make an untenable choice. If climate change presented a terrible threat to the future, writers could mount an impassioned paean to the preservation of the current order. Such is the impetus of Cormac McCarthy's *The Road* and several Hollywood films, but few authors could swallow the conservative duplicity of defending "capitalism's second contradiction." Faced with the problem, most novels elided their present, even as they depended on a deep nostalgia for the individual rights, safeties, and comforts of late-twentieth-century capitalism.

On the other hand, writers could condemn the "system" tout court, losing any purchase on its nuances. Foucault's own account of power rejected the supremacy of economic relations, the state, or human nature in determining human outcomes.[34] Instead, power is understood as a set of alliances and contests between parties. This model seems to describe the economics of climate change much more clearly. Oil companies have viewed emissions reductions as a threat to their survival, while reinsurance groups have viewed political inaction as a threat to *their* survival. Universities have capitalized on grant money to fund climate change studies, and sustainable industries have been awarded major subsidies. Car companies have profitably engaged (Toyota's Prius) and evaded (General Motors' Hummer) the issue of emissions. Manufacturers agitate for cheaper, dirty energy and seek tax breaks to make more efficient plants. Property owners clamor for defense of their land from "natural" disaster. States' posture to climate change is not determined by the relentless expansion of capital, so much as whether they are major emitters, whether they export carbon-intensive products, whether they believe they could receive competitive advantages or subsidies from climate accords, and how they assess climate change's impacts on local geography. Reducing these conflicts to a monolithic account of global capital eliminated any meaningful engagement with the terms of the real economy.

Through much of the twentieth century, activist movements were characterized by attempts to find liberatory positions outside regimes of power.

While the aims of these movements remain essential, their tactics are implicitly out of step with the need to create new systems of regulation in the name of climate change. In the late 1990s, critics could condemn sustainable development and Al Gore's environmental proposals as "boil[ing] down to a new form of economic rationality," a kind of magical thinking that reaffirmed the "existing premises of . . . advanced corporate capitalism."[35] Four elections later, Gore's unsuccessful presidential bid seems a catastrophe: the United States would likely have led the path toward meaningful, global emissions reductions. Climate change is not the latest fight in liberation, but a fight for greater governmentality. In short, climate change would seem to demand the systematic and just limitation of publics and capital.

The final contradiction of the period is its continual deferral of climate change itself. Time and again, global warming is positioned as a catastrophe foretold, rather than a transformation that has already begun. During the entire period, novels were interpreted as warnings, threats, jeremiads, rather than accounts of a new geological and historical period. Of course, emissions had already reached levels not seen in human history, and scientists had already found increasingly certain evidence that global temperatures had already risen, causing major changes to weather and ecosystems. Of equal importance, climate change was already exerting a profound influence on global economies. When George W. Bush declared the United States was addicted to oil, or BP adopted the slogan "Beyond Petroleum," the ventriloquism of these statements was astonishing, forcing some of the world's most powerful entities to speak in the language of their greatest enemies. When critics dismissed these expressions as mere hypocrisy, they underestimated the *normative* force climate change had already come to possess.

Climate change also named a profound shift in the organization of knowledge, the "range of methodologies . . . [used] to think about certain subjects."[36] Foucault's work traced the interrelated organization of knowledge about living beings, language, economics, and philosophy in historical epistemes.[37] In a similar way, climate change began to reconfigure the successors of these disciplines, forcing meteorology to map weather at new temporal and spatial scales, biosciences to develop models to account for species in the future, economics to account for geological processes and to discount futures far beyond traditional investment horizons, philosophy to account for the ethics of collective action in relation to future generations, and criticism to reevaluate literary aesthetics, not to mention dozens of other disciplines that were reorganized to address the new problems, data, analytic challenges, and urgency of the phenomenon. The human ecology of eating, reproduction, habitation, and travel; the historical legacy of industry, consumption, and progress; and expectations of the future were reconfigured under the same name. Corporations, bureaucracies, charities, armies, voters, and artists demonstrably reconfigured themselves to changing climates. Because climate change is not internally consistent, the results of this shift are uneven, even contradictory, but climate change names a massive, sudden restructuring of the processes of knowledge across all these different domains.

At the outset of the period, it seemed certain that the system could step in and see off the threat of climate change. Over two decades, the free market remained the most significant protagonist, a hero, clown, or villain that ought to address the future threat. And then, quite late in the decade, the Anthropocene finally arrived.

Eco-nomic Novels

The first decade of the twenty-first century might be characterized as a series of political catastrophes for emissions reductions. Particularly in the United States, a pattern of dashed hopes slowly drained away belief that a solution could be found to avert catastrophic climate change, despite the oft-repeated goal of limiting temperature rises to 2 degrees Celsius. Al Gore's loss of the American presidency to George W. Bush in 2000 and Bush's reelection in 2004 effectively torpedoed hopes of executive leadership for most of the decade. Despite US disinvolvement, the Kyoto Protocol finally came into force in 2005, amid widespread recognition that its targets were insufficient to prevent catastrophic climate change. In 2006, Bush declared in his State of the Union speech that the United States was addicted to oil, raising widespread hopes that foreign and domestic policy would be directed toward renewable sources, but sufficient action did not materialize. In 2007, over five hundred US cities ratified the Kyoto Protocol, although this had a negligible effect on international negotiations. The widespread financial crisis of 2008 gave birth to the sense that a new, more sustainable financial system might be implemented. At the same time, the economic slowdown was sufficient to reduce greenhouse gases for a short period of time. The ensuing presidential election indicated a new moment of hope, with both the Republican and Democratic nominees professing a need to address climate change. After Barack Obama took office, the American Recovery and Reinvestment Act of 2009 included significant clean energy investments and tax credits as part of a wider stimulus package; much of this spending was later criticized as ineffectual. At COP 15, in Copenhagen, Denmark, in December 2009, the stated goal of reaching an ambitious global climate accord was discarded. President Obama, the Chinese delegation, and twenty-three other parties reached a political accord but were widely condemned for circumventing the process in order to reach an empty agreement. A more meaningful accord was thwarted by economic disagreements among China, the United States, and developing countries on how the costs of emissions reductions should be borne by producing and consuming, wealthy and developing nations. In the UK, the 2010 election of a center-right coalition led by the conservative David Cameron insured emissions reductions would not be a major priority there. Within the United States, the 2010 midterm election saw the rise of the Tea Party movement and the return of climate denial in the US political discussion. Partisan fights over health care and the economy pushed climate change from the agenda for much of Obama's first term. Although there have been other initiatives to reduce emissions in the United States, a transformation in global energy consumption has not materialized.

The decade from 2000 to 2009 was also the warmest ever recorded. Across different fields, scientists recorded the effects of higher temperatures: more droughts, wilder weather, melting glaciers, warmer oceans, and rising sea levels. The economic and biological effects of these changes were directly measured in countless studies. The political failure to take meaningful action on emissions, coupled with this irrefutable data, precipitated a wide shift in fiction at the end of the decade. Instead of writing about a future crisis that might yet be deferred, novelists began to describe the Anthropocene as a moment that had already begun.

The most striking feature of novels written in the last several years is that they have sought to explore the complex economic and social adaptations necessary in a period of anthropogenic global warming. Science fiction, teen novels, and "literary" works took a new interest in economics. Survival in the Anthropocene is not, as McCarthy's *The Road* imagines, a lone man and his son battling the elements and cannibals, so much as a differentiated crisis for different people. How humans live depends on the economic system in which they find themselves and where they fit into that social order. Just as important, their lives depend intimately on the biological, meteorological, and *social* changes that have been wrought by climate change. This demands a rearticulation of the basic assumptions of human ecology, the reimagination of how humans live without fossil fuels, stable weather, common sources of food, and so on. In this sense, these novels are doubly "eco," economic and ecological, while returning to the original meaning of "home" that spawned both disciplines. By imaginatively addressing these questions, such eco-nomic novels examine what it means to live after climate change can no longer be deferred.

The Carbon Diaries 2015 (2008), by Saci Lloyd, describes a society transforming itself, without minimizing the tremendous resistances to emission reductions.[38] The novel is a fictional memoir intended for teen readers, but its diary form conveys the humor and emotional ambivalence of carbon rationing. In response to a devastating storm, the slowing down of the Gulf Stream, and global changes to weather patterns, the UK government enacts legislation to create an immediate 60 percent reduction in greenhouse gas emissions. Every individual is issued with a carbon card that keeps track of the points spent, and every home is fitted with a smart meter that prevents overconsumption of energy. These disciplinary devices force immediate emissions calculations in every household:

> The car's gonna be cut way back, all of us get access to the PC, TV, HD, stereo for only 2 hours a day, heating is down to 16°C in the living room and 1 hour a day for the rest of the house, showers max 5 minutes, baths only at weekend. We've got to choose—hairdryer, toaster, microwave, smartphone, de-ioniser (Mum), kettle, lights, PDA, e-pod, fridge or freezer and on and on. Flights are a real no-no and shopping, travelling and going out not much better. It's all kind of a *choice.* (6)

The legislation creates a mechanism whereby the atmosphere, the government, and the smallest individual choices are drawn together. Carbon credits force individuals into a new economic consciousness, making choices to balance their well-being against the environmental cost. As Laura observes, "It's not about money any more, it's about keeping your card low" (47).

Carbon Diaries also explores how climate change precipitates problems that are not purely "natural." In previous decades, floods and storms appeared as outside forces, even if they were spurred by human activity. Lloyd shows the more intricate interplay between Anthropocene weather and humans' constructive choices. When the mayor and water utility introduce water rationing, it feels like a democratic betrayal. Later, heavy rains create quotidian effects: Laura is forced to help clear gutters and drains; neighbors gossip about London's flood defenses; leaks and drips must be plugged. But when a storm surge finally overwhelms the Thames Barrier, the crisis becomes acute: the Brown family is separated; Laura's sister goes missing; the neighborhood is flooded; the family home is filled with "the most massive, grossest, stinking pile of mud" (369); the army and UN soldiers pump water out of the city; cholera threatens greater disaster. Abroad, droughts in North Africa precipitate a refugee crisis in Spain while forest fires cannot be extinguished in France. In the United States and Europe, popular demands for major emissions reductions lead to political recriminations, the violent suppression of protests, and depression as the actual effects of rationing begin: "big celebrations across France, Germany, Holland and Belgium" fail because "no one turned up. It's like celebrating poking yourself in the eye" (301). Climate change appears not as a singular, catastrophic event, but rather as an interplay between climate and communities.

The Carbon Diaries uses a strong, likeable first-person narrator to capture the emotional ambivalence arising from carbon rationing. On the one hand, Laura Brown recognizes the desperate need for carbon rationing in the face of a tipping climate. She marches for climate action, deplores US political hypocrisy when it fails to act, and cheers when Europe joins the UK in carbon rations. On the other hand, she experiences rationing as a fundamental deprivation. She reacts with bitter sarcasm when politicians express concern for people's hardship, finds the smart meters "disgusting," and feels like a rat in a lab when politicians consider deeper cuts (42, 49, 84). After the basic goods she depends on are no longer available, she is depressed and frustrated; protests by lorry drivers also attract sympathy. Instead of holding an artificially unified view, Laura Brown describes the inherent tensions in emissions reduction. Laura's friends pull her in different directions as they become politicized, immerse themselves in school to survive a shrinking economy, or adopt radical, punk aesthetics, but Laura never fully identifies with these directions. She does attend protests and sours to authority when she is kettled, is charged by mounted police, and witnesses police making mass arrests using antiterror legislation. Mainstream aesthetics also lose their appeal: MTV videos of boy bands driving Ferraris seem like "sci-fi" after five months of carbon rationing (134). In her own band, Laura writes lyrics that politicize both the scarcity and the necessity of carbon rationing. Instead of implausible coherence, *Carbon Diaries* captures the natural ambivalence between politicization and privacy, the resistance to an unthinking mainstream and a militant subculture, and the antipathy toward politicians who create a new scarcity and those who refuse to address a climate crisis.

Laura Brown's diary also sketches the transformation of a fossil fuel economy. These effects are simultaneously domestic and social. Laura's father loses his job as a tourism teacher, since carbon rationing all but eliminates the industry. The family is mortified when he goes "self-sufficiency crazy," turning the back garden into a vegetable patch, installing solar panels, reusing bath water, and trading in his wife's car for tools and livestock. Laura's mother has a different relationship to carbon rationing. At first, she struggles to give up driving her Saab and pathetically cadges carbon points from her daughter. Later, she is invigorated by a renewal of radical protest, joining a cultish women's empowerment group tailored to the carbon rationing era. Laura's sister, Kim, is even more resistant to rationing. Early on, she bankrupts the family's credits by taking secret flights to Ibiza. After being sent to the "Carbon Offenders Rehabilitation Outreach Centre," Kim helps sell black-market electrical goods, hiding her self-interest as political resistance. The characters in the Brown family are fundamentally economic, their identities unthinkable without labor, consumption, and leisure. Even within a family, carbon rationing affects different characters differently, and new forms of poverty pull the family apart. As the economy begins to price emissions, the family's civic identities shift as well: the father becomes hyper-compliant; the mother is radicalized in a group that would exceed the demands of state rationing; and Laura's sister offers a cunning, intransigent resistance. Overall, the intimacy of the diary form shows the pervasiveness of fossil fuels in everyday activities and self-identity.

Other effects emerge as Laura observes her neighbors' adaptations. The block's thuggish, working-class family finds new purchasing power selling hacked white goods to middle-class carbon cheaters. Indeed, the carbon economy creates a new black market in premium petrol, imported wine, and consumer electronics. Another neighbor starts a matchmaking business, "Carbon Dating," after the romantic gestures of exotic flowers, fine restaurants, and cheap weekend getaways have become impossibly expensive (200). A third, elderly neighbor is delighted to discover he is now a "carbon creditor," materially augmenting his poor pension. He also endows Laura with a historical perspective, describing how rationing during the Second World War brought rich and poor together and also created a thriving black market (150). For other families, strict cultural norms are overturned when women contribute in new ways. After the climactic storm, Laura sees evidence of new social harmony: "Everywhere you look there's people zooming about with wheelbarrows, chopping, digging, clearing, slinging sandbags. We look like medieval peasants . . . and the strange thing is everyone keeps throwing back their heads and laughing" (370–71). Carbon rationing rebalances the "normal" economy, creating new winners and losers, not to mention new terms for social exchange.

Although it is a mere teen novel, *Carbon Diaries 2015* accomplishes something the novels of ten years before simply could not. Instead of imagining that capitalism would suddenly, responsibly transform itself, or that the system would lurch unconsciously to ultimate destruction, Lloyd's novel describes an economy divided against itself. The interests of lorry drivers, gardeners, teenagers, travel guides, and pensioners are in a complex tension. Moreover, carbon rationing prizes apart the parts of the self, setting personal freedom, security, familial affection, friendship, and self-expression at odds. Living within the Anthropocene means tracing these intricate contests.

Another important example of this literary moment is Bruce Sterling's *The Caryatids* (2009), which indicates that the conflicts endemic to the Anthropocene may not be resolved in a single, evaluable outcome. Written fifteen years after *Heavy Weather, The Caryatids* is experimental, speculative science fiction that directly addresses climate crisis. The novel develops a complicated account of the future through multiple points of view and economic organizations, suggesting the Anthropocene will be characterized by multiple economic strategies and uneven results. Sterling himself has been outspoken about the inadequacy of utopia and dystopia as analytical frameworks:

I don't even *do* "positive" and "negative" potential. I sincerely think that attitude makes people actively stupid about the future. . . . Major change-drivers, true historical forces, they have little to do with people's innate need for pep-talk. If you want to help people deal with futurity, you need to think talk and act in a way that clarifies the situation—not within mental frameworks that are dystopian, utopian, miserabilist, hunky-dory, apocaphiliac, Singularitarian, millennialist.[39]

Instead of imagining a once-and-for-all disaster, the novel describes a world in the grips of ongoing environmental catastrophes, even as global groups embrace new technology to address the problems. Sixty years in the future, climate change has made colossal areas of China, Australia, India, and central Asia uninhabitable (162). Over a billion people have died in Asia as a direct result of climate crisis. Hurricanes, plagues, famines, and water wars reduce millions more to misery. Other disasters are nearly forgotten: New York was annihilated by a nuclear weapon and has become an afterthought for characters (198). Overall, disaster is neither natural nor human controlled: China kills billions with geoengineering projects; the son of a real estate family sparks burning riots to level and rebuild the uninhabitable slums of Los Angeles; droughts turn peaceable neighborhoods into sites of small wars fought with small arms; new farms grow grain in Antarctica; engineers dream of restoring rain to Australia. Humans act self-interestedly, exacerbating and alleviating crises. Disaster is conspicuously uneven: "The world couldn't possibly fall apart, all over, at the same speed, at the same moment. There simply had to be lags, holes, exceptions, safe spots, and black spots" (277). In short, humanity lacks a singular fate. Different characters foretell a long boom in global business, a population crash that only nomadic groups and bubbled communities will survive, and a world that is "radically unimaginable" (285). Despite these uneven fortunes, greenhouse gas emissions have left their mark in every place. Gazing at a simulation of the medieval sky, characters find it "scarily blue and clean": smokestacks and continental fires cloud every future horizon.

This tension between a universal disaster and uneven effects is embedded in an innovative narrative structure. Instead of adopting the point of view of a single, sympathetic character or attempting an imperfect omniscience, *The Caryatids* has as its protagonists seven cloned sisters and a brother, all created by a megalomaniacal Balkan politician exiled to an orbiting space station. One sister earnestly operates heavy machinery to clean up a devastated island in the Balkans, wearing neural hardware that lets coworkers see each other's emotions; a second is a Hollywood star fronting a plutocratic family firm with financial interests in home-decor products, "real estate, politics, finance, retail, water interests . . . and of course entertainment" (92); the third is a freedom fighter and operative for the Chinese government in the Gobi desert; the fourth is a self-absorbed international criminal. The three other sisters never even appear, having been killed by a panicked, drunken pack of young soldiers on the Balkan island where they were all raised for world domination; their brother is a "normal" businessman living in Vienna, having found a rare economic and geographical space where climate crisis can almost be forgotten. Despite their individual ambitions, the sisters are visually identical and share a homicidal hatred of each other. As each follows a different approach to a world fractured by climate crisis, the novel refuses to endorse any single vision.

The Caryatids glimpses a complex, global future that is continuous with our own moment. Sterling's novel supersedes the simple structures of the cautionary dystopia or the implausible Anthropocene hero. Sixty years in the future, nation-states and formal politics have broken down and been replaced with a stable, two-party, global system: the Dispensation is an entrepreneurial, capitalist society led by celebrity families, while Acquis is a global collective that uses technology to share authenticity and common labor.[40] In a subsequent interview, Sterling explained, "If the market was in the business of saving its best customers from extinction, then it might look like the Dispensation. If a global standards board existed, then it might look like Acquis."[41] The societies dwell alongside each other, with the Dispensation strongest in Hollywood and Acquis emerging from Europe.[42] Instead of vying to be a "one-world government," the parties compete, collaborate on projects, and balance each other's latent extremism.

The first half of the novel explicates their different approaches to environmental remediation on Mljet, the small Adriatic island home of the Caryatids before they were forced to flee.[43] At the opening of the novel, Vera works in an Acquis advance-guard cadre that lives in a labor camp with strict, even totalitarian social rules. Mechanized exoskeletons turn the workers into construction cyborgs, and scanner helmets display their feelings and attach halos of "glory"—the currency of social esteem. (For Dispensation onlookers, the helmets amount to sensory totalitarianism.) The

Acquis workers use extensive "sensorwebs" to map the island's ecosystem, with the goal of restoring Mljet as an authentic, natural place: "nobody's tool or pawn or property" (68). Their success in environmental remediation triggers the attention of the Dispensation. Vera's Dispensation brother-in-law, John Montalban, uses venture capital to transform the island into an elite tourist destination, developing the Acquis sensorweb into an augmented-reality vision of the island in the Dark Ages. Vera loathes capitalism, but he explains, "History *is* a business. History is the *only* business. It's abnormal to do business without history as the absolute and final business bottom line. That's why industry wrecked this planet: because people ran the world like a fire sale" (68–69). When Vera accuses him of disbelief in nature and reality, he counters that he believes in ecotourism and heritage, "two major, wealth-creating industries" (68). Together, the parallel economies of financial capital and social esteem address the climate crisis by rewarding the adaptation of devastated ecosystems.

The two-party schema is not absolute: China persists as a "ubiquitarian" state dominated by "computational infrastructure, plus the fallible human beings supposedly controlling that." The Acquis and the Dispensation share a belief in global regulation and transparency and hate China's state secrets. While the parties are obsessed with "rogue technologies spun out of control"—internal combustion, electric light, and fossil fuels—China has a grander belief in technological projects to escape climate crisis (230). Thus, the Chinese state sponsors massive projects to reinstitute rainfall by dropping hydrogen bombs in the Himalayas, pioneer sustainable settlements on Mars, develop bacterial paddies for food and fuel, map the DNA of every citizen, manufacture furniture and carpets and homes with bioplastics, and eliminate starvation by reengineering the human gut to produce protein and energy. At the same time, water wars and rogue groups continually threaten Chinese order, and hundreds of millions of Chinese people die from climate change and the state's attempts to overcome it.

Despite their differences, the Dispensation, the Acquis, and the Chinese state share an unyielding commitment to technology. Spreading deserts, uncontrollable wildfires, and social instability demand innovations that can reinflate the carrying capacity of ecosystems. The novel is most interested in an "internet of things": the mapping of living things and inanimate objects with miniscule identifying devices, enabling networks to inventory and manage the material world. (Advanced factories, warehouses, and stores already use these tools: items are tagged so that they "speak" to networks that monitor systems, order replacements, manage inventories, predict breakdowns, and sustain commercial ecosystems.) The meaning of these advanced, posthuman economies varies between societies. For the Acquis, they are a means of renewing nature and authenticity. For the Dispensation, they enable more intensive "development," marrying entertainment, capital improvement, and profitability. And for the Chinese state, they are a means to exert ubiquitous social *and* environmental control. Surprisingly, Sterling does not wholly share in these societies' optimism: an epilogue describes the collapse of such distributed, ubiquitous systems, arguing their complexity and need for maintenance will quickly render them unsustainable (295). Ultimately, the "science" of the novel works to imagine Anthropocene economies, as well as their climatic, social, and technological limits.

Instead of proposing a single disaster and precipitating an ideal human organization, *The Caryatids* is notable for its distributed account of the future. Climatic effects are subject to geography, not cultural capitals. Future economic and social organization is inevitably shaped by climate but also by current cultural and political ideas. Consensus is unlikely, even as the "climate crisis" forces human adaptation. *The Caryatids* seems flawed by twentieth-century literary standards, even in comparison to Sterling's *Heavy Weather*. Characters are cartoonish and inscrutable. Historical events and future disasters are hinted at and then forgotten. Despite massive info-dumps, future technology remains opaque. Human and climatic history is relayed through patchy, nonsequential asides. The reader can never be sure where to position herself. But these difficulties emerge from a real attempt to address a distributed, indeterminate problem. *The Caryatids* successfully makes the metamorphosis from the literary jeremiad to an exploration of a deepening, current crisis and the interlocking and competing strategies humans might use to survive within it.

Other recent novels, spanning the continuum between contemporary realism and speculative science fiction, have explored similar questions. Barbara Kingsolver's gentle, incisive *Flight Behavior* (2012) traces the effects of climate-induced mass migration on a poor, rural community in the American South, adjusting the interrelations among domesticity, land rights, eco-consumption, Christianity, and science in the process. Robert Edric's *Salvage* (2010) describes the dynamics of reconstruction for local politicians and businessmen, national initiatives, engineers, farmers, and low-skilled workers, finding an endemic tension among business development, sustainability, and personal justice. Kim Stanley Robinson's Nebula-prize winning *2312* (2012) describes humanity after three centuries' progress in bioengineering, medicine, planetary exploration, and terraforming. Humanity's modes of life are radically expanded, but the interrelated problems of poverty and climate on Earth remain central. By indicating the economics of climate change in the present, imagining new economic organizations in the future, challenging twentieth-century accounts of nature, humanity, and modernity, and rearticulating the niche humans dwell within on Earth and beyond, these novels all address a central question: How will humans live in the Anthropocene? And attendant on this question, how does it feel, what are the aesthetics and ethics, what is to be feared, and for what might we hope, when it is recognized that Earth has been turned from the perfect other into a series of chaotic systems operating beyond the parameters of human history?

The Windup Girl: Integrating Agents in the Anthropocene Economy

The Windup Girl (2010), by Paolo Bacigalupi, is one of the most sophisticated accounts yet written of a future economy transformed by climate change. *The Windup Girl* was called one of the best novels of the year by *Time, Locus,* and *Publishers Weekly,* and it also won the Hugo, Nebula, Locus, and Compton Cook awards. Bacigalupi's novel richly describes a world after the "Contraction," a century in the future, when oil supplies have been exhausted, extreme climate change has taken hold, many key species have gone extinct, and globalization has failed. Future Bangkok struggles to feed its population, keep the rising ocean at bay, and maintain security in the face of waves of refugees and colonizing capital. The novel manages to describe a disastrous future without alienating the reader and without simplifying the material or moral complexities of climate change. Future Bangkok is distinctly contiguous with our own moment, reflecting contemporary dilemmas between global trade and environmental regulation, altruism and self-interest, technology and reversion. Novels of the previous two decades tended to adopt the point of view of either capital's privilege or climate change's victim, simplifying the future into "positive or negative," utopia or dystopia. By contrast, *The Windup Girl* complicates the idea that climate change can be told through a single point of view, without devolving into empty formalism. The novel raises and then rejects the reader's identification with familiar characters and ideals, relentlessly exposing the limits of received points of view. Unlike so many anthropocentric novels, *The Windup Girl* also foregrounds the persistent, inseparable agency of nonhumans. Thus, the novel relentlessly examines its narrative strategies, suggesting how the aesthetics and identifications of twentieth-century fiction must be adapted to the moral world of the Anthropocene.

In the first instance, the reader is set up to think that the hero will be Anderson Lake, an American factory manager in Bangkok. White, wealthy, virile men have repeatedly been figures for Anglo-American wish fulfillment, even more so when they lead technological enterprises. In Bova's *Empire Builders*, Dan Randolph is a heroic, American executive who leads humanity's response to climate change. In McEwan's *Solar,* nearly two decades later, egotistical, libidinous privilege remains the best hope for humanity. Early on, Anderson Lake's virility is foregrounded: he gallantly fights a rampaging megodont (a GM elephant) and possesses the novel's main love interest, a rogue Japanese concubine. Lake even seems alluring when the narrative reveals he is a spy for AgriGen, an agricultural corporation that has long superseded the US government in global importance. The reader's moral identification with Lake is gradually stripped away as details of his mission emerge: he is intent on stealing Thailand's seedbank, enriching his corporation and enabling it to force sterile, genetically modified seedstock on the independent Kingdom. The results of private bioengineering have already been disastrous, leading to invasion, compliant colonies, and genetically based diseases that have decimated populations and made today's fruits and vegetables extinct. Lake would believe that AgriGen has shared interests with the Kingdom's Trade Ministry, but his counterpart pointedly dismantles Lake's claim, describing a clear history of economic exploitation, first through religion, then through foreign ownership, then through the loss of self-sufficiency during globalization, and finally through genetically engineered scarcity (150). Despite the trade minister's belief in an international economy, there can be no illusions about Lake's character. Too often, white, virile Americans are the heroes of science fiction novels, but *The Windup Girl* demands the examination of other points of view.

Perhaps, then, aesthetic beauty or identification with the vulnerable could provide a more reliable moral compass in the Anthropocene. Emiko, the "windup girl" of the title, appears to be a figure that could provide morally acceptable identification. Emiko is a kind of latter-day geisha, genetically modified by Japanese engineers to have perfect skin; to be impervious to diseases; to move with a stutter-stop, *"heechy-keechy"* motion; and to be as subservient as a Labrador retriever. Wanting to save the expense of returning her to Japan, her Japanese corporate keeper sells her into sex slavery in a Thai brothel, where she is violently raped again and again. When cornered, Emiko discovers that her genes also allow her to move with lightning-fast speed. In a moment, Emiko unleashes breathtaking violence, ripping the throat from a major political figure and killing all his bodyguards, sparking a political crisis. Her superpowers are compelling in a science fiction novel, but Emiko is deeply vulnerable. Her subservient conditioning makes her fall in love with Anderson, even though he uses her as a sexual pawn in his political intrigue. Also, her pores have been genetically modified to be tiny: she has beautiful skin, but any exertion leads her to overheat and collapse. She remains dependent on ice and air-conditioning in a world that simply cannot supply the energy. As she observes, "I was not designed for this climate" (44). Emiko's self-judgment extends beyond herself. Many have hoped that the aesthetic and the beautiful will be a reliable guide to value, creating identification with the natural or the ecologically sound. But in *The Windup Girl,* the aesthetic turns out to be intimately linked to violence and subservience, and it depends on an exoticism that is wholly unsustainable. Emiko's example suggests that identification with art or subservience cannot provide answers in the Anthropocene.

Often, critics have hoped climate change could be addressed by a strong, principled state that would police environmental infractions for the greater good. Captain Jaidee Rojjanasukchai of the Environment Ministry is such a hero. Called the Tiger of Bangkok, Jaidee is the visible face of the White Shirts, a former Muay Thai figher who cannot be bribed by business interests. In the Kingdom, the Environment Ministry is extraordinarily powerful, precisely because environmental crisis constantly threatens to overwhelm the nation:

> At every turn the ministry's purview was expanding. The plagues were but the latest insult to the Kingdom's survival. First came the rising sea levels, and the need to construct the dikes and levees. And

then came the oversight in power contracts and trading in pollution credits and climate infractions. The white shirts took over the licensing of methane capture and production. Then there was the monitoring of fishery health and toxin accumulations in the Kingdom's final bastion of calorie support. . . . And there was the tracking of human health and viruses and bacteria. . . . There was no end to the duties of the Ministry. (121)

In the future, environmental threats justify extraordinary powers. Jaidee's integrity positions him as an eco-avenger, raiding illegal importers and shutting factories that exceed their carbon allowance. Nevertheless, there are too many similarities to Mussolini's Brown Shirts.[44] Most of the Environment Ministry is corrupt, shaking down businesses for bribes and demanding tribute from the very poor so they can warm their food over methane fires. Jaidee is incorruptible but brutal: he beats businessmen, orders the slaughter of tens of thousands of animals, and burns villages at the suspicion of infection. In a moment of introspection, he realizes he is terrified of infection and pollution and recognizes himself as a bully (122, 125). Jaidee's uncompromising assault on enterprise leads him to attack the Ministry of Trade; when he fails, he is ritually humiliated and then killed, halfway through the novel. So much for militant environmentalism.

Perhaps, in the climate-changed future, rational self-interest is the only way to survive. Hock Seng manages Anderson Lake's factory, where he first appears as a sullen, craven, and disloyal old man. As his backstory is revealed, Hock Seng is shown to have a more compelling past and greater inner resources than it first appeared. Hock Seng is actually a Chinese refugee after Malaya has expelled all foreigners. He once presided over a fleet of clipper ships before his family was killed and his fortune lost when the political climate turned. He longs for his large family, wives and children and grandchildren, "the marble-floored halls and red lacquer pillars of his ancestral home." Living in a wood shack secured only with a leather thong, he hides away money and jewels, hoping to rebuild his family and wealth, and views his lot as a kind of luck. Despite his loss, Hock Seng is grateful not to live with most of the other yellow-card refugees in the abandoned, rotting skyscrapers that are nearly uninhabitable without elevators and air-conditioning. Even so, the unfolding plot reveals the repugnance of Hock Seng's moral calculations: when he first arrived, starving, he killed another hungry refugee by shoving a broken bottle into his throat; he stays at the factory only to steal its technology; and when the factory's algae baths inadvertently breed a new disease, he covers up the dead bodies and allows a pandemic to spread. It is not that Hock Seng is unaccountably immoral, but that calculated self-interest in a ruthless world inexorably leads to unforgiveable violence.

Hero narratives, aesthetic beauty, environmental fundamentalism, and self-interest cannot counteract climate change or guide the economy that is already emerging from it. Such an economy should not be confused with the imaginary space described by free-market economists, who defend the idea that a system of rational, self-interested human agents will maximize efficiency. When the civil war between the Ministry of Trade and the Ministry of Environment starts, Hock Seng can see such an economy for what it is: "'We're like little monkeys, trying to understand a huge jungle.' The thought frightens Hock Seng. They're piecing together clues, but they have nothing to provide context. No matter how much they learn, it can never be enough. They can only react to events as they unfold, and hope for luck" (315). Climatic instability means that a comprehensible environmental context may be slipping out of reach forever. None of the characters, with their moral flaws and limited points of view, can understand the whole. Imagining that these issues can be reduced to a political binary or entrusted to a single authority is foolhardy. Nor is there a disinterested, omniscient point of view that can encompass the Anthropocene. Instead, the Anthropocene economy binds together technology, nature, and culture in ways that are unpredictable and unbalanced. Unlike the purified "free market," this economy is also shaped by the agency of technologies, plants, and animals. Human organizations, political groups, and ideological forces radically shape both production and consumption. Ultimately, the Anthropocene economy is a collection of agencies—businessmen, governmental ministries, populations, storms, species, fuels—reforming each other in a shifting climate. *The Windup Girl* traces these economic transformations with remarkable foresight.

First, Bangkok's economy and culture have been dramatically rebalanced by the global exhaustion of oil deposits and strict emissions limits on burning coal. Characters allude to the recent past as "the Contraction," meaning the collapse of global trade when a dearth of fuel for internal combustion engines brought ships, planes, and lorries to a halt. The novel is set in a moment of renewed expansion: dirigibles dock on anchor pads in Bangkok's airfield (47), and clipper ships, with palm-oil polymer hulls and tall white sails, have begun to move goods between continents (47). Wind power and simple flotation have been renewed. For local travel, most people use rickshaws and bicycles, even the Tiger of Bangkok. Nevertheless, there are functions that can only be performed by fossil fuels. Sea walls and levees surround Bangkok, and twelve coal-fired pumps consume nearly all the kingdom's carbon credits (276). After rising sea levels have made the city all but untenable, only the continued use of coal can keep it from drowning.

Climate change has also transformed the class structures of the city. A small community of wealthy expats manages the country's trade and exploit local conditions, even as they face deportation and arrest. The constant threat of crop failure and contagion, alongside the Environment Ministry's far-reaching limitations on energy and trade, has impoverished the country. Even wealthy factory owners fume over permit letters that make "a bribe look like a service agreement" (15). Market sellers live in fear of the ministry as they forge certificates to sell fruit; basic trade has become politically and environmentally hazardous. More broadly, the wealth of the twentieth-century city has been replaced by an underclass of refugees:

> Overhead, the towers of Bangkok's old Expansion loom, robed in vines and mold, windows long ago blown out, great bones picked clean. Without air conditioning or elevators to make them habitable, they stand and blister in the sun. The black smoke of illegal dung fires wafts from their towers, marking where Malayan refugees hurriedly scald *chapatis* and boil *kopi* before the white shirts can storm the sweltering heights and beat them for their infringements. (7)

Of course, the death of the high-rise—and with it the urban middle class—has been a trope in climate fiction since J. G. Ballard and George Turner, but Bacigalupi replaces a distinctly bourgeois panic of class regression with the real likelihood of endemic refugee crises.[45] The Malayan refugees who now live in future Bangkok are doubly oppressed by the White Shirts, first because they are marginal "yellow cards" with little legal protection and second because their poverty does not allow them to participate in the legal fuel trade. The yellow cards are also related to a gray trade in energy, collecting dung and fruit rinds around the city that are then composted. The resulting methane lights the city at night, casting a green glow overseen by the shadowy Dung Lord, the kingpin of recycling (22). Instead of presenting a sustainable utopia, critical environmental measures impoverish the city, creating shadow economies that serve only the powerful.

Energy scarcity has also reformed industry and labor. Often, dystopian fiction imagines that extreme climate change will send humans back to a new Victorian, medieval, or Stone Age era, while optimistic early science fiction foretold a new era of supermodernity.[46] *The Windup Girl* offers a more sophisticated view of the teleology of technology. Anderson Lake's factory is trying to perfect the "kink spring," which can be wound like an extraordinarily flexible rubber band, storing gigajoules of energy, with the hope of finally rivaling petroleum as a compact, moveable fuel. To do so in the post-Contraction world, the factory assembles half a dozen technologies into a single production line. A cutting press uses a precision blade and a hydraulic jack. Burning lamps depend on electricity, necessitating massive bribes to siphon off "a portion of the Kingdom's own global carbon budget" (10). In a different area, genetically modified algae are cultivated in vats by women and children wearing triple-filter masks (9). But "the living heart of the factory's drive system" is a team of genetically modified elephants chained to enormous teak spindles, encouraged and beaten by Union handlers, the "megodonts" in turn driving conveyor lines, venting fans, and manufacturing machinery (8). In the office, computers with fifteen-centimeter displays are powered by treadles, like old sewing machines, while telephones are powered by hand crank. Far from superannuating the past, the factory combines medieval animal power, Victorian presses and labor conditions, early-twentieth-century assembly lines, late-twentieth-century computing, and futuristic biotechnology into a single system, all to replicate the density of energy taken for granted in the late twentieth century. The factory also assembles different aesthetics: industrial clockwork, Far Eastern exoticism, medieval drudgery, and futuristic ambition. Humans are altered by these technologies: office workers must sustain steady, aerobic effort; the mahout union is able to exert considerable political pressure; unskilled laborers crank out joules for industrial and domestic devices; child labor has become "valuable" once again; workers die in droves when a new contagion is inadvertently created. Ultimately, the factory suggests a vision of sustainable, local practices, while also tracing the cruel demands of an energy-scarce economy.

The Windup Girl is noteworthy, as well, for the agency it attributes to nonhuman actors. Unlike character-driven fiction, Bacigalupi's novel describes the unintended consequence, costs, and hazards that transform human calculation. The most obvious examples are disasters. The genes of Emiko, hybridized from multiple species, lead Japanese manufacturers, Thai politicians, and the American spy to assume they can perfectly exploit her. When she rebels, they similarly assume a logical, human strategy is behind her killing. In actuality, Emiko acts from her hybridized instincts, precipitating a political crisis with far wider ramifications. Other agents also foil human calculation. After a calorie executive creates "Cheshires" for his Alice-obsessed daughter, the shape-shifting animals push cats into extinction (26–27). A megodont rampages Anderson Lake's factory. Genetically modified fruit bear deadly diseases, and the factory's algae baths breed a new plague. These agents are neither natural nor artificial, and their origins don't safely predict what they will do. Instead, *The Windup Girl* indicates that the categories of natural and artificial have long been superceded. Human agency itself can only be described as an alloy of plants, animals, bacteria, machines, capital, and weather.

This posthuman framework allows *The Windup Girl* to trace the value of biodiversity. In Bacigalupi's future, unpredictable weather and gene warfare have caused mass extinctions and countless food-borne plagues, severely depleting the species available for human use. After peak oil and mass starvation, calories are the primary measure of value. Regional survival now depends on genetic material, whether a national gift of tilapia or the corporate dumping of proprietary SoyPro or UTex rice. The novel opens in a market, with Anderson Lake encountering new varieties of fruit and vegetables long thought to be extinct, resuscitated by a secret Thai seedbank. When he researches these mysterious calorie sources in books from our time, the scale of ecological loss emerges:

> Anderson has spent enough time poring over ancient pictures that they seldom affect him. He can usually ignore the foolish confidence of the past—the waste, the arrogance, the absurd wealth—but this one irritates him: the fat flesh hanging off the *farang*, the astonishing

abundance of calories that are so obviously secondary to the color and attractiveness of a market that has thirty varieties of fruit: mangosteens, pineapples, coconuts, certainly . . . but there are no oranges, now. None of these . . . these . . . dragon fruits, none of these pomelos, none of these yellow things . . . lemons. None of them. So many of these things are simply gone. But the people in the photo don't know it. (64)

Suddenly, the reader, who can take for granted thirty varieties of fruit in a local supermarket, who can take for granted the mere existence of a lemon, must view the world through Lake's eyes. Even for an industrial spy, the Kingdom's seed bank is a treasure trove allowing humanity to beat back plague mutations, develop food stocks, and ensure survival for a few more generations (86). Environmental critics have often distinguished between the anthropocentric and the intrinsic value of species. For Lake, it is clear that these arguments are indistinguishable: a mere lemon can influence humanity's survival, while its extinction is felt as an irreparable loss. The open-air market values individual fruits, but it also charts the hopes of the human species.

Finally, *The Windup Girl* revalues the economy of the present. There is a strong sense of irony when Anderson Lake comes across his predecessor's collection of books, stacks of titles like *Global Management in Practice, Intercultural Business, The Little Tigers of Asia, Supply Chains and Logistics, Exchange Rate Considerations in Business*, "stolen from libraries and business schools across North America . . . a careful pillaging of Alexandria that had gone entirely unnoticed because everyone knew global trade was dead" (62). If capitalism now structures the hegemonic, global order, *The Windup Girl* indicates the final vulnerability of this structure in the face of climate change. There is more room for environmental justice in Bacigalupi's future, but more oppression and poverty, as well. Lake's own books, with pictures of the fruits and vegetables we take for granted, represent another Alexandria, whose value can only be perceived when it is made scarce. The threat of climate change exceeds individual points of view, but it paradoxically indicates the wealth we all still share.

Over thirty years, there has been remarkable growth in fiction's ability to describe the impacts of climate change on human ecology. The novel is unlikely ever to be suited to predicting the specific data of crisis, whether it is measured in parts per million, property loss in dollars, meters of flooding, or accurate casualty figures. But what fiction can do is conceptualize complex, heterogeneous systems: how national pride, bioengineering, aesthetics, familial love, social resistance, species loss, job loss, local food, and flooding might combine to create a way of life in the future. Even when a novel's account is spectacular or extreme, it evaluates the complex agents of the Anthropocene to provide an overall account of human life. To do so is to conceptualize human ecology under climate change, whether in the present or the distant future.

Early novels described climate change in terms of economic scarcity, creating unconscionable poverty and leading eventually to the extinction of *Homo bourgeois*. After the fall of communism, capitalism became the primary subject in many climate change novels: it alone had agency, either to save the world or to destroy it. Recent fiction radically complicates this account of capital and climate. Instead of taking capitalism to be a unitary system, recent novels provide a framework to explore the complex interactions between a multitude of agents. In Saci Lloyd's *Carbon Diaries*, climate-change induced scarcity cuts through the center of people, splitting their loyalties between carbon reduction and self-interest, environmental activism and resistance to authority, and old versus new forms of labor and consumption. Bruce Sterling's *The Caryatids* suggests the economic systems of the future will almost certainly respond to human failure to control emissions, as well as a changed physical climate. These systems, however, are not *determined* by climate; nor can they be characterized as simply good or bad. A radically altered climate is just as likely to permit the coexistence of ecological and economic styles. Paolo Bacigalupi's *The Windup Girl* amplifies these tensions, suggesting that no existing agent has the answers to address anthropogenic global warming but that any provisional solution must include a multitude of agents, human and hybrid.

Markets are specific, not abstract, mechanisms for exchange, spanning from a local, open-air fruit and vegetable market to the abstract system of international trade; from the energy use of a single household to the international mix of coal, natural gas, wind, solar and nuclear power plants; from legally protected contracts to gray and black markets. The national character of much fiction is overrun as political boundaries and systems are transformed and refugees surge across. Underpinning all of these transformations is the real scarcity of energy and human goods and the inevitability of a pattern of distribtion. Markets should not be understood as a framework for purified, rational humans, but rather as a terrain to test the uneven, heterogeneous forces of corporations, self-interested individuals, national trade objectives, and environmental restrictions. Plants, animals, bacteria, machines, financial capital, and weather all materially shape markets as well, in ways that are not precisely predictable, even if they are often decisive. As it has grown, climate fiction has begun to recognize these agents, turning even a humble lemon into a sign of all that has been lost and all that might yet be preserved.

CONCLUSION
The Real and the Future

What does the future hold for climate fiction? Assessing this future is unusually difficult, because of the dual uncertainties of climatic and political feedback loops. Yet it seems clear that we have reached a new present, in which both authors and critics can respond to the contemporary reality of anthropogenic global warming.

For most of the history of climate fiction, catastrophic global warming was a distant, hypothetical future. Four decades ago, when Ursula LeGuin wrote *The Lathe of Heaven* (1971), climate change was but one of a number of alternative contingencies for dimension-traveling characters. Through the 1970s, 1980s, and 1990s, climate change appeared most in science fiction, thrillers, dystopias, and apocalyptic narratives. Science fiction could capture the science underpinning climate change as a distant prospect. Thrillers could describe the countdown to a heroic rescue. Dystopias found a new reason for material scarcity and totalitarianism. Apocalyptic narratives could repurpose greenhouse gases to speculate about the end of time, a novelty to replace nuclear holocausts, pandemics, and the Second Coming. Other literary approaches became possible around the turn of the millennium, as the scientific consensus became stronger, accounts of climate change circulated more widely, and calls for political action became more strident.

Despite these conditions, climate change stubbornly resisted literary realism. Of course, realism is a literary effect, an illusion whereby fiction "reflects life and the social world as it seems to the common reader."[1] Realism makes a pointed investment in the aesthetics of representation (in contrast to the mediation common to fiction more generally).[2] But realism also depends on depicting specific types of people, places, and social milieus: "an ordinary citizen of Middletown, living on Main Street, perhaps, and engaged in the real estate business."[3] When literary authors have tried to depict climate change, disasters disassemble the illusion of realism, rupturing quotidian experience, devastating towns, fracturing the economy, and severing the connections of bourgeois ecosystems. In the hands of some authors, such as Maggie Gee, George Turner, and Jeanette Winterson, climate change systematically deconstructs greenhouse culture, necessitating a new narrative space that is "beyond" the destroyed world, an afterlife, the deep future, or another planet.[4] For other authors, such as T. C. Boyle, Will Self, and Ian McEwan, the deconstructive force of climate change produces comedy. Whether black humor, satire, or ribaldry, this comedy also indicates the uncomfortable gaps between recognizable realism and global warming's forceful reconfiguration of late-twentieth-century ways of life.

And yet, the absence of the realist climate change novel could be a symptom of a deeper cultural resistance to the Anthropocene itself. Through the 1970s, 1980s, and 1990s, much climate fiction treated the present elegaically. Cormac McCarthy's *The Road* is a noteworthy example, conflating the man's grief at the loss of his wife and at the loss of familiar, beautiful landscape. Other novels, like Jeanette Winterson's *Stone Gods* and T. C. Boyle's *A Friend of the Earth,* reminisce from the future on the loss of love and late modernity. This temporal structure indicates a difficulty in experiencing our "greenhouse culture" as an end point, rather than a moment in a longer narrative of progress. Richard Kerridge has argued realism cannot, in fact, "explore the emotional complexity of our responses to the threat [of climate change]," because "we are, collectively, evading its emotional import." Under these circumstances, perhaps the best fiction can do is show us, "in artistic form, the feelings we do not yet dare to have."[5] If we are no longer at this point of elegy and evasion, this likely has less to do with collective emotional maturity and more to do with the insistent agency of a global climate.

Throughout the early 2000s, further temperature data, alongside disastrous floods, fires, and storms, suggested that the age of innocence had expired and that global warming could no longer be deferred to the future. As a critic in the *New Yorker* recently observed, "Today, novels that would once have been called science fiction can be read as social realism."[6] Realism's "here and now" had strayed into the Anthropocene. A handful of very recent novels by Jonathan Franzen, Barbara Kingsolver, and Robert Edric indicate the literary transition that is taking place.

Jonathan Franzen's *Freedom* (2010) begins to address the problems with realism in the Anthropocene, without fully resolving them.[7] The novel is a remarkably nuanced portrait of American liberalism in the first decade of the twenty-first century, tracing the extended relationships and intertwined lives of an environmental executive, Walter, his competitive wife, Patty, and his best friend, the rock musician Richard, from their first meeting in college through middle age. Freedom is a recurrent ideal in American life, but characters continually encounter freedom's limits in early sexual encounters, marriage, suburban neighborhoods, private enterprise, and global empire. The novel's discussion of limitations is particularly apropos in the Anthropocene: the young, studious Walter is influenced by the Club of Rome, believing that the endless growth assumed by Marxist and free-market economics cannot be sustained (151). As an idealist, the young Walter expects the American bourgeoisie to voluntarily accept increasing restrictions on its personal freedom, while Richard views Marxist revolution as much more likely (126–27). Of course, neither occurs.

Over the subsequent decades, characters in *Freedom* confront America's failure to address its own global impacts. Richard turns to sarcasm, claiming his music is mere bubble gum, not "meaningful labor or social justice or wisdom," and that the Republican Party is the party of liberty and individualism (252). Walter, always more earnest, founds an environmental trust devoted to saving a single species, the cerulean warbler. Backed by a Houston oil-and-gas magnate, the trust takes the novel approach of creating an immense nature preserve in southern West Virginia, funded by first permitting mountaintop removal mining to strip the area's coal reserves. Walter's attempt to marry the interests of capitalism and conservation is underpinned by a belief that billionaires "tend to care" about biodiversity, since they and their heirs have a stake in the planet's future (266). Walter makes considerable concessions to justify his backer, cynically claiming coal has environmental benefits over nuclear and wind energy (406). Privately, he is contemptuous of the loutish, bellowing vox populi (575) and of governments "elected by majorities that don't give a shit about biodiversity" (266). Eventually, even Walter must concede that he has been used to push through devastating mining practices. In response, he mounts a wider campaign against overpopulation, calling humans "A CANCER ON THE PLANET" (611). Little comes of any of Walter's actions, indicting the public's freedom to disengage and the economic discretion of the elite, not to mention the misanthropy that underpins Walter's environmental rhetoric.

Franzen's novel offers pleasures rarely found in the corpus of climate fiction. *Freedom* gives a rich, detailed account of the political, economic, and social milieu of a host of characters, providing a deep sense of recognition and insight into George W. Bush–era liberalism. And yet, the novel can be read as a criticism of its own, realist aesthetic. Unlike the other novels discussed in *Anthropocene Fictions, Freedom* fails to articulate the things involved in climate change or extinction. Instead of circulating through the characters of the novel, the environment is merely a *psychological* preoccupation, never meaning much to Walter's wife, their children, or most of their extended circle. Cerulean warblers never appear *or* disappear; the imminent devastation glimpsed by Walter is never gathered into a flood of reality. Despite a nuanced account of early twenty-first-century politics, the Iraq war, federal scandals, and the attendant media, *Freedom*'s aesthetics ultimately treat political organization as a symptom of poor character, pathologizing attempts to address environmental issues. Nor is the environment ever really connected to Walter's class position: in this novel, economic interests are thoroughly human. The cerulean warbler, coalfields, and changing climates are never allowed to intervene into characters' fortunes. Despite its engagement with environmental crisis, Franzen's realism prevents scientific predictions from circulating, refuses to locate the agency of the nonhuman world, atomizes and reifies character, and declines to engage with the ecosystems that support them. And yet, the novel's indictment of freedom and reaction, which thoroughly suffuses the form of the novel, conveys the continued resistance to making the Anthropocene real.

The difficulties faced by Franzen's realism suggest subtle yet profound innovations in Barbara Kingsolver's *Flight Behavior*.[8] Kingsolver's novel builds a complex, moving portrait of the contemporary Anthropocene, integrating science, place, politics, and economics in unexpected ways. Instead of drawing on common disaster tropes, *Flight Behavior*'s crisis is the unexpected arrival of millions of monarch butterflies on a small mountain in rural, southern Appalachia. Dellarobia, the protagonist, first experiences the butterflies as a burning vision, a warning from God, but it soon becomes clear the butterflies are a roosting colony representing a significant proportion of the entire North American monarch population. Waylaid by changing weather patterns on their way to Mexico, the entire species faces extinction in the freezing Tennessee winter. In the majority of climate change novels, a local disaster makes global warming undeniable and immediate, rupturing quotidian life and suppressing questions of belief.

By contrast, this flood of orange wings makes climate change gently, gorgeously palpable, without simplifying human characters' inner lives.[9]

Kingsolver's realism shows its fragility where many novels attempt to render climate science improbably certain. Soon after Dellarobia discovers the roosting colony, a leading lepidopterist named Ovid Brown arrives, creates a temporary laboratory in the farm's barn, and hires Dellarobia to work alongside his research assistants, collecting data. Privately, Ovid's scientific explanations, personal warmth, and rich Caribbean accent win over Dellarobia. Publicly, the scientist is tragically constrained: "After decades of chasing monarchs and their beautiful mysteries, he would now be with them at the end, for reasons he had never in his whole life foreseen" (245). The lepidopterist denies he is a physician or superhero able to save the patient with special powers; biology must be distinguished from matters of conscience; scientists who address the public are ridiculed by their colleagues for being imprecise or theatrical; Ovid's personal magnetism and composure never appear on camera. Ovid is an imperfect vessel of climatic truth, conveying the limits of science in the contemporary world.

These limits allow *Flight Behavior* to trace the complex circulation of scientific knowledge through a small Tennessee community. Characters' understanding of climate change is shaped by the complicated terms of their own identity. Dellarobia's preoccupation with quotidian life makes climatic disaster hard to absorb: "Getting the kids to eat supper, getting teeth brushed. No cavities the next time. Little hopes, you know? There's just not room at our house for the end of the world" (283). Dellarobia is gradually enlisted by Ovid's charm, rationality, and the laboratory evidence she gathers, leading her to connect his explanations to her more immediate experiences of weather "turned weird" over recent years (260–61). Dellarobia's mother-in-law, Hester, quietly believes the monarchs must be protected, though family dynamics make her reluctant to side visibly with Dellarobia. On the other hand, Hester's husband, Bear, is more concerned with the impending default of the farm's debt and views harvesting the mountain's timber as his duty, regardless of any impact on the butterflies. Dellarobia's husband, Cub, dismisses global warming as a liberal fantasy, quoting the local talk radio show host. Dellarobia's best friend is sympathetic to her but more preoccupied with dating. By contrast, the family's pastor views the mountain's timber in terms of stewardship and frugality, ultimately pressuring Bear not to clear-cut the area where the butterflies have landed.

More broadly, the media is interested in human-interest stories, not climate change, while activists who descend onto the farm all but ignore local perspectives. Through these nuances, *Flight Behavior* does the good work of literary realism, complicating the stereotypical certainty of scientists and the ignorance of rural southerners while unpacking the cultural nuances of contemporary climate change.

Kingsolver's realism is underpinned by an account of Anthropocene economics for the working poor. The portrait of Dellarobia, her family, and the town is effective in large part because of the detailed rendering of their financial struggles, without ever falling into pity or condescension. The family farm makes little money; Cub finds insufficient work; and Dellarobia struggles to look beautiful, provide for her children, and maintain domestic comforts with second-hand clothing, processed food, and dollar-store goods. Dellarobia's quiet and principled efforts imbue her character with depth and dignity, even when her respectability is undercut. At the same time, Dellarobia's immediate circumstances can make climate change seem irrelevant. A visitor tries to get Dellarobia to sign a "Sustainably Pledge," but his lifestyle suggestions are laughable: she hasn't eaten in a restaurant in two years, is bemused that anyone would buy bottled water, doesn't have a computer to use Craigslist, already economizes on gas and shops at thrift stores, and couldn't "fly less" or make "socially responsible investments" even if she so wanted (326–29). The implication is clear: blame for carbon emissions falls disproportionately on bourgeois consumers, not the working poor. On the other hand, Dellarobia describes how antienvironmental positions have been "assigned to people," leading her neighbors to conclude, "If I'm the redneck in the pickup, fine, let me just go burn up some gas" (323). Another character argues that climate change denial has been incorporated into people's identity, and condescension only galvanizes it (395).[10] Ultimately, the effects of climate change are disproportionately borne by those who cannot afford them, even as their economic niche leads them to deny its existence.

Nevertheless, Kingsolver's realism does not prevent her from expressing indignation at the politics of global warming. The novel captures the outrage of a neutral person finding out about climate change for the first time. When Dellarobia learns from Ovid that atmospheric levels of carbon dioxide have long passed the level needed for thermal balance and continue to climb without pause, she is floored, feeling she never had a chance to address the problem (277–78). Later, Ovid confronts a news anchor who avoids the cause of the monarchs' arrival, falling back on the old tale of scientific disagreement. Ovid plainly tells her that scientists only disagree on "how to express our shock," indicting the American media for its complicity (367). *Flight Behavior* is also critical of climate activists. When the local community college's Environment Club pickets the farm for "trying to kill all the butterflies," they show up at the wrong house, have barely legible signs, and miss the most salient issues: local economic hardship is the force behind the logging, while global emissions are the more significant cause of extinction (236–37). Other activists come from further afield, including a group of women who craft pretty butterflies out of recycled yarn, to no noticeable effect. Sympathy for the activists is also qualified by their unconscious entitlement to the family farm: Cub views them as "trespassers . . . unwilling to respect private property," while Dellarobia views their ignorance as a symptom of news reports of the butterflies treating the farm like it was "anyone's business" (253). Thus, *Flight Behavior*'s realism complicates the oppositional politics of other climate change novels, showing the many parties to climate change in a small town, as well as the influence of national news media, science, activism, and party politics on local situations. Even so, contemporary realism seems unable to imagine political innovations or new ways of living that could address the challenges of the Anthropocene.

A third recent novel, Robert Edric's *Salvage*, addresses these political problems indirectly.[11] Its realism shows the difficulty of articulating the political and economic transformations needed in the Anthropocene. Set a century in the future, primarily in a single Yorkshire town, *Salvage* lacks the trenchant cultural observation of Franzen's *Freedom* or the complex interiority of Kingsolver's *Flight Behavior*. What makes the novel realist is its refusal of fanciful technologies or spectacular disaster. Endemic flooding is a *bureaucratic* problem, leading to "policies of widespread, organised abandonment," refugee populations demanding the restoration of middle-class life, and a national government obsessed with rehousing (90). The plot stages the nonhuman forces of climate change and shows the conflicts between human interests that arise. These conflicts are simultaneously political, creating new configurations of human beings, and eco-nomic, altering the lived environments of these people.

At a superficial level, *Salvage* presents a predictable cast of economic villains capitalizing on the scramble for adaptation. A derelict municipality is to receive the "overspill" of flooding—up to three hundred thousand people in a decade—necessitating the creation of new roads, leisure centers, shopping malls, entertainment, "everything" (91–92). Greer, the mayor and self-styled "Chief Executive," negotiates for the revival of the city and ensures his far-reaching investments in local land and businesses "[go] in some way towards the betterment of this place and the people who live here," not to speak of the meteoric rise of his own bank balance (88–89). Greer's right-hand man, Stearn, is the police chief and provides private security for the vast tracts of land that are to be turned into a vision of country living. The town's newspaper's editor, "Good News Fischer," garners advertising revenue by selling a vision of local progress, while Reverend Pollard hopes to preside over a vast flock from his new cathedral. Behind these men, another dozen investors own the town and expect it to appreciate. Together, local government, media, religion, and business align their interests to form a regenerated future.

In an era of critique, it would be easy to interpret the novel as an unmasking of these interests. However, their interests are bald, and the Anthropocene demands a more complex social network. The novel's protagonist, Quinn, an auditor for the national Planning and Development Ministry, is sent to prepare the town for its influx of capital. Quinn's ambitious boss, Webb, describes the assignment by positioning Quinn and himself over a map of the town and "repeatedly [jabbing] at the place from above as though his finger were a falling stick of bombs dropped on to the town from a great height to strike and obliterate its centre" (40). Quinn's audit is needed to bring together destructive and creative impulses, local leaders and national government, monetary and bureaucratic interests. This work is quite different from critique or the assignation of blame. At the Centre for Library and Archive Services, where the city's public records are held, Quinn knows not to look for "anything as simplistic or as misleading as innocence or guilt" and is dismissive of conspiracies that hold that those in positions of authority and trust are "wasteful, or fraudulent, or profligate, or imprudent" (55). Quinn understands that he is a mere "facilitator" and that neither Greer nor Webb will allow the deal to fail. Quinn recognizes a deeper truth: that the Anthropocene demands something more than mere interruption.

Outside of his official duties, Quinn meets others with different perspectives on the town, interests that lie beyond the official development organization. The friendly foreman of a road crew tries to clear drainage channels, struggling to maintain his men's jobs and an access road that continually threatens to be washed out. An alcoholic, unemployed journalist shows Quinn a photograph of a flood fifty years before that submerged the town to its rooftops (132–33). Bored teenagers work the government-rationed petrol pumps, not daring to wish for better jobs. The terminal owner of a family farm describes the collapse of the countryside through the story of his own land: a pathetic history of repeated livestock culls, the arrival and disappearance of thousands of illegal immigrants, and the inevitable withdrawal of subsidies that made fashionable crops, wind farms, and biofuels temporarily profitable (96–101). And Anna Laing, a chief vet from the Agriculture Ministry, digs up ever more toxic waste, despite pressure to stop digging and declare a "safe" plague pit. In these encounters, Quinn is torn among feelings of solidarity, contempt, pity, and attraction as others try to entangle him in their material relationships to the town. Quinn might recognize these people as the representatives of a climatic proletariat and determine his duty is to give them voice, against the interests of the local elite. To do so would be to obscure their need for economic regeneration, an independent media, farmland, and the remediation of devastating pollution.

In the third chapter, boundary work is described as a process of bringing together distinct interests into a new agency. This process depends on boundary objects, things that are real but also subject to different, mutually productive interpretations by different groups. In *Salvage*, the town itself is a boundary object: it is known in distinct ways by the mayor, police chief, editor, reverend, and investors, but their action is harmonized through complementary interpretations. But the town is also the site of power struggles between local and national interests, conducted in the subtle terms of bureaucratic procedure and disrespectful informality, bursts of profanity and official apologies. Other, local characters recognize the town's history of flooding, irrigational problems, underlying toxicity, need for productivity, and limits of development. Struggles are not resolved through pure social power but instead as that power interfaces with real, nonhuman things with their own, compelling agency: Quinn's dismissal of the drunken journalist's conspiracy is overturned when he is confronted with photographic evidence; Greer and Stearns can suppress, but not remake, the toxic dumps and human remains of fifty years before; Wade, the foreman, struggles to clear the flooded roads and keep his men employed based on poorly drawn plans. Rather than merely labeling characters dominant or marginal, critical interpretation of objects reveals uneven, yet unstable, distributions of power.

In *Salvage*, the existing politics of adaptation are vulnerable, exposing the need for new kinds of organization. Often, it has been suggested that an "iconic extreme" can galvanize a community into action.[12] At the novel's climax, a flood disintegrates the careful linkages forged between characters, leaving development plans, national and local alliances, cleanup efforts, employment, families, and friendships fragmented. In earlier fiction, spectacular, apocalyptic disasters are used as a device to connect all people, but *Salvage* suggests a different outcome: Quinn and his love interest watch a blizzard in "wonder" and "awe," but their private emotions join no one together and lead to no action. The unsustainable development of the town is merely deferred until spring, when better photo opportunities will be available. Of course, the reader knows only greater disaster can come of this deferral. Such hypocrisy emphasizes the perspectives of civil servants, engineers, farmers, road workers, unemployed workers, and reporters, as well as the laws, waste pits, waterways, crops, roads, labor, and stories that also must be considered in the adaptation to climate change. In *Salvage*, these things are an externality to the plans of government and business, and Edric's novel is unable to articulate a realistic path through which they could be addressed. At the same time, these things are included in the architecture of the narrative. The realist plot, then, erects a scaffold for the political assembly we cannot, yet, imagine.

Interpreting fictional things yields an outcome that is fundamentally different from a unified thesis. Theories of boundary objects suggest that it can be productive for different groups to interpret things in different ways. Fiction is able to show these multiple approaches through characters, holding open the potential for collaboration, even when differences remain unresolved. Meaningful adaptation to climate change will require action from developers and farmers, national bureaucrats and local leaders, and they need not wait for an impossible political organization or final version of truth to begin collaboration. On a practical basis, these parties are already interconnected through human economies and ecosystems. Critical practice can contribute to adaptation when it articulates how parties outside the climate regime also share in our bounded climate.

The rise of realist fiction about the Anthropocene shows a wider transformation of human culture. For most of its cultural existence, climate change was imagined as a final disaster that could be endlessly deferred. The political subtext of such novels was that such a disaster should force total, human agreement, leading to widespread change. But climate change is not structured as a final, local disaster: its effects are incremental, widespread, and various. Just as important, climate change is not just in the future: it began with the rise of human agriculture, gained pace during the Industrial Revolution, and has had demonstrable effects for decades. Human society is unlikely ever to agree and certainly will never understand climate change in the way atmospheric scientists do. Meaningful action on climate change will not look like a popular political uprising, even if unrest should trigger greater progress. The creation of Anthropocene realism marks a profound shift in the understanding of climate change itself, from something that ought not to exist to something that already does.

And yet, there remain real limits to realist fiction. It cannot imagine novel technological, organizational, and political approaches to climate change. Its focus on a narrow locale and set of characters compresses distributed, global events. It struggles to understand the devastating potential of climatic disaster. For these reasons, novels like *Flight Behavior* and *Salvage* are but one branch of an evolving literary phenomenon.

In the next decades, humanity may or may not take greater steps to draw down existing greenhouse gases and reduce further emissions. In either case, the influence of climate change will only grow in the twenty-first century, as we transform our consumption of energy or are forced to adapt to climate change's ever-greater effects. As this process plays out, climate change will become more and more a part of everyday life, influencing authors to come. Climate change is not just a "theme" in fiction. It remakes basic narrative operations. It undermines the passivity of place, elevating it to an actor that is itself shaped by world systems. It alters the interactions between characters and introduces entirely new things to fiction. Finally, it mutates the ecological systems that underpin any novel's world. In a very real sense, contemporary fiction is becoming climate fiction, insofar as all fiction mediates the world, has a setting, organizes characters, and also mobilizes things. Of course, there is a limit to the number of "ignorant" novels that can be interpreted productively through climate change. Aside from such a project, the narrower category of climate fiction is likely to grow for the foreseeable future.

One of the ironies of climate science is that continued emissions make the effects of warming more difficult to predict. In a similar way, as the body of Anthropocene fiction grows, and as its texts influence more authors and readers, its significance becomes more difficult to describe. By incorporating new energy technologies, political organizations, places, peoples, and disasters, climate fiction will alter the capacities of the novel in ways that cannot yet be predicted. As we saw in the first chapter, there is a distinct need to read against the "message" of climate change literature. This need is perhaps more acute because the evident authorial intent of so much climate fiction is to preach to a choir of environmentally committed readers. Despite the intentions of authors, climate fiction becomes innovative as it incorporates new things into preexisting genres. Anthropocene technologies are unprecedented in the history of humanity, and they redraw the interconnections between facts and literary fabrications. Climate change changes the literary potentialities of setting, conflict, the organization of characters, and the fundamental way that diverse characters and nonhumans interact in narratives. These developments will demand new readers to trace the more complicated networks among science, things, and societies.

This book has always been intended as a provocation to further research. During its composition, there was an outpouring of journal numbers and essay collections attempting to theorize climate change. Most often, these essays develop existing continental theory to address the "new" problem of global warming. *Anthropocene Fictions* engages with this theory as it bears on particular issues. However, this "theory" has been remarkably untethered to the practices of literature over the last forty years. Unlike the issues of gender, national identity, and philosophy (for example), there is not a centuries-old body of texts and interpretations that are commonly associated with climate change. Critical climate change "theory" is closer to "hypotheses" at this stage. Specific theories need further testing against climate science, politics, and literature before their utility is proved.

This is not to suggest that investigations of climate fiction should defer to scientists. As the first chapter shows, the creation of "facts" depends on their circulation beyond the laboratory and scientific journal, into funding bodies, political arenas, and publics. Fiction is not just an impure reflector of scientific knowledge. It models the entire process of circulation and, in some cases, traces new paths for circulation. Public understanding of science is an important field of research, and literature could be used as crude tool to trace the imperfect dissemination of climate knowledge from academic to literary circles. A more interesting approach would explore how different works of fiction articulate the overlapping categories of science and public. There is a historicist component to this project, tracking different models of circulation through different literary periods. However, it is also speculative, showing how fiction seeks to reimagine both scientific practice and public organization in the future. Above all, this research should not devolve into a history of ideas: things like global climate models, ice cores, wind turbines, and tipping points have specific histories that shape both scientific and literary practice.

Both places and disasters also have a longer, literary history. The second chapter traces the most dominant disaster, the deluge, as a specific, literary means of interrupting fictional settings to account for climate change. Other forms of disaster have a distinct rhetoric. Erosion, for example, has a very different structure: while deluge presents as a disaster from without, erosion dissolves the ground we stand on, perhaps presenting a more apt transformation of the climate on which we depend. Other disasters deserve more investigation, particularly as more fictional examples emerge. In addition, more research is needed on the impact of climate change on specific places. Places have specific histories that are simultaneously cultural and geographic. The meaning of places also changes as real disasters befall them. Climate novels about New York, London, and Washington, DC, work within a longer literary and urban history that deserves negotiation, no less than nonurban places like the English countryside, the Australian outback, the Scottish highlands, Alaska, and Antarctica. So, too, the science fiction roots of much climate fiction means that outer space appears in a multitude of Anthropocene novels, acting as both a foil and a continuation of Earth-bound environmental practices. Hopefully, more fiction about places beyond North America and Britain will emerge, particularly more fiction about specific developing countries where climate change is already having a disastrous effect. Also, Ursula Heise has described the importance of postlocal ways of knowing the world. In fiction, climate models, media reports, and traveling characters perform these functions, while local places often act as a synecdoche of the planet. New literary strategies for understanding planetary systems continue to emerge in climate fiction.

There is a fundamental relationship between new ways of knowing the planet and new ways of organizing human responses to it. For most of its history, climate fiction's political subtext was that the threat of global warming necessitated a tremendous, common response from humanity. Either political unity would fix the problem, or the devastation would make the world unrecognizable. Adaptation remained all but unthinkable, because addressing it could undermine the apocalyptic rhetoric or concede political failure. More recently, fiction has begun to address the political crises likely to result from "adaptation" itself. Matthew Glass's *Ultimatum* describes a United States redrawn due to mass exoduses, before diverting the narrative to a more conventional nuclear thriller. Yet other recent novels, including those by Kim Stanley Robinson, Paolo Bacigalupi, and Saci Lloyd, begin to describe a world in which politicians must lead massive adaptation efforts while conceding that some problems are irreversible. In addition, such novels begin to assemble new forms of political agency, spanning insurance companies, scientific organizations, governmental groups, international businesses, zoos, spiritual leaders, technology companies, refugees, homeless people, and stay-at-home parents. By necessity, these affiliations go well beyond the formal structures of a representative democracy, imagining new kinds of interconnected action in the Anthropocene. Another fundamental question for future research is how the Anthropocene is experienced by individuals of different genders, sexual orientations, racial and cultural origins, and religious affiliations. Similarly, more must be done to articulate the political connections among people across nation-states, actively rejecting the parochialism also found in climate denial. We have seen how novels by Crichton, Gee, Robinson, Bacigalupi, Bova, Butler, and Sterling address identity in the Anthropocene, but much more research is needed in this area. Formally, realism is unlikely to imagine novel political affiliations because of its commitment to a desultory status quo. For this reason, it seems likely that the most interesting fiction and criticism about the politics of climate change will dwell in the speculative future, inventing new ways of connecting diverse human beings.

To engage with the Anthropocene, literary criticism must also attend more closely to the material practices that produce unsustainable emissions. The fourth chapter traces fiction's developing relationship with the economic and ecological systems of the Anthropocene. Novelists and critics have often attempted to circumvent specific engagement with energy sources, global industrial production, transportation, logistics, agriculture, and an unsustainable system of prioritizing delivery of goods. To be bald, too many environmentalists have assumed that if humans moved back toward tribal living, or if government legislation mandated massive emission cuts on industry, catastrophic climate change could be avoided. Not only are these strategies politically naive, but they also radically underestimate the need for greater productive efficiency and massive retooling, neither of which can be delivered by the most extreme neoprimitivism or authoritarian state. Fiction can productively engage with the politics of animal welfare, crops, energy, and biodiversity, as well as the nuances of genetically modified organisms, nuclear power, clean coal, fracking, and the ongoing history of petro-culture. Additionally, fiction can examine the current and future effects of these things on different human lives. By necessity, fiction's formal operation will also change as it articulates different forms of human ecology. Environmental criticism has an ongoing duty to situate these literary and technological changes in the context of the Anthropocene.

It has already been observed that such a critical practice will be founded on a number of ironies.[13] Not only does climate change refuse to provide a unitary subject for investigation, but it also emphasizes the circulation of artifacts outside of academic study. Climate change defies scales from local places to global spaces, but it is also recognizable as a category of effects that dissolve both place and space. While criticism continues to be founded on the politics of opposition and personal choice, climate change seems to demand the sharing of agency and, with that, the expansion of bureaucracy. Markets have often been blamed for climate change while market-based approaches to emissions have been derided, as climate change deniers have invoked markets as a cure for bureaucracy and a locus of freedom. And yet, tracing human economies may be the only way to map the complex effects of climate change and to describe the loss of that which is priceless. Climate novels have a role to play in our collective accounting of the Anthropocene, even those that were written in the hope that such a day would never come to pass.

NOTES

Introduction

1. *Anthropocene* was coined by Eugene F. Stoermer in the 1980s. See also Will Steffen, Jacques Grinevald, Paul Crutzen, and John McNeill, "The Anthropocene: Conceptual and Historical Perspectives," *Philosophical Transactions of the Royal Society A* 369:1938 (13 Mar. 2011): 842–67.

2. Paul Crutzen, "Geology of Mankind," *Nature* 415 (3 Jan. 2002): 23.

3. Joseph Stromberg, "What Is the Anthropocene and Are We in It?" *Smithsonian Magazine*, Jan. 2013, http://www.smithsonianmag.com/science-nature/What-is-the -Anthropocene-and-Are-We-in-It-183828201.html.

4. These impacts have been drawn from S. H. Schneider et al., "Assessing Key Vulnerabilities and the Risk from Climate Change," in *Climate Change 2007: Impacts, Adaptation and Vulnerability*, ed. M. L. Parry et al. (Cambridge: Cambridge University Press), 779–810.

5. See Spencer Weart, *The Discovery of Global Warming*, rev. and exp. ed. (Cambridge, MA: Harvard University Press, 2008).

6. Absent, of course, significant greenhouse gas draw-down projects, likely at the scale of the twentieth-century proliferation of the automobile.

7. Robin McKie, "Read All about the End of the World," *Observer*, 16 Aug. 2009, http://www.theguardian.com/books/2009/aug/16/cold-earth-ultimatum-rapture-flood.

8. Rose Fox, "Good Worlds and Bad," *Publishers Weekly*, 13 Apr. 2009, http://www .publishersweekly.com/pw/print/20090413/17277-good-worlds-and-bad.html.

9. Andrew Dobson, "The Fiction of Climate Change," *openDemocracy*, 17 Sept. 2010, http://www.opendemocracy.net/andrew-dobson/fiction-of-climate-change.

10. Chris Ross, "I'm with the Bears Edited by Mark Martin—Review," *Guardian*, 11 Oct. 2011, http://www.guardian.co.uk/books/2011/oct/11/im-with-the-bears-review; Daniel Kramb, "Climate Change Fiction Melts Away Just When It's Needed" *Guardian*, 18 Oct. 2012, http://www.guardian.co.uk/books/booksblog/2012/oct/18/climate-change-fiction.

11. John DeNardo, "A Flood of Science Fiction," *Kirkus*, 8 Aug. 2012, http://www .kirkusreviews.com/features/flood-science-fiction/#continue_reading_post.

12. Angela Evancie, "So Hot Right Now: Has Climate Change Created a New Literary Genre?" *NPR Books*, 20 Apr. 2013, http://www.npr.org/2013/04/20/176713022/so-hot -right-now-has-climate-change-created-a-new-literary-genre; Husna Haq, "Climate Change Inspires a New Literary Genre: Cli-Fi," *Christian Science Monitor*, 26 Apr. 2013, http:// www.csmonitor.com/Books/chapter-and-verse/2013/0426/Climate-change-inspires-a

-new-literary-genre-cli-fi; Rodge Glass, "Global Warning: The Rise of 'Cli-Fi,'" *Guardian,* 31 May 2013, http://www.guardian.co.uk/books/2013/may/31/global-warning-rise-cli-fi; Pilita Clark, "Global Literary Circles Warm to Climate Fiction," *Financial Times,* 31 May 2013, http://www.ft.com/intl/cms/s/0/8a8adf10-c9e3-11e2-af47-00144feab7de.html#ax zz2Ybg3Cdzd; Brian Merchant, "Behold the Rise of Dystopian 'Cli-Fi,'" *Vice,* June 2013, http://motherboard.vice.com/blog/behold-the-rise-of-cli-fi; Carolyn Kormann, "Scenes from a Melting Planet: On the Climate-Change Novel," *New Yorker,* 3 July 2013, http://www.newyorker.com/online/blogs/books/2013/07/scenes-from-a-melting-planet.html.

13. For example, see Arthur Herzog, *Heat* (1977; rpt., New York: Authors Choice Press, 2003) (hereafter cited in the text).

14. For a prominent example, see Kunstler's *World Made By Hand,* describing a village economy after widespread social collapse.

15. For example, see Maggie Gee, *The Ice People* (London: Telegram, 1998); Saci Lloyd, *Carbon Diaries 2017* (London: Hodder Children's Books, 2009); Mike Resnick, *Kirinyaga: A Fable of Utopia* (New York: Ballantine Pub. Group, 1998); Ian McDonald, *Cyberabad Days* (Amherst, NY: Pyr, 2009); and Paolo Bacigalupi, *The Windup Girl* (San Francisco, CA: Nightshade, 2010) (hereafter cited in the text). Also see chapter 3.

16. Frank Schatzing, *The Swarm: A Novel of the Deep,* trans. Sally-Ann Spencer (New York: Regan Books, 2006).

17. Jostein Gaardner, *The Castle in the Pyrenees,* trans. James Anderson (London: Weidenfeld & Nicolson, 2010).

18. Yrsa Sigurdardóttir, *The Day Is Dark,* trans. Philip Roughton (New York: Minotaur, 2013).

19. Javier Sierra, *The Lost Angel,* trans. Carlos Frias (New York: Atria, 2011).

20. Johanna Sinisalo, *Troll: A Love Story,* trans. Herbert Lomas (New York: Grove 2004).

21. Peter Verhelst, *Tongue Cat: A Novel,* trans. Sherry Marx (New York: Farrar, Straus & Giroux, 2003).

22. David Brauner, *Contemporary American Fiction* (Edinburgh: Edinburgh University Press, 2010), 206.

23. See "Print Isn't Dead, Says Bwoker's Annual Print Production Report," Bowker, 18 May 2011, http://www.bowker.com/en-US/aboutus/press_room/2011/pr_05182011.shtml.

24. Harold Bloom, *The Western Canon* (London: Macmillan, 1995), 10–11.

25. Dominic Head, *The State of the Novel: Britain and Beyond* (Oxford: Blackwell, 2008), 5.

26. Peter Childs, *Contemporary Novelists: British Fiction since 1970* (Houndmills, Basingstoke: Palgrave, 2005), 274.

27. Head, *State of the Novel,* 15.

28. Rod Mengham, "General Introduction: Contemporary British Fiction," in *Contemporary British Fiction,* ed. Richard J. Lane, Rod Mengham, and Philip Tew (Cambridge: Polity, 2003), 1.

29. See Adeline Johns-Putra, "Ecocriticism, Genre, and Climate Change," *English Studies* 91.7 (2010): 744–60.

30. See Adam Trexler and Adeline Johns-Putra, "Climate Change in Literature and Literary Criticism," *Wiley Interdisciplinary Reviews: Climate Change* 2.2 (Mar.–Apr. 2011): 185–200.

31. George Monbiot, "Civilisation Ends with a Shutdown of Human Concern: Are We

There Already?" *Guardian,* 30 Oct. 2007, www.guardian.co.uk/commentisfree/2007/oct/30/comment.books.

Graulund argues climate change is not at the center of the novel, while Kunsa and Warde ignore the possibility. See Rune Graulund, "Fulcrums and Borderlands: A Desert Reading of Cormac McCarthy's *The Road,*" *Orbis Litterarum* 65.1 (2010): 57–78; Ashley Kunsa, "'Maps of the World in Its Becoming': Post-Apocalyptic Naming in Cormac McCarthy's *The Road,*" *Journal of Modern Literature* 33.1 (2009): 57–74; Anthony Warde, "'Justified in the World': Spatial Values and Sensuous Geographies in Cormac McCarthy's *The Road,*" in *Writing America into the Twenty-First Century: Essays on the American Novel,* ed. Elizabeth Boyle and Anne-Marie Evans (Newcastle: Cambridge Scholars Publishing, 2010), 124–37.

32. Paul William Gleason, *Understanding T. C. Boyle* (Columbia: University of South Carolina Press, 2009).

33. Gillen D'Arcy Wood, "Eco-Historicism," *Journal for Early Modern Cultural Studies* 8.2 (2008): 1–7.

34. Timothy Morton, *Ecology without Nature* (Cambridge, MA: Harvard University Press, 2007), 166–68.

35. Ursula Heise, *Sense of Place and Sense of Planet: The Environmental Imagination of the Global* (New York: Oxford University Press, 2008), 206.

36. Scott Slovic, "The Story of Climate Change: Science, Narrative, and Social Action," in *Going Away to Think* (Reno: University of Nevada Press, 2008), 117–33.

37. Richard Kerridge, "Environmental Fiction and Narrative Openness," in *Process: Landscape and Text,* ed. Catherine Brace and Adeline Johns-Putra (Amsterdam: Rodopi, 2010), 65–85.

38. Greg Garrard, "*Endgame:* Beckett's Ecological Thought," *Samuel Beckett Today/ Aujourd'hui* 23 (2011): 383–97.

39. "Environmental Change—Cultural Change," University of Bath, 1–4 September 2010.

40. "Culture and Climate Change," Bath Spa University, 31 July 2010.

41. *English Studies* 91.7 (2010); Laurenz Volkmann, Nancy Grimm, Innes Detmers, and Katrin Thomson, eds., *Local Natures, Global Responsibilities: Ecocritical Perspectives on the New English Literatures* (Amsterdam: Rodopi, 2010).

42. Among these were the Association for the Study of Literature and Environment Conference, Indiana University, June 2011; New Climes: Critical Theory, Environmentalism, and Climate Change, Tremough, Cornwall, June 2011; the Environment and Identity Conference, Pendennis Castle, Cornwall, July 2011; and Climate Change: A Challenge for Literary Criticism?, workshop, Lund University Centre for Sustainability Studies, Sweden, Jan. 2012.

43. Timothy Clark, "Some Climate Change Ironies: Deconstruction, Environmental Politics, and the Closure of Ecocriticism," *Oxford Literary Review* 32.1 (2010): 141.

44. See Joseph Carroll's *Evolution and Literary Theory* (Columbia: University of Missouri Press, 1994).

45. Dana Phillips, *The Truth of Ecology: Nature, Culture and Literature in America* (Cambridge: Cambridge University Press, 2003), 45.

46. See, respectively, Jonathan Bate, *The Song of the Earth* (Cambridge, MA: Harvard University Press, 2002); Jonathan Levin, "Between Science and Anti-Science: A Response to Glen A. Love," *Interdisciplinary Studies in Literature and Environment* 7.1 (2001):

6–7; Dana Phillips, "Ecocriticism, Literary Theory, and the Truth of Ecology," *New Literary History* 30.3 (Summer 1999): 577–602.

47. Bruce Clarke, "Science, Theory, and Systems: A Response to Glen A. Love and Jonathan Levin," *Interdisciplinary Studies in Literature and Environment* 8.1 (Winter 2001): 150, 151–52.

48. Clarke, "Science, Theory, and Systems," 155–56.

49. Molly Wallace, "'A Bizarre Ecology': The Nature of Denatured Nature," *Interdisciplinary Studies in Literature and Environment* 7.2 (2000): 137–53.

50. Phillips, *Truth of Ecology*, 2003.

51. Eric L. Ball, "Literary Criticism for Places," *symplokē* 14.1–2 (2006): 232–51.

52. Robert Markley, "Monsoon Cultures: Climate and Acculturation in Alexander Hamilton's *A New Account of the East Indies*," *New Literary History* 38 (2007): 527–50.

53. Emily Potter, "Climate Change and the Problem of Representation," *Australian Humanities Review* 46.1 (2009), http://www.australianhumanitiesreview.org/archive/Issue-May-2009/potter.htm.

54. Gert Goeminne and Karen François, "The Thing Called Environment: What It Is and How to Be Concerned with It," *Oxford Literary Review* 32.1 (July 2010): 109–30.

55. See also Phillips, *Truth of Ecology*.

ONE. Truth

1. William Howarth, "Imagined Territory: The Writing of Wetlands," *New Literary History* 30.3 (Summer 1999): 515.

2. Glen Love, "Ecocriticism and Science: Toward Consilience?" *New Literary History* 30.3 (Summer 1999): 561.

3. Levin, "Between Science and Anti-Science," 7.

4. Phillips, "Ecocriticism, Literary Theory." See also Phillips, *Truth of Ecology*, 5–11; Lawrence Buell, *The Future of Environmental Criticism* (Oxford: Blackwell, 2005), 30–44.

5. Jonathan Bate, "Culture and Environment: From Austen to Hardy," *New Literary History* 30.3 (Summer 1999): 558.

6. Daisy Maryles, "Crichton's State," *Publishers Weekly*, 20 Dec. 2004, http://www.publishersweekly.com/pw/print/20041220/24307-crichton-s-state.html.

7. Michael K. Janofsky, "Michael Crichton, Novelist, Becomes Senate Witness," *New York Times*, 29 Sept. 2005, http://www.nytimes.com/2005/09/29/books/29cric.html.

8. Bruce Barcott, "'State of Fear': Not So Hot," *New York Times*, 30 Jan. 2005, http://www.nytimes.com/2005/01/30/books/review/30BARCOTT.html; Sam Leith, "A Tsunami of Silliness," *Telegraph*, 19 Dec. 2004, http://www.telegraph.co.uk/culture/books/3633626/A-tsunami-of-silliness.html.

9. Myles Allen, "A Novel View of Global Warming," *Nature* 433 (20 Jan. 2005): 198.

10. James Hansen, "Michael Crichton's 'Scientific Method,'" http://www.columbia.edu/~jeh1/2005/Crichton_20050927.pdf (accessed 15 Mar. 2011); Peter Doran, "Cold Hard Facts," *New York Times*, 27 July 2006, http://www.nytimes.com/2006/07/27/opinion/27doran.html.

11. Michael Crichton, "'Aliens Cause Global Warming': A Caltech Lecture by Michael Crichton" (unpublished), 2003, https://www.cfa.harvard.edu~scranmer/SPD/crichton.html (accessed 3 Sept. 2014).

12. Bruce Barcott, in "'State of Fear,'" usefully compares Crichton's NERF to the NRDC and the Environmental Liberation Front to the Earth Liberation Front.

13. Michael Crichton, *State of Fear* (New York: Harper Collins, 2004), 57 (hereafter cited in the text).

14. The real-life model for Kenner is Peter Huber, who holds similar degrees and is cited in Crichton's bibliography.

15. Crichton, "'Aliens Cause Global Warming.'"

16. Michael B. McElroy and Daniel P. Schrag, "Overheated Rhetoric: A New Novel Misrepresents Global Warming and Distorts Science," *Harvard Magazine,* Mar.–Apr. 2005, http://harvardmagazine.com/2005/03/overheated-rhetoric.html.

17. Gregory Kirschling, "Review of 'State of Fear,'" *Entertainment Weekly,* 15 Dec. 2004, http://www.ew.com/ew/article/0,,955669,00.html.

18. Admittedly, Crichton more often describes the failure of conservation efforts due to insufficient research and overdependence on the purity of nature (*State of Fear,* 575–77).

19. Ryan Roberts, ed., *Conversations with Ian McEwan* (Jackson: University of Mississippi Press, 2010), 103. See also especially Patricia Waugh, "Science and Fiction in the 1990s," in *British Fiction of the 1990s,* ed. Nick Bentley (Oxford: Routledge, 2005).

20. Laura Salisbury, "Narration and Neurology: Ian McEwan's Mother Tongue," *Textual Practice* 24.5 (2010): 895. See also Roberts, *Conversations with Ian McEwan,* 103. For ecocritics, see the work of Joseph Carroll, Glen Love, and Greg Garrard.

21. Ian McEwan, *Solar* (New York: Nan A. Talese/Doubleday, 2010), 6 (hereafter cited in the text).

22. In particular, see Richard Dawkins, *The Selfish Gene,* 2nd ed. (Oxford: Oxford University Press, 1976, 1989) 67.

23. If Jung is squarely rejected, *Solar* does seem open to a notional Freudianism: both Beard's and Melissa Browne's libidos are determined by their relationship to the parent of the opposite sex.

24. Amigoni traces McEwan's relationship to Dawkins, Dennett, Pinker, and E. O. Wilson: David Amigoni, "'The Luxury of Storytelling': Science, Literature and Cultural Contest in Ian McEwan's Narrative Practice," in *Literature and Science,* ed. Sharon Ruston (Cambridge: D. S. Brewer, 2008), esp. 156.

25. See Salisbury, "Narration and Neurology," 896; Waugh, "Science and Fiction," 62.

26. Walter Isaacson, *Einstein: His Life and Universe* (London: Simon and Schuster, 2007), 173.

27. See ibid., 41, 274–75.

28. In *Solar,* Melissa's genius for balancing stock between fads and long-term demand is a likely model (161).

29. See also Waugh, "Science and Fiction," 65.

30. Amigoni, "'Luxury of Storytelling,'" 157.

31. Jan Golinski, *Making Natural Knowledge: Constructivism and the History of Science* (London and Chicago: University of Chicago Press, 1998, 2005), 4.

32. Ibid., 7.

33. Ibid., xix, 6.

34. While some science studies scholars have found useful ideas in postmodernism,

Latour has been scathing of postmodern reductivism and the aims of critique. See Bruno Latour, *Pandora's Hope: Essays on the Reality of Science Studies* (Cambridge, MA: Harvard University Press, 1999) (hereafter cited in the text); Bruno Latour, "Why Has Critique Run Out of Steam?" *Critical Inquiry* 30 (Winter 2004): 225–48.

35. For the use of heterogeneous explanation in other fields, see Lennard J. Davis and David B. Morris, "Biocultures Manifesto," *New Literary History* 38 (2007): 413, 418.

36. Clarke, "Science, Theory, and Systems," 155–56.

37. Bruno Latour, *We Have Never Been Modern*, trans. Catherine Porter (Cambridge, MA: Harvard University Press 1993), 283.

38. Clarke, "Science, Theory, and Systems," 150.

39. Wallace, "'Bizarre Ecology'"; Phillips, *Truth of Ecology*, 39, 133; Buell, *Future of Environmental Criticism*; Ball, "Literary Criticism for Places"; Potter, "Climate Change and the Problem of Representation"; Goeminne and François, "Thing Called Environment."

40. Latour, *We Have Never Been Modern*, 287.

41. For a recent survey, see Peter T. Doran and Maggie Kendall Zimmerman, *Eos* 90.3 (20 Jan. 2009), http://tigger.uic.edu/~pdoran/012009_Doran_final.pdf.

42. See also Susan M. Gaines's *Carbon Dreams* (Berkeley, CA: Creative Arts, 2001).

43. When they land on an island that has been studied by anthropologists to prove the existence of cannibalism, the parallels between adventure and field research become even more pointed.

44. Allen, "Novel View," 198.

45. Crichton, "'Aliens Cause Global Warming.'"

46. In contrast to Crichton's reductivist account, many detailed studies have traced how the IPCC is a new kind of social organization, bringing together the differing aims of politicians, scientists, and bureaucrats.

47. Crichton, "'Aliens Cause Global Warming.'"

48. Roberts, *Conversations with Ian McEwan*, 160, 151.

49. Peter Childs has described the importance of children to McEwan's work, mostly as sites of trauma, violence, and anxiety. Catriona isn't abused, but her future environment is called into question. See Peter Childs, "'Fascinating Violation': Ian McEwan's Children," in Bentley, *British Fiction of the 1990s*, 123–34.

50. Roberts, *Conversations with Ian McEwan*, 151.

51. Joseph Rouse uses a nondiscursive version of Baudrillard's simulacra: see "Understanding Scientific Practices: Cultural Studies of Science as a Philosophical Program" (1998), in Mario Biagioli, ed., *Science Studies Reader* (London: Routledge, 1999), 449–50.

TWO. Place

1. Buell, *Future of Environmental Criticism*, 63.

2. Bate, *Song of the Earth*, 225–37.

3. Michael Bennett, "From Wide Open Spaces to Metropolitan Places: The Urban Challenge to Ecocriticism," in *The ISLE Reader: Ecocriticism, 1993–2003*, ed. Michael P. Branch and Scott Slovic (Athens: University of Georgia Press, 2003), 296–317.

4. Robert Kern, "Ecocriticism: What Is It Good For?" in Branch and Slovic, *ISLE Reader*, 259–60.

5. For summaries of these developments to ecocritical theories of place, see Buell, *Future of Environmental Criticism*, 77; Heise, *Sense of Place*, 45–47, 61.

6. Heise, *Sense of Place*, 205.

7. Ibid., 206.

8. M. L. Parry, O. F. Canziani, J. P. Palutikof, P. J. van der Linden, and C. E. Hanson, eds., *Contribution of Working Group II to the Fourth Assessment Report of the Intergovernmental Panel on Climate Change, 2007* (Cambridge: Cambridge University Press, 2007), chapter 6.2.2., http://www.ipcc.ch/publications_and_data/ar4/wg2/en/ch6s6-2-2.html.

9. S. Solomon, D. Qin, M. Manning, Z. Chen, M. Marquis, K.B. Averyt, M. Tignor, and H. L. Miller, eds., *Contribution of Working Group I to the Fourth Assessment Report of the Intergovernmental Panel on Climate Change, 2007* (Cambridge: Cambridge University Press, 2007), FAQ 5.1., http://www.ipcc.ch/publications_and_data/ar4/wg1/en/faq-5-1.html.

10. Parry et al., *Contribution of Working Group II*, 6.6

11. Juliet Jowett, "Flooding Rated as Worst Climate Change Threat Facing UK," *Guardian*, 25 Jan. 2012, http://www.guardian.co.uk/environment/2012/jan/26/floods-worst-climate-change-uk.

12. This account of early-twentieth-century deluge novels is very much indebted to Nicholas Ruddick, "Deep Waters: The Significance of the Deluge in Science Fiction," *Foundation* 42 (Spring 1988): 49–59.

13. Ibid., 49.

14. Ibid., 50.

15. J. G. Ballard, *The Drowned World* (London: Berkley, 1962) (hereafter cited in the text). For another account of Ballard in terms of ecocriticism, see Rudolphus Teeuwen, "Ecocriticism, Humanism, Eschatological Jouissance: J. G. Ballard and the Ends of the World," *Tamkang Review* 39 (2009): 39–57.

16. Richard Cowper, *The Road to Corlay* (London: Gollancz, 1978) (hereafter cited in the text). Indeed, Cowper's novel is among the first to directly address anthropogenic climate change. Only Ursula LeGuin's *The Lathe of Heaven* (1971), a parallel history novel, is earlier.

17. Marcus Sedgwick, *Floodland* (London: Faber, 2009), 56.

18. Julie Bertagna, *Exodus* (London: Young Picador, 2002).

19. See Donald Bingle, *Greensword: A Tale of Extreme Global Warming* (Waterville, ME: Five Star, 2009); Terry Brooks, *Armageddon's Children (Genesis of Shannara)* (London; Orbit, 2007); Charles deLint, *Svaha* (New York: Ace Books, 1989); Ian R. MacLeod, *The Great Wheel* (New York: Harcourt Brace, 1997); and Robert J. Rubis, *Mai Shangri-La* (CreateSpace, 2008).

20. Hunter Hayes, *Understanding Will Self* (Columbia: University of South Carolina Press, 2007), 169.

21. See, for example, Will Self, "Demotic English in *The Book of Dave*," in *Voices and Silence in the Contemporary Novel in English*, ed. Vanessa Guignery (Newcastle: Cambridge Scholars Publishing, 2009), 23.

22. Will Self, "In the Beginning: Will Self on the Genesis of *The Book of Dave*," *Guardian*, 15 June 2007, http://www.guardian.co.uk/books/2007/jun/16/willself.

23. Will Self, *The Book of Dave: A Revelation of the Recent Past and Distant Future* (London: Viking, 2006), 59 (hereafter cited in the text).

24. John Mullan, "Broken English: John Mullan on Readers," responses to Will Self's *The Book of Dave, Guardian*, 22 June 2007, http://www.guardian.co.uk/books/2007/jun/23/featuresreviews.guardianreview3.

25. Self's predictions are consistent with the IPCC's 2001 projections.

26. The height of the water seems to be quite precisely measured by the amount the Centrepoint building protrudes from the ocean, forty men high, or approximately seventy meters higher (131).

27. Future towns correspond closely with current cities.

28. See Steven Barfield, ed., "Psychogeography: Will Self and Iain Sinclair in conversation with Kevin Jackson," *Literary London* 6.1 (Mar. 2008), http://www.literarylondon.org/london-journal/march2008/sinclair-self.html; Magdalena Maczynska, "This Monstrous City: Urban Visionary Satire in the Fiction of Martin Amis, Will Self, China Miéville, and Maggie Gee," *Contemporary Literature* 51.1 (Spring 2010): 58–86. Also see Will Self, *Psychogeography,* illus. Ralph Steadman (London: Bloomsbury, 2007).

29. Barfield, "Psychogeography."

30. Self, "In the Beginning."

31. François Gallix, Didier Girard, and Vanessa Guignery, "Conversation with Will Self," 15 Dec. 2007, La Sorbonne, Paris, in Guignery, *Voices and Silence,* 27.

32. Barfield, "Psychogeography."

33. Timothy Clark, "Towards a Deconstructive Environmental Criticism," *Oxford Literary Review* 30.1 (2008): 53.

34. Self, "Demotic English," 21.

35. On the novel's argot, see Hayes, *Understanding Will Self,* 172.

36. Self, "Demotic English," 21.

37. See also Self, *Psychogeography.*

38. T. Clark, "Towards a Deconstructive Environmental Criticism," 61.

39. Liorah Anne Golomb, "The Fiction of Will Self: Motif, Method and Madness," in *Contemporary British Fiction,* ed. Richard J. Lane, Rod Mengham, and Philip Tew (Cambridge: Polity, 2003), 82.

40. See Frederick Buell, *From Apocalypse to Way of Life: Environmental Crisis in the American Century* (New York: Routledge, 2004).

41. George Turner, *The Sea and Summer* (London: Faber, 1987), 110 (hereafter cited in the text).

42. Kim Stanley Robinson, *Forty Signs of Rain* (London: HarperCollins, 2004, 2005), 332 (hereafter cited in the text).

43. Maggie Gee, *The Flood* (London: Saqi, 2004) (hereafter cited in the text); John Sears, "'Making Sorrow Speak': Maggie Gee's Novels," in *Contemporary British Women Writers,* ed. Emma Parker (Woodbridge, Suffolk: D. S. Brewer, 2004), 55.

44. Susie Thomas, "Literary Apartheid in the Post-War London Novel: Finding the Middle Ground," *Changing English* 12.2 (Aug. 2005): 321.

45. The formulation is John Sears's. Sarah Dillon traces the origin of *The Flood*'s characters: Sarah Dillon, "Imagining Apocalypse: Maggie Gee's *The Flood,*" *Contemporary Literature* 48.3 (Fall 2007): 380.

46. Mr. Bliss actively advocates for invasion of "Loya," declaring, "We have to be prepared for germ warfare," and "We think they've got nuclear as well" (37).

47. Sears, "'Making Sorrow Speak,'" 66.

48. Ibid., 61.

49. Ibid., 63.

50. Dillon, "Imagining Apocalypse," 375.

51. Ibid., 377.

THREE. Politics

1. For one influential version of these arguments, see Nigel Lawson, *An Appeal to Reason: A Cool Look at Global Warming* (New York: Overlook Press, 2009).

2. Dieter Helm, "Climate-Change Policy: Why Has So Little Been Achieved?" in *The Economics and Politics of Climate Change*, ed. Dieter Helm and Cameron Hepburn (Oxford: Oxford University Press, 2009), 31–33.

3. Cameron Hepburn and Nicholas Stern, "The Global Deal on Climate Change," in Helm and Hepburn, *Economics and Politics of Climate Change*, 38.

4. Octavia Butler, *The Parable of the Sower* (New York: Four Walls Eight Windows, 1993); Margaret Atwood, *Oryx and Crake* (London: Virago, 2004) and *The Year of the Flood* (New York: Nan A. Talese/Doubleday, 2009); Cormac McCarthy, *The Road* (New York: Alfred A. Knopf, 2006); Self, *Book of Dave*. For more on McCarthy, see chapter 2; on Self, see chapter 2; on Atwood, see chapter 4.

5. Michael Glass, *Ultimatum* (London: Atlantic Books, 2009); Paul McAuley, *The Quiet War* (London: Gollancz, 2008) (hereafter cited in the text).

6. Bruce Sterling, *The Caryatids* (New York: Del Rey/Ballantine Books, 2009).

7. George Marshall, *The Earth Party: Love and Revolution at a Time of Climate Change* (Brighton: Pen Press, 2008) (hereafter cited in the text).

8. T. Coraghessan Boyle, *A Friend of the Earth* (London: Bloomsbury, 2000) (hereafter cited in the text).

9. Clive Cussler, *Arctic Drift* (New York: Putnam, 2005).

10. See Kim Stanley Robinson's *Forty Signs of Rain, Fifty Degrees Below* (London: HarperCollins, 2005), and *Sixty Days and Counting* (London: HarperCollins, 2007) (all hereafter cited in the text).

11. David G. Victor, *Victor Proposal: Fragmented Carbon Markets and Reluctant Nations: Implications for the Design of Effective Architectures*, policy brief, 5 Sept. 2007, Harvard Project on International Climate Agreements, Belfer Center for Science and International Affairs, Harvard Kennedy School, http://belfercenter.ksg.harvard.edu/publication/17331/victor_proposal.html. For a summary of Victor's arguments, see Anthony Giddens, *The Politics of Climate Change* (Cambridge and Malden, MA: Polity, 2009), 192. For a defense of the process, see Joanna Depledge and Farhana Yamin, "The Global Climate-Change Regime: A Defence," in Helm and Hepburn, *Economics and Politics of Climate Change*, 433–53.

12. Helm, "Climate-Change Policy," 9–13, 29.

13. Ibid., 18–19.

14. Giddens, *Politics of Climate Change*, 14.

15. Heise, *Sense of Place*, 206.

16. Timothy Clark, *The Cambridge Introduction to Literature and the Environment* (Cambridge and New York: Cambridge University Press, 2011), 132, 136.

17. Ibid., 121.

18. Giddens, *Politics of Climate Change*, 182–83.

19. See Helm, "Climate-Change Policy," 13–14, summarizing many other studies. Helm also repeats the familiar statistic that China has added an average of two large coal power stations per week.

20. Ibid., 31–32.

21. McKie, "Read All about the End of the World."

22. "Tidal Fear: A Thriller for Our Age," *Economist*, 4 June 2009, http://www.economist.com/node/13777094.

23. David G. Victor, "The Green in the Machine," *National Interest* 106 (Mar.–Apr. 2010): 84, http://nationalinterest.org/bookreview/the-green-in-the-machine-3387.

24. Ibid., 84.

25. Ibid., 84.

26. See Giddens, *Politics of Climate Change*, 168.

27. This passage is discussed in more detail in chapter 1.

28. Buell, *Future of Environmental Criticism*, 11; see also Buell, *The Environmental Imagination: Thoreau, Nature Writing and the Formation of American Culture* (Cambridge, MA: Harvard University Press, 1995), 430n20.

29. Lawrence Buell, contribution to "Forum on Literatures of the Environment," *PMLA* 114.5 (1999): 1091.

30. Phillips, *Truth of Ecology*, 139, 160; Richard Kerridge, "Introduction," in *Writing the Environment: Ecocriticism and Literature*, ed. Richard Kerridge and Neil Sammells (London and New York: Zed Books, 1998), 16.

31. T. Clark, *Cambridge Introduction*, 89.

32. Ibid., 77.

33. Ibid., 74–75.

34. Kjetil Rommetveit, Silvio Funtowicz, and Roger Strand, "Knowledge, Democracy and Action in Response to Climate Change," in *Interdisciplinarity and Climate Change: Transforming Knowledge and Practice for Our Global Futures*, ed. Roy Bhaskar, Cheryl Frank, Karl Georg Høyer, Petter Næss, and Jenneth Parker (Abingdon and New York: Routledge, 2010), 159–61.

35. Giddens, *Politics of Climate Change*, 6.

36. Ibid., 72.

37. Gemma Malley, *The Declaration* (London: Bloomsbury, 2007).

38. Patrick Cave, *Sharp North* (New York: Atheneum Books for Young Readers, 2006).

39. Sarah Hall, *The Carhullan Army* (London: Faber, 2007).

40. For a policy-based version of this argument, see Giddens, *Politics of Climate Change*, 5.

41. Unfortunately, it is entirely possible to conceive of authoritarian governments wholly refusing to engage with climate change, but the argument here is that such novels are limited in their ability to engage with its political dimensions.

42. Moreover, climatologists have ceased understanding climate as static, indicating the stability proposed here is likely to prove as shaky as the authoritarian regime that has created it.

43. Tierwater's voice occasionally interjects in the third-person narration. There is some suggestion that the 1989–97 account is related to the book written by April Wind, with interjected explanations by Tierwater explaining his own point of view, but this is not positively confirmed in the novel.

44. Richard Kerridge, "Narratives of Resignation: Environmentalism in Recent Fiction," in *The Environmental Tradition in English Literature*, ed. John Parham (Aldershot: Ashgate, 2002), 87–99.

45. Elisabeth Schäfer-Wünsche, "Borders and Catastrophes: T. C. Boyle's Californian

Ecology," in *Space in America: Theory History Culture,* ed. Klaus Benesch and Kerstin Schmidt (Amsterdam: Rodopi, 2005), 401–17.

46. Kerridge, "Narratives of Resignation," 99.

47. After Mac dies, Tierwater gives Chuy, his assistant, "fifteen hundred dollars cash," apparently all his money (231).

48. In a sense, this accords with Giddens's critique of the "unrealistic assumption . . . that everyone is willing and able to live like the small minority of 'positive greens'" (*Politics of Climate Change,* 105–6), even as he concedes that changes in the purchasing and lifestyle decisions of the public can significantly decrease greenhouse gas emissions.

49. Schäfer-Wünsche has criticized the novel's satire for relying on the perspective "of the aging, ethnocentric white male" ("Borders and Catastrophes," 414), but this misses the destructive, totalizing critique Tierwater mounts against his earlier self. Schäfer-Wünsche's point seems to be that the "other" is excluded from the satire's first-person perspective, but to include it—on her terms—would have been for Boyle to satirize the other. Of course, the novel also pays careful attention to nonhuman animals.

50. In the 2008 US presidential election, both candidates supported cap-and-trade policies to curb emissions, although subsequently Tea Party Republicans have led to a resurgence of denial. See Bryan Walsh, "Who's Bankrolling the Climate-Change Deniers?" *Time,* 4 Oct. 2011, http://www.time.com/time/health/article/0,8599,2096055,00. html; Coral Davenport, "Retired Republicans Push GOP to Confront Climate Change," *Atlantic,* 1 Oct. 2011, http://www.theatlantic.com/politics/archive/2011/10/retired -republicans-push-gop-to-confront-climate-change/246029/1/.

51. Hepburn and Stern, "Global Deal," 36.

52. See Rommetveit, Funtowicz, and Strand, "Knowledge, Democracy and Action," building on the work of Ulrich Beck, Michel Callon, and Sheila Jasanoff.

53. Giddens, *Politics of Climate Change,* 8, 68.

54. Ibid., 68.

55. Ibid., 4–5, 91, 211.

56. For a version of this proposal, see Helm, "Climate-Change Policy," 34.

57. Giddens, *Politics of Climate Change,* 7.

58. For a critique of the precautionary principle, see Cass R. Sunstein, *Laws of Fear* (New York: Cambridge University Press, 2005); for further discussion of the precautionary principle in the light of climate change, see Giddens, *Politics of Climate Change,* 57.

59. *Heat* interestingly suggests that postdisaster solidarity is not sustainable as a basis for climate change prevention, particularly since Kim Stanley Robinson views this collective mood as a basis for a new society. See Herzog, *Heat,* 218, and the discussion of "Science in the Capital" following.

60. Herzog's "solution" is partly related to a misunderstanding of global warming. The novel attributes a significant portion of it to human energy production itself, creating "thermal waste." By generating energy beyond Earth's atmosphere, this "problem" is solved. See Herzog, *Heat,* 234, for more details.

61. Although *Heat* is resolutely focused on America, a United Nations antithermal effort is mentioned as an afterthought; see Herzog, *Heat,* 242.

62. Kim Stanley Robinson, *Pacific Edge* (New York: Tor, 1990); Lisa Garforth, "Green Utopias: Beyond Apocalypse, Progress, and Pastoral," *Utopian Studies* 16.3 (2005): 405–6.

63. Kim Stanley Robinson, *Red Mars* (New York: Bantam, 1992), *Green Mars* (New

York: Bantam, 1993), and *Blue Mars* (New York: Bantam; 1996). For a discussion of the Mars trilogy's successive revolutions, see K. Daniel Cho, "Tumults of Utopia Repetition and Revolution in Kim Stanley Robinson's Mars Trilogy," *Cultural Critique* 75 (2010): 65–81. For a discussion of the "eco-economics" of the series, see Robert Markley, "Falling into Theory: Simulation, Terraformation, and Eco-Economics in Kim Stanley Robinson's Martian Trilogy," *Modern Fiction Studies* 43 (1997): 773–99.

64. Kim Stanley Robinson, *Antarctica* (New York: Bantam, 1999).

65. Tom Moylan, "'The Moment Is Here . . . and It's Important': State, Agency, and Dystopia in Kim Stanley Robinson's *Antarctica* and Ursula K. Le Guin's *The Telling*," in *Dark Horizons: Science Fiction and the Dystopian Imagination*, ed. Tom Moylan and Raffaella Baccolini (London: Routledge, 2003), 135–54.

66. Heise, *Sense of Place*, 207.

67. Roger Luckhurst, "The Politics of the Network: The Science in the Capital Trilogy," in *Kim Stanley Robinson Maps the Unimaginable: Critical Essays*, ed. William J. Burling (Jefferson, NC: McFarland, 2009), 171–72.

68. Gib Prettyman, "Genes, Genres, and Utopia in the Science in the Capital Trilogy," in Burling, *Kim Stanley Robinson Maps the Unimaginable*, 190.

69. Ibid., 199.

70. Johns-Putra, "Ecocriticism, Genre and Climate Change."

71. Kim Stanley Robinson, "Redefining Utopia: Kim Stanley Robinson Interviewed," *Yatterings*, 17 Apr. 2007, http://www.yatterings.com/2007/04/17/redefining-utopia-kim-stanley-robinson-interviewed/.

72. Giddens, *Politics of Climate Change*, 11.

73. Ibid., 98–99.

74. Gerry Canavan, Lisa Klarr, and Ryan Vu, "Science, Justice, Science Fiction: An Interview with Kim Stanley Robinson," *Polygraph* 22 (2010), http://www.duke.edu/web/polygraph/poly22.html.

75. Jennifer Rohn, "The Day after Today: Interview with Novelist Kim Stanley Robinson," *Lablit.com*, 4 Feb. 2007, http://www.lablit.com/article/208.

76. In *Forty Signs of Rain*, scientists claim carbon dioxide levels are at six hundred parts per million, a level that will not be reached for several decades. In the subsequent two novels, the figure is silently revised downward to five hundred parts per million, a level that will be reached in the 2010s. The novel is not contemporaneous with its moment of composition: Robinson has denied that the Republican president is George W. Bush (Rohn, "Day after Today"). Other clues, particularly a mention of Clinton and the age of Viet Nam veterans (Phil Chase and Frank's Rock Creek Park friends), suggest the novels are set in the early or mid-2010s.

77. Robert Markley has traced the historical contingency of this weather situation, finding it was a plausible scenario when the novels were composed but less likely in 2011; see Robert Markley, "Climate Change and Consciousness in Kim Stanley Robinson's Science in the Capital Trilogy," Society for Literature, Science and the Arts Annual Conference, Delta Hotel, Kitchener, 24 Sept. 2011.

78. Ernest J. Yanarella and Christopher Rice, "Global Warming and the Specter of Geoengineering: Ecological Apocalypse, Modernist Hubris, and Scientific-Technological Salvation in Kim Stanley Robinson's Global Warming Trilogy," in *Engineering Earth: The Impacts of Megaengineering Projects*, ed. Stanley D. Brunn (London: Springer, 2011), 2233–52.

79. Prettyman, "Genes, Genres, and Utopia," 189–90.

80. Luckhurst, "Politics of the Network," 177.

81. Giddens identifies these as significant obstacles to be overcome in the shift to nonemitting sources of electricity (*Politics of Climate Change*, 138–41, 145). Remarkably, "Science in the Capital" convincingly shows that the National Science Foundation could implement, or cause the implementation of, all of them.

82. Susan Leigh Star and James Griesemer, "Institutional Ecology, 'Translations' and Boundary Objects: Amateurs and Professionals in Berkeley's Museum of Vertabraate Zoology, 1907–39," *Social Studies of Science* 19.3 (1989): 387–420.

83. This discussion of boundary objects is also indebted to Simon Shackley and Brian Wynne, "Representing Uncertainty in Global Climate Change Science and Policy: Boundary Ordering Devices and Authority," *Science, Technology, and Human Values* 21.3 (1996): 275–302.

84. Ibid.; Clark Miller, "Hybrid Management: Boundary Organizations, Science Policy, and Environmental Governance in the Climate Regime," *Science, Technology, and Human Values* 26.4, special issue, *Boundary Organizations in Environmental Policy and Science* (Autumn 2001): 478–500; Myanna Lahsen, "Seductive Simulations? Uncertainty Distribution around Climate Models," *Social Studies of Science* 35.6 (Dec. 2005): 895–922; Sheila Jasanoff, "A New Climate for Society," *Theory, Culture and Society* 27.2–3 (Mar.–May 2010): 233–53.

85. Robinson has himself claimed that climate change necessitates more governmental control of the economy, while acknowledging the relationship necessarily fluctuates; see Canavan, Klarr, and Vu, "Science, Justice, Science Fiction."

86. Heise, *Sense of Place*, 207.

87. Specifically, they help Frank shake off a black-ops agent chasing him, and he teaches them techniques to survive the extreme winter.

88. Nick Gevers, "Wilderness, Utopia, History: An Interview with Kim Stanley Robinson," *Infinity Plus*, 30 Oct. 1999, http://www.infinityplus.co.uk/nonfiction/intksr.htm.

89. Heise, *Sense of Place*, 207.

90. For example, a number of American cities pledged to meet Kyoto targets independently of the federal government's refusal to participate.

FOUR. Eco-nomics

1. On "eco-nomics," see Markley, "Falling into Theory."

2. Giddens, *Politics of Climate Change*, 5.

3. J. G. Ballard, *High-Rise* (London: Harper Perennial, 2006 (1975)) (hereafter cited in the text).

4. Daniel Bodansky, "The History of the Global Climate Change Regime," in *International Relations and Global Climate Change*, ed. Urs Luterbacher and Detlef F. Sprinz (Boston: Massachusetts Institute of Technology, 2001), 23–40.

5. Ibid., 30.

6. This account is heavily indebted to ibid., 30–31.

7. Ben Bova, *Empire Builders* (New York: Tor, 1995) (hereafter cited in the text). Specifically, Bova anticipated space exploration would bring raw materials, isotopic fuel, electronics crystals, medicines and vaccines, solarvoltaic cells, and solar power satellites

beaming energy to earth (18). This vision of a solar-powered future isn't wholly squared with the novel's climate change problem.

8. Bodansky, "History of the Global Climate Change Regime," 37.

9. Ibid., 38.

10. See chapter 3.

11. Bodansky, "History of the Global Climate Change Regime," 37.

12. T. Clark, "Some Climate Change Ironies," 141.

13. Ben Dibley and Brett Neilson, "Climate Crisis and the Actuarial Imaginary: The War on Global Warming," *New Formations* 69.1 (2010): 148–49.

14. Leerom Medovoi, "A Contribution to the Critique of Political Ecology: Sustainability as Disavowal," *New Formations* 69.1 (2010): 131–32, 142.

15. Sian Sullivan, "'Ecosystem Service Commodities'—A New Imperial Ecology? Implications for Animist Immanent Ecologies, with Deleuze and Guattari," *New Formations* 69.1 (2010): 121.

16. Karen Pinkus, "Carbon Management: A Gift of Time?" *Oxford Literary Review* 32.1 (2010): 56.

17. Tom Cohen, "The Geomorphic Fold: Anapocalyptics, Changing Climes and 'Late' Deconstruction," *Oxford Literary Review* 32 (July 2010): 74–75.

18. Goeminne and François, "Thing Called Environment," 125. Actor network theory was constructed as an alternative to paradigmatic thinking.

19. James O'Connor, "The Second Contradiction of Capitalism," in *The Greening of Marxism,* ed. Ted Benton (New York and London: Guilford Press, 1996), 205–6.

20. By contrast, O'Connor's intellectual heirs have often viewed "market" solutions to climate change as abhorrent (see the journal *Capitalism, Nature, Socialism*).

21. O'Connor, "Second Contradiction," 206–10.

22. As T. Clark has argued, climate change has no "unitary object *directly* to confront or delimit, let alone to 'fix' as such" ("Some Climate Change Ironies," 144–45). Blaming capital is a preeminent example of this error.

23. Ibid., 134.

24. Robyn Eckersley, "Socialism and Ecocentrism: Toward a New Synthesis," in Benton, *Greening of Marxism,* 289.

25 Bruce Sterling, *Heavy Weather* (New York: Bantam, 1994) (hereafter cited in the text).

26. James Herbert, *Portent* (London: New English Library, 1997).

27. Susanna Waters, *Cold Comfort* (London: Doubleday, 2006).

28. John Minichillo, *The Snow Whale* (Kensington, MD: Atticus Books, 2011).

29. See Éric Darier, "Foucault and the Environment: An Introduction," in *Discourses of the Environment,* ed. Éric Darier (Oxford: Blackwell, 1999), 1–34.

30. Sara Mills, *Discourse* (London: Routledge, 1997), 57.

31. See, for example, Timothy W. Luke, "Environmentality as Green Governmentality," in Darier, *Discourses of the Environment,* 133.

32. Darier, "Foucault and the Environment," 22.

33. Regarding the ontology of the future and carbon management, see Pinkus, "Carbon Management," 51–70.

34. See Mills, *Discourse,* 38; Darier, "Foucault and the Environment," 19.

35. Luke, "Environmentality as Green Governmentality," 133.

36. This definition of the episteme is from Mills, *Discourse,* 57.

37. Michel Foucault, *The Order of Things*, 2nd ed. (London: Routledge, 2001), x.

38. Saci Lloyd, *The Carbon Diaries 2015* (London: Hodder Children's, 2008) (hereafter cited in the text).

39. Paul Raven, "Interview: Bruce Sterling on Caryatids, Viridian and the Death of Print," *Futurismic,* 11 Feb. 2009, http://futurismic.com/2009/02/11/interview-bruce-sterling-on-caryatids-viridian-and-the-death-of-print/.

40. For a concise summary of the geopolitics of *The Caryatids*, see Matt Dawson, "The Caryatids by Bruce Sterling," *Prometheus Unbound,* 15 Feb. 2011, http://prometheus-unbound.org/2011/02/15/book-review-the-caryatids/.

41. Adam-Troy Castro, "Before the Climate Crisis Kills Us All, We'd Better Listen to Bruce Sterling," *Blastr,* 16 Mar. 2009, http://www.blastr.com/2009/03/interview_bruce_sterling_unleashes_clone_sisters_on_climate_change_in_the_caryatids.php.

42. The novel indicates that Acquis also emerged from Seattle, Raleigh, Madison, Austin, San Francisco, and Canada: current centers of liberal culture (70).

43. Several reviews and interviews suggest that Mljet is Cyprus, renamed for its post-disaster condition. However, Mljet is the name of an actual Balkan island, which is consistent with the political geography of the novel and the apparent scale of Mljet. Castro's interview ("Before the Climate Crisis") may have begun the Cyprus theory, as it appears to put it in the mouth of Sterling.

44. Colored shirt parties have a distinct history in Thailand as well.

45. Beyond Ballard and Turner, Maggie Gee's *The Flood* and Adam Roberts's *The Snow* feature the high-rise.

46. In *We Have Never Been Modern*, Latour also describes how human culture has always blended technologies of different eras.

Conclusion

1. M. H. Abrams, *A Glossary of Literary Terms*, 5th ed. (San Francisco: Holt, Rinehart and Winston, 1988), 152–54.

2. See chapter 1. Also see Adam Trexler, "Mediating Climate Change: Ecocriticism, Science Studies," in *Oxford Handbook of Ecocriticism*, ed. Greg Garrard (Oxford: Oxford University Press, 2014).

3. Abrams, *Glossary of Literary Terms*, 152–53.

4. For climate change as a deconstructive force, see T. Clark, "Some Climate Change Ironies," 131–49.

5. Richard Kerridge, "The Single Source," *Ecozona* 1.1 (2010), http://www.ecozona.eu.

6. Kormann, "Scenes from a Melting Planet."

7. Jonathan Franzen, *Freedom: A Novel* (New York: Picador, 2010) (hereafter cited in the text).

8. Barbara Kingsolver, *Flight Behavior* (New York: Harper, 2012) (hereafter cited in the text).

9. In fact, there is a flood in the final scenes of *Flight Behavior*, but it is far less central to the novel's account of climate change than in the deluge novels described in chapter 2.

10. In making the point, Ovid's wife traces the origins of climate change denial to corporate motives introduced by conservative media.

11. Robert Edric, *Salvage* (London: Black Swan, 2011) (hereafter cited in the text).

12. Lynch, Tryhorn, and Abramson have proposed the "iconic extreme" as an ideal

boundary object, linking the goals of participants such as scientists and community members, "even as they embody different meanings." See Amanda H. Lynch, Lee Try-horn, and Rebecca Abramson, "Working at the Boundary: Facilitating Interdisciplinarity in Climate Change Adaptation Research," *Bulletin of the American Meteorology Society* 89.2 (Feb. 2008): 169–79.

13. This account consciously builds on the ironies located by Timothy Clark in "Some Climate Change Ironies." Clark cites three that are developed in the current account: scale-framing problems for a global, multiplicitous problem; lack of a unitary object that makes climate change an all-but-impossible area of study; and the obsolescence of a liberatory method in climate change politics.

INDEX